Facts On File Encyclopedia of

Black Women

IN AMERICA

Literature

Encyclopedia of
Black Women in America

Facts On File Encyclopedia of

Black Women

IN AMERICA

Literature

Darlene Clark Hine, Editor

Kathleen Thompson, Associate Editor

☑® Facts On File, Inc.

Facts On File Encyclopedia of Black Women in America: Literature

Facts On File, Inc.
11 Penn Plaza
New York NY 10001

Library of Congress Cataloging-in-Publication Data

Facts on File encyclopedia of Black women in America / Darlene Clark
Hine, editor ; Kathleen Thompson, associate editor.
p.   cm.
Includes bibliographical references and index.
Contents: v. 1. The early years, 1619–1899 — v. 2. Literature —
v. 3. Dance, sports, and visual arts — v. 4. Business and professions —
v. 5. Music — v. 6. Education — v. 7. Religion and community —
v. 8. Law and government — v. 9. Theater arts and
entertainment — v. 10. Social activism — v. 11. Science, health, and
medicine.
ISBN 0-8160-3424-9 (set : alk. paper)
ISBN 0-8160-3430-3 (Literature)
1. Afro-American women—Biography—Encyclopedias. I. Hine,
Darlene Clark. II. Thompson, Kathleen.
E185.96.F2   1996
920.72'08996073—dc20   96-33268

Text design by Cathy Rincon
Cover design by Smart Graphics

Printed in the United States of America

RRD FOF 10 9 8 7 6 5 4 3 2 1

This book is printed on acid-free paper.

Contents

How to Use This Volume

SCOPE OF THE VOLUME

The *Literature* volume includes entries on individuals in the following subject areas: poetry, fiction, criticism, autobiography, and biography.

RELATED OCCUPATIONS

Professionals in related occupations addressed in other volumes in this encyclopedia include the following: playwrights (*Theater Arts and Entertainment*), screenwriters (*Theater Arts and Entertainment*), journalists (*Business and Professions*), and scholars and educators (*Education*).

HOW TO USE THIS VOLUME

The introduction to this volume presents an overview of the history of black women in literature. A chronology following the entries lists important events in the history of black women in American literature.

Individuals and organizations are covered in alphabetically arranged entries. If you are looking for an individual or organization that does not have an entry in this volume, please check the alphabetically arranged list of the entries for all eleven volumes of this encyclopedia that appears at the end of this book.

Names of individuals and organizations for which there are entries in this or other volumes of the encyclopedia are printed in **boldface.** Check the contents list at the back of this book to find the volume where a particular entry can be found.

Facts On File Encyclopedia of

IN AMERICA

Literature

Introduction

In the first week of October 1993, something truly remarkable happened: **Rita Dove**, a black woman, became Poet Laureate of the United States of America, the highest honor this country bestows on a poet. In the same week, something even more remarkable occurred: **Toni Morrison**, another black woman, won the Nobel Prize in literature, the highest honor the world bestows on any writer.

That week was extraordinary but, to anyone who had been paying attention to American literature in the previous decade, it was not a surprise. One by one, black women have risen above the crowd of poets and novelists to take commanding positions in the world of books. In addition to Dove and Morrison, there is **Maya Angelou,** who more and more becomes the poetic voice of America. There is **Alice Walker,** author of the Pulitzer Prize–winning novel *The Color Purple.*

Among fiction writers, there are **Toni Cade Bambara, Gloria Naylor, Marita Golden, Bebe Moore Campbell,** and **Terry McMillan.** Among poets, the distinguished **Gwendolyn Brooks** continues to make clear why she was the first African American to win a Pulitzer

While the world watched Maya Angelou read her poem "On The Pulse of Morning" at President Bill Clinton's inauguration, those who knew anything about American literature were aware that she was part of a tradition of black women writers stretching back for centuries and forward to Toni Morrison's Nobel Prize and beyond.

Prize. **Jayne Cortez, Lucille Clifton, Sonia Sanchez, Nikki Giovanni, Margaret Walker,** and the late **Audre Lorde** are everywhere in the anthologies.

These women—these splendid women—are not finding readers only in the black community, nor are they finding approval only among critics: In spring of 1992, Morrison's novel *Jazz*, Walker's *Possessing the Secret of Joy*, and McMillan's *Waiting to Exhale* were on the *New York Times* best-seller list at the same time. America has writers who are consistently producing books the critics praise and millions of people read, and those writers are black women.

THE BEGINNING OF THE JOURNEY

The first written literature by African-American women, which appeared in the middle 1700s, was not slave literature, even though the women who wrote it were slaves. It was written by women who felt themselves to be citizens and who were identified, to a great degree, with their white neighbors. In their own way, they accepted the American dream and participated in it, and they used the English language in its traditional forms.

This makes them difficult for modern readers to evaluate. For some time, they were dismissed as "not black." In fact, their situation was much more complex than that. They were slaves, but they were writing at a time before slavery had overwhelmed the nation and tainted all relations between white and black people.

Before cotton became the critically important crop of the American South, slavery was on its way out. It did not fit into a society that prided itself on its democratic love of freedom and justice. Slavery could never be other than a terrible crime against those principles.

Also, in New England, slaves had always been known as servants and had often been treated as such. Free blacks usually remained servants, but some became landowners and tradespeople and were dealt with on that level by their neighbors. Shortly after the Revolutionary War, the gradual elimination of slavery began in the North.

However, with the rise of the plantation South, slavery suddenly became a tremendous economic issue. More and more African people were enslaved to work for King Cotton, and the South's obsession with slavery and race began to poison race relations in the rest of the country. Those who practiced slavery and those who tolerated it had to justify themselves, and the only way they could do that was to create, and spread, a terrible lie about the African people: This lie of inferiority became something that every black person, slave or not, had to deal with every day in every circumstance of life.

A black consciousness arose out of this history, fed by continuing racism after the Civil War. To those who have lived with this consciousness, the work of the early black poets may seem, in some way, lacking in "soul." That work has, on the other hand, a straightforward confidence and dignity that is undeniable.

The very first known work of literature by a black woman—indeed, by any African American—is a poem written by **Lucy Terry [Prince]** when she was sixteen years old. Terry was brought to Deerfield, Rhode Island, on a slave ship, in about 1730 when she was a baby. She was purchased by Deacon Ebenezer Wells when she was five years old and baptized in the Christian faith. Wells taught her to read and write. The only poem of hers that has come down to us is one that describes an Indian attack on some white townspeople at a plateau outside town called "The Bars."

The tone of this poem makes it quite clear that young Lucy Terry thought of the people she describes as friends and neighbors; there is certainly no suggestion that she thought of them as her superiors in any way or that there was any barrier between them because of race or status. Indeed, one of the most appealing qualities of the poem is the obvious affection the poet feels for her subjects.

Bars Fight

August, 'twas the twenty-fifth,
Seventeen hundred forty-six,
The Indians did in ambush lay
Some very valient [sic] men to slay,
Samuel Allen like a hero fout,
And though he was so brave and bold,
His face no more shall we behold.

Eleazer Hawks was killed outright,
Before he had time to fight, —
Before he did the Indians see,
Was shot and killed immediately.

Oliver Amsden he was slain,
Which caused his friends much grief and
  pain
Simeon Amsden they found dead
Not many rods distant from his head.

Adonijah Gillett, we do hear,
Did lose his life which was so dear.
John Sadler [sic] fled across the water,
And thus escaped the dreadful slaughter.

Eunice Allen see [sic] the Indians coming,
And hopes to save herself by running;
And had not her petticoats stopped her,
The awful creatures had not catched her,
Nor tommy hawked her on the head.
Young Samuel Allen, Oh, lack-a-day!
Was taken and carried to Canada.

Although this is quite a respectable effort for a teenager, its value lies primarily in the story it tells. In fact, Lucy Terry became a well-known storyteller in Deerfield after her marriage to Abijah Prince. Either before or at her marriage, she was freed. (All of her six children were born free, and at that time the slave or free status of the mother determined the status of the child.) The young people of the town often gathered at her house to hear her tell stories. Many of the stories, apparently, were African in origin. Because she was an infant when she was brought to America, she must have heard them from other African Americans in the area and decided to keep them alive.

Everything we know of Lucy Terry Prince confirms the impression the poem gives of a confident woman for whom race was not an overriding issue. One of her sons fought in the Revolutionary War and then married a white woman and lived on a farm near his parents. Prince and her husband received land grants; her husband was a founder of the town of Sunderland, Vermont. The Princes even took a white man to court for trying to claim some of their property. Lucy herself argued the case and won. One of her sons was refused entrance to Williams College because of his race, but only after she made a three-hour argument to the trustees.

Transported by slave ship to the American colonies in 1761, Phillis Wheatley eventually became a master of eighteenth-century poetic forms, producing work that gained recognition in England and Europe as well as in America. Her book Poems on Various Subjects, Religious and Moral *was the first published book by a black women in America.* (SCHOMBURG CENTER)

It seems clear from everything she did that Prince believed in justice and expected it; she also usually got it. The racism she faced was significant, but it was not of overwhelming importance in her life.

"Bars Fight" was not published during Prince's lifetime. In fact, it was not published until 1855. Until that year, it was believed that the first black woman writer in America was **Phillis Wheatley.**

Wheatley was also brought to the United States on a slave ship as a child. She was about seven or eight when she was purchased as a personal servant for Susanna Wheatley, the wife of a Boston tailor. She was taught to read and write by a daughter of the family and within sixteen months, according to John Wheatley, had "attained the English language, to which she was an utter stranger before, to such a degree, as to read . . . the most difficult parts" of the Bible.

The Wheatleys proceeded to teach young Phillis anything and everything she could absorb, including Latin, astronomy, ancient history, and modern geography. She remained legally a slave, but she had her own room, only light duties, and the freedom to write whenever the muse inspired her. Her first published poem was an elegy on the death of the English evangelist George Whitefield. As other poems appeared, Wheatley became a celebrity in Boston and beyond.

In 1773, the Wheatleys sent Phillis on a sea voyage to England, in part because of her health and in part so that she could be introduced to London society. When she returned to America, because Mrs. Wheatley was ill, she was freed. Shortly thereafter, Susanna Wheatley died. Phillis lived with the Wheatley family by choice for four more years.

An ardent patriot, Phillis Wheatley wrote often in support of the American Revolution. Because John and Susanna Wheatley were Loyalists, this was clearly a conscious, individual choice on the part of the young poet. The style she chose to write in was, on the other hand, simply the style of the day; that is, she wrote the way virtually everyone else who took poetry seriously was writing, and she did it very well.

Indeed, Wheatley was highly skilled in what is called the "neoclassical" style; in addition, she was a born poet. So, while she wrote quite a few mediocre elegies when famous people died, she also wrote some excellent poetry, as seen in this extract from her poem "Thoughts on the Works of Providence:"

Infinite love, where'er we turn our eyes,
Appears: this ev'ry creature's want
  supplies;
This most is heard in nature's constant
  voice;
This makes the morn, and this the eve,
  rejoice;
This bids the fostering rains and dews
  descend
To nourish all, to serve one gen'ral end.
The good of man; yet man ungrateful pays
But little homage, and but little praise.
To Him whose works arrayed in mercy
  shine,
What songs should rise, how constant,
  how divine!

Along with black male poet Jupiter Hammon, Phillis Wheatley and, to a lesser degree, Lucy Terry Prince form a special group in black literature. While they have not influenced those who come after them because they lived in a different world, they are important because, for so many years, they represented what African Americans could accomplish and because they sometimes, in flashes here and there, speak to readers two centuries into the future.

FOLKLORE

While Phillis Wheatley was writing in the style of English poet Alexander Pope, other black Americans were telling stories in the style of African folktales, singing songs in the style of African chants, and giving Christian sermons filled with parables and proverbs from their African past.

This body of folklore is almost entirely anonymous. No one knows which tale was first told by a woman and which by a man. All we know for certain is that both men and women sat in the slave compound at night and spoke of Br'er Rabbit and his tricks.

Slave owners tried very hard to root out African customs and language among the slaves, but animal stories must have seemed harmless to them. They failed to see the parallels to slave life, never understood how frustration, anger, and fear could be expressed in the stories that made their own children laugh.

In African folklore, the hare is not a major character; he appears only now and then as a trickster. In America, the hare became a rabbit and stepped into the limelight. The African jackal became a fox; the African hyena became a wolf or bear.

Br'er—that is, Brother—Rabbit was an animal with virtually no real strength or power. In fact, there is no weaker hero-animal in world folklore than Br'er Rabbit. He was chosen to represent the slave, who had so little control over his or her life. However, by being smarter and more wily than his enemies, Br'er Rabbit could win out over Br'er Fox (the slave owner) and Br'er Bear (the overseer).

Other folktales featured a human trickster named John or Jack. Jack did not always win, but when he did, he escaped a beating or even won his freedom through outwitting Ole Master, Ole Miss, and the "patterollers" (patrolers). Sometimes, he even went up against the devil.

The "preacher tale" was another traditionally African-American folktale. These stories were mildly satirical at the expense of the preacher.

Written black literature draws on all of these sources as well as spirituals, sermons, "why" stories, and tall tales—or "lies." Along with black music, they provide texture and richness to novels written in the twentieth century, and their echoes can be heard in twentieth-century poetry. There is another source of inspiration, however, for those remarkable black women writing today.

The autobiographical tradition began for black women with the 1836 publication of Jarena Lee's Life and Religious Experience of Jarena Lee. *(LIBRARY OF CONGRESS)*

EARLY AUTOBIOGRAPHY

Autobiography is important in the literature of black women and men for many reasons. For one thing, it is a significant genre for all Americans. In the seventeenth century, as people explored new frontiers, they wrote about their discoveries, knowing that the very newness of their experience would make this interesting to their readers. For another, black Americans have written about the circumstances of their lives for very pressing reasons—to protest them, to denounce them, to get them changed. Finally, black women and men have felt the need to define themselves, to make clear their own identities separate from those enforced upon them.

Those who wrote of their lives in the nineteenth century began a tradition of autobiography in the literature of African-American women that continues into the twentieth century with works such as Maya Angelou's *I Know Why the Caged Bird Sings* and its four companion volumes. They also influenced the novels, such as *The Color Purple*, that today express so much of the rich culture of black women.

The earliest autobiographies to emerge from the African-American community were usually by free blacks. Narratives of slave life would come later, as the abolitionist movement grew stronger and the Civil War approached. After the war, too, many former slaves would write of their lives in slavery. However, in the 1830s, there were many autobiographies published by women that do not fit into the slave narrative tradition. Two of these books were spiritual autobiographies, written by women who wanted to relate their religious journeys.

The first of these spiritual autobiographies was by **Jarena Lee,** who was born at Cape May, New Jersey, in 1783. Her book, published in 1836, was *The Life and Religious Experiences of Jarena Lee, a Coloured Lady, Giving an Account of Her Call to Preach the Gospel. Revised and Corrected from the Original Manuscript, Written by Herself.* In it, she describes her repeated attempts to obtain permission to preach within the African Methodist Episcopal (AME) Church; she was eventually given permission by Bishop Richard Allen to hold prayer meetings in her home. Later, she traveled around the Northeast, preaching wherever she went.

In 1846, a second spiritual autobiography by a black woman was published. **Zilpha Elaw,** too, was a traveling evangelist. Her book was entitled *Memoirs of the Life, Religious Experience, Ministerial Travels, and Labours of Mrs. Zilpha Elaw: An American Female of Colour.* For a time, Elaw was a preaching partner of Jarena Lee's.

Both Elaw and Lee gained the courage to defy convention from the belief that they were called by God. Their autobiographies emphasize their belief that women, in divine inspiration, are in no way inferior to men.

In 1838, *The Memoirs of Elleanor Eldridge* told a different sort of story. A free black woman, **Elleanor Eldridge** began to work when she was ten years old. By the time she was sixteen, she was skilled in spinning, weaving, arithmetic, and housekeeping. She later became a cheesemaker, whose product was considered to be of exceptional quality. After Eldridge's father died, leaving her a small estate, she went into business with her sister and became quite successful. All of this she describes in her memoirs, along with real-estate deals and

legal problems. It's a fascinating record of the life of an early-nineteenth-century black woman who was not only free but independent.

As the antislavery movement became stronger, in the decades just before the Civil War, there began to appear slave narratives, records of life within the institution of slavery that were often published by abolition groups as a way of educating the public and encouraging them to oppose that institution. Most of the early narratives were written by men; however, in 1831, the autobiography of a West Indian slave, Mary Prince, was published in the United States and told a terrible story of slavery in the Caribbean.

The most important slave narrative published by a black woman was probably *Incidents in the Life of a Slave Girl: Written by Herself,* which first appeared in 1861. At the time, it was mistaken for a work of fiction, produced by a white writer; it was not until 1987 that the book was shown to be the work of **Harriet Ann Jacobs,** a black woman and a slave.

Incidents is particularly significant because it deals with the way a black woman's oppression in slavery is intensified by her owner's sexual aggression. It also details the lengths to which one woman went to resist and finally escape that aggression. At one point in her life, Jacobs lived in a crawl space in her grandmother's attic for seven years in order to get away from her owner and be near her children by another man.

Jacobs finally escaped and, with her children, lived in New York for many years. One of her white employers, without her knowledge, "purchased" her and her children from her former master and then freed them. When she learned of this, Jacobs decided to write her story. With the help of African-American abolitionist William C. Nell and white abolitionist Lydia Maria Child, she published it herself.

After the Civil War, many more slave narratives were published. Certainly one of the most unusual is **Elizabeth Keckley's** *Behind the Scenes: or Thirty Years a Slave and Four Years in the White House*. Keckley was born into slavery and writes about her slave experiences, but most of the book is dedicated to her years as dressmaker and confidante to Mary Todd Lincoln, President Abraham Lincoln's wife. The book caused a furor when it was written because it revealed a great deal about the personal lives of the Lincolns and contained forty letters written by Mrs. Lincoln to Keckley.

Together, the narratives of Jarena Lee, Zilpha Elaw, Elleanor Eldridge, Elizabeth Keckley, and Harriet Ann Jacobs present a vivid picture of life for black women in the late eighteenth and early nineteenth centuries, both inside slavery and out. Their treatment by the black literary establishment presents a vivid picture of what black women writers have often had to contend with.

In a history of African-American literature published as recently as 1989, Lee, Elaw, and Eldridge go entirely unmentioned. Jacobs is dismissed in one condescending paragraph that begins with the words "It was probably inevitable that at least one abolitionist slave narrative, if not more, would focus on sex . . ." and then manages to confuse Jacobs' real name with her pseudonym and uses the word *claim* more than once to refer to the sexual harassment she describes. It's difficult to imagine a black literary historian referring to "the beating he *claims* he got."

In discussing the history of black women in literature, this is a problem that cannot be ignored. Black women writers have faced discrimination from the white literary establishment and the black. They have had difficulty being published and having their work taken seriously, but they have continued to write.

Slave narratives were written and published up to the end of the nineteenth century. In 1879, **Julia A. Foote** published *A Brand Plucked from the Fire! An Autobiographical Sketch*; in 1898, **Kate Drumgold's** *A Slave Girl's Story* appeared; and in 1902, **Susie Taylor** published *A Black Woman's Civil War Memoirs: Reminiscences of My Life in Camp*, about her life as a slave and, later, a nurse for the Union army.

Slave narratives and other autobiographies were not the only writings of nineteenth-century black women; among free black Americans, there were many who turned to literature as a way of expressing deeply felt beliefs or their most personal thoughts and emotions.

POLITICS AND POETS

The abolition movement brought to light a great many black women with something to say and the ability to say it. Some of these women were political leaders and speechmakers. Others recorded their work behind the scenes. Still others were poets who expressed their urgent hatred of slavery in verse published in abolition journals.

As early as 1831, **Maria Stewart**, the first American-born woman to lecture publicly on political subjects, published a small pamphlet of her writings. In 1832, she published a larger work, *Meditations from the Pen of Mrs. Maria W. Stewart*, which included political speeches, essays, and religious meditations. Stewart was a strong advocate of black self-determination and economic independence from white society. She also wrote in favor of women's rights.

In mid-century, **Sojourner Truth** began to lecture for abolition and woman's rights. She was a powerful speaker who vividly represented the evils of slavery and the injustices suffered by women of all races. Little of what she said was recorded, but the words we have are among the most powerful in black literature.

Never has the special plight of black women been more forcefully stated than in the "Ain't I a Woman?" segment of a speech made to a woman's rights conference in May 1851: "That man over there," she declared in part, "says that women need to be helped into carriages and lifted over ditches and to have the best place everywhere. Nobody ever helps me into carriages and over mud-puddles or gives me any best place! And ain't I a woman? Look at me! Look at my arm! I have ploughed and planted and gathered into barns and no man could head me! And ain't I a woman?"

As she goes on to talk of hard work done, beatings received, and children borne and lost to slavery, she uses the powerful repetitions and rhythms of sermons and spirituals to build tension. A reader can almost hear her powerful voice growing louder and more demanding with every repetition until it reaches that dramatic conclusion—". . . and when I cried out with my mother's grief, none but Jesus heard! And ain't I a woman?"

All of the instances of Truth's oratory that we have bear the stamp of eloquence. When leaders of the abolitionist movement, including the great Frederick Douglass, asked that she stop pressing for the rights of women until those of black men had been guaranteed, she replied with frankness and common sense. "There is a great deal of stir about colored men getting their rights," she said, "but not a word about the colored women theirs. You see, the colored man will be masters over the women, and it will be just as bad as it was before. So I am for keeping the thing going while things are stirring, because if we wait 'til it is still, it will take a great while to get it going again."

It is a terrible pity that more of Truth's speeches have not come down to us. Fortunately, she did dictate an autobiography, which was published in 1850. It was entitled *The Narrative of Sojourner Truth* and was written down by Olive Gilbert. A memoir of Truth written by Frances Dana Gage was added in the 1875 edition of the book and also published in Elizabeth Cady Stanton's *History of Woman Suffrage*.

Another political leader whose words stirred people into action was **Mary Ann Shadd Cary**, whose special concern was self-reliance and financial independence for former slaves and, indeed, all black citizens. In 1853, she founded the *Provincial Freeman*, a newspaper dedicated to her campaign against those she thought were bringing shame to her people. Her prose, as she attacked the representatives of the Refugee Home Society, was filled with such scathing phrases as *moral pest, petty despot, priest-ridden people*, and *nest of unclean birds*.

The various antislavery journals and literary magazines were an outlet for many black women of the time. **Sarah Forten** Purvis, a member of the prominent Forten family, wrote eloquently against slavery in the *Liberator* magazine in articles that had such titles as "The Abuse of Liberty" and "The Slave Girl's Address to Her Mother."

A more striking example, however, is **Charlotte Forten Grimké**, Purvis' niece who was born into the elite black Forten family.

Frances Ellen Watkins Harper was the most prominent black woman author of the nineteenth century.

She was educated at home by tutors and began to write poetry early in life. Her work was published almost exclusively in abolitionist journals such as the *Liberator,* the *Christian Recorder,* the *Anglo-African Magazine,* the *National Anti-Slavery Standard,* the *Atlantic Monthly,* and the *New England Magazine,* but it was not all about slavery.

Grimké wrote about loneliness and love in the same style as her white contemporaries. Prominent poet John Greenleaf Whittier praised her work and encouraged her career. She also wrote about her experiences as a teacher on South Carolina's Sea Islands. Her essays about teaching recently freed black citizens were published in the *Atlantic Monthly* in 1864. It was the only time she was published in the mainstream white press.

There was no place for her outside the abolitionist movement and no place for her work outside the abolitionist press. Her diaries, which are perhaps her most important writings, tell a story of dedication and frustration that must have been common to other free black women of the time.

The most prominent black woman author of the nineteenth century also published in the abolition journals. The first poems of **Frances Ellen Watkins Harper** appeared in the *Liberator* and the *Christian Recorder.* A popular speaker against slavery and for equal rights, Harper recited her poetry on the platform. When her first volume of poetry, *Poems on Miscellaneous Subjects,* came out in 1854, she already had a loyal audience. The book sold more than 10,000 copies in three years and was revised and reissued in 1857; in fact, 20 editions of it were published within 20 years of its first appearance.

Harper's work covers a variety of subjects, usually "improving" subjects such as heroism, religion, woman's rights, black achievement, and temperance. But Harper was not just a black version of the white sentimental writers who littered the literary scene in England and America during the Victorian Era. She was a powerful advocate for her people.

In her epic poem "Moses: A Story of the Nile," Harper recounts the escape of the people of Israel from slavery. The parallel to the black people of the American South was not pointed out, but it was unmistakable, and Harper showed great insight into the effects that slavery would have long after it ended:

> If Slavery only laid its weight of chains
> Upon the weary, aching limbe, e'en then
> It were a curse; but when it frets through
>   nerve
> And flesh and eats into the weary soul,
> Oh then it is a thing for every human
> Heart to loathe, and this was Israel's fate,
> For when the chains were shaken from
>   their limbs,
> They failed to strike the impress from their
>   souls.

Harper was also the first black woman to publish a short story in this country: "Two Offers" appeared in 1859, six years after Frederick Douglass' "The Heroic Slave," and yet, it was only the second published by a black writer.

Harper's first novel, entitled *Minnie's Sacrifice*, appeared in serial form in 1869 in the *Christian Recorder*; her most famous novel, *Iola Leroy*, was published in 1892. Between those dates, she wrote poetry and essays and also lectured throughout the country. After *Iola Leroy*, she published five collections of poetry. Her writing spanned more than fifty years.

Important as Harper is to the history of black women in American literature, she was not the first to write a novel. That distinction belongs to **Harriet E. Wilson**, the first African American of either gender to publish a novel in the United States and one of the first two black women to publish a novel in any language. Yet, for more than a century to come, this achievement was ignored.

Harriet Wilson's novel, *Our Nig*, published in 1859, was a remarkable achievement: It is well-plotted and more than competently written, and although it has elements of autobiography—as do most first novels—it is significantly a work of the imagination.

However, it was never reviewed and is almost never included in the important bibliographies of black literature. Until Henry Louis Gates, Jr., prepared a new edition of the book in 1983, *Our Nig* might as well never have existed.

Gates suggests that there are two reasons for this. First, the book is "not about the horrors of slavery in the South but about the horrors of racism in the North." That fact probably alienated a large portion of those who might have been expected to buy, read, and praise the novel—white Northern abolitionists. Second, the book treats sympathetically the marriage of its main character's parents, who are a black man and a white woman; this almost certainly alienated the rest. It was a book that dared greatly, and its daring earned it obscurity.

Perhaps the most startling fact about the literature of black women before the twentieth century is that its two most important works—*Incidents in the Life of a Slave Girl* and *Our Nig*—were both assumed for more than a century to have been written by white authors. Nothing could illustrate more clearly the lack of regard for black women that was widespread in both the black and white literary worlds.

WOMEN OF A NEW ERA

As the century turned, the new writers were not people who had personally experienced slavery or fought against it in the abolition movement; slave narratives—factual or fictional—faded as the primary form of black literature. Where slavery entered in now, it was usually as part of a larger narrative. Nonetheless, black literature remained a literature of protest. When slavery had been destroyed, racism had remained alive.

One of the first novels of the new era was **Pauline Elizabeth Hopkins'** *Contending Forces: A Romance Illustrative of Negro Life North and South*. Cast in the form of that period's historical romances, the novel follows the black Smith family from before the Civil War in the South to later life in the North and deals with such serious topics as slavery, lynching, and discrimination.

Anna Julia Cooper's book A Voice from the South by a Black Woman of the South *(1892) has been called the first black feminist publication.* (SCURLOCK STUDIO)

All of Hopkins' novels share this combination of romantic form and serious content; they also tend to have well-educated, light-skinned heroes and heroines, many of whom pass for white. Some pass deliberately and some are stunned to discover their true racial identities. Hopkins uses the ambiguity of color to attack lynching and other forms of oppression. She shows that those terrible persecutions are inspired by slavery and its racist legacy, rather than any inborn qualities of black men and women.

In other words, whites in the South needed to keep proving that what they did to black people during slavery was justified.

That could only be true if African Americans were beasts rather than human beings. In her novels, Hopkins kept pointing out that it often wasn't even possible to tell who was black and who wasn't. "The slogan of the hour," she writes, "is 'Keep the Negro down!' but who is clear enough in vision to decide who hath black blood and who hath it not? . . . No man can draw the dividing line between the two races, for they are both one blood!"

Hopkins' final novel celebrates African culture. *Of One Blood: or The Hidden Self*, published in 1902, once again introduces a hero who has never identified as black. However, during a visit to Africa, he discovers and begins to value his African heritage.

Hopkins was also a major force at the magazine *The Colored American*, which published her short fiction and three of her novels in serial form; The fourth was published by the magazine's parent company. Her influence there, as well as the importance of her novels, was greatly underestimated between the early decades of the century and 1972. In that year, **Ann Allen Shockley** rediscovered her work and brought her to the attention of the literary world. As more people read and pay attention to her novels, Pauline Elizabeth Hopkins will probably be considered one of the most important black novelists of the early twentieth century.

There were other black women who wrote fiction at this time, but they often wrote "nonracial" novels. In their stories of love, marriage, children, and family life, it was virtually impossible to tell that the characters were black, and yet, these characters carried much the same message that Hopkins' mulattoes did—"We are all alike."

Portraying black people as simply human was, for this time, a radical act.

Most of the poetry being written by black women at this time also avoided dealing with race directly and for the same reason. Perhaps for that reason, it seldom rises above the level of good greeting-card verse. Poets who are unable, for whatever reason, to write of the specific realities of their lives cannot create poetry that speaks to the lives of their readers.

Yet, in spite of the limitations, **Anna Julia Cooper** could write that simply to be a woman in this era was "sublime" and "to be a woman of the Negro race in America, and to be able to grasp the deep significance of the possibilities of the crisis, is to have a heritage, it seems to me, unique in the ages," and she was right.

Cooper was part of a new and remarkably exciting movement among black women called the women's club movement, but that phrase doesn't summon up the right picture at all. These weren't ladies in flowered hats sitting around sipping tea.

The members of black women's clubs came from the black middle class. They were the black elite, but they certainly weren't the idle rich. The members of the Bethel Literary and Historical Association in Washington, D.C., for example, were almost all teachers. **The Woman's Loyal Union** in New York was founded by a teacher and a journalist. The Woman's Era Club of Boston was founded by a journalist who had also served on the United States Sanitation Commission. Some of these women were also the wives of prosperous business and professional men, and many were not.

The club movement was rooted in the black church and in the benevolent societies that worked in the North before the Civil War to keep black communities together; it grew out of the literary societies that had promoted social improvement and the advancement of the race; it was a product of free-born black society in Northern cities, but eventually it spread around the country.

The purpose of all of the club activities was to advance African-American people in every way. Every literary or artistic activity was considered political. Every time a member gave a talk on English poetry, it was proof of the intellectual and artistic abilities of the race. Each performance of concert music on the piano was an opportunity for a musician who would never find a public arena.

The clubs founded schools and raised funds for hospitals, orphanages, and homes for the aged just as their white counterparts did. But there was a special consciousness behind their efforts, an awareness that they were serving their own people—and that no one else was going to.

The clubs also addressed serious social concerns: They confronted segregation in housing and transportation, were in the forefront of the antilynching movement, and worked constantly for the rights of women.

The women of these clubs were a powerful intellectual force, and many of them wrote books that still have power today. Among these are Anna Julia Cooper's *A Voice from the South by a Black Woman of the South*, published in 1892; Gertrude Mossell's *The Work of the Afro-American Woman*, published in 1894; and Virginia W. Broughton's *Women's Work, as Gleaned from the Women of the Bible*, published in 1904. All of these books deal with the position of black women in American society.

The last of the important slave narratives was also written by a clubwoman: Susie Taylor had a different kind of background than did most of the others, but she had the one asset that made any woman welcome in club circles—an education. Taylor was born a slave, but she was brought up free. She was taught to read by two white children. Later, she became a teacher of freed slaves and then a nurse for the Union army during the Civil War.

Taylor's book, *A Black Woman's Civil War Memoirs: Reminiscences of My Life in Camp with the 33rd United States Colored Troops, Late 1st S.C. Volunteers*, did more than just tell about her work as a nurse during the war; it also spoke out about American society after the war. On hearing that the Daughters of the Confederacy were circulating petitions to ban the theatrical productions of *Uncle Tom's Cabin* because its "exaggerated" portrayal of slave life would be harmful to children, Taylor wrote, "Do these Confederate Daughters ever send petitions to prohibit the atrocious lynchings and wholesale murdering and torture of the Negro? Do you ever hear of them fearing this would have a bad effect on the children?"

The black clubwomen were ladies, every one of them, but clearly, they were ladies who could throw a punch.

In the same interval, three periodicals for black women were founded—*Ringwood's Afro-American Journal of Fashion*, *The Woman's Era*, and the *Colored Woman's Magazine*—and **Charlotta Bass** became owner and publisher of the *California Eagle* newspaper.

Black women, then, had not turned away from writing. They had, however, turned very much toward the advancement of their people and themselves. The more radical **Ida B. Wells-Barnett**, during this period, carried on her antilynching campaign, and most of her writing concerned violence against black people. She was as powerful a writer as she was a speaker and had a tremendous impact on the political scene.

This extraordinary intellectual flowering has often been overlooked by historians of black literature and culture, and yet, many of the ideas and issues that black male thinkers would promote in the early twentieth century had already been brought up in the writing of these nineteenth-century black women. Cooper's *Voice from the South* spoke of the need for an African-American culture that did not depend on that of white American society. Hopkins' novels raised the question of Pan-Africanism, and they did it years before W. E. B. DuBois and Marcus Garvey.

It does not diminish the achievement of those remarkable men to pay just tribute to these equally remarkable women. It is important to acknowledge all those who contributed to the creation of a true African-American heritage.

THE HARLEM RENAISSANCE

There has been endless speculation about what caused the blooming of black art and culture that occurred in the 1920s and 1930s. Most say the large numbers of black Southerners who moved north, bringing with them their folklore and music, had something to do with it. The emphasis on culture of such leaders as W. E. B. DuBois and Marcus Garvey was certainly part of the explanation. Coincidence may have brought together some of the remarkably talented people who lived within the borders of New York's Harlem. But whatever the reasons, black literature, art, music, and theater became startlingly alive.

Part of the excitement of the time came from the sheer number of gifted writers creating lasting works. Then there were the night life and the music, the parties where the best and brightest came together to talk about life and art. But the most exciting aspect of the Harlem Renaissance was the redefining of black culture in America.

Encouraged by DuBois and others, young black artists looked to Africa, to the folklore of African America, to their own lives and experiences. They shook off the standards of European-American literature and began to celebrate their own cultural heritage. They also began to write realistically and fiercely about the oppression of their people.

These writers published in two magazines put out by black civil-rights organizations: *The Crisis*, with DuBois as editor, was sponsored by the **National Association for the Advancement of Colored People** (NAACP); *Opportunity*, with Charles Johnson as editor, was sponsored by the Urban League. In these publications, there was no need to tailor the work for a white audience; black writers could say what needed to be said as they wanted to say it.

They were also encouraged by two white literary figures of stature—Carl Van Doren and Carl Van Vechten. They were entertained at parties by such influential white women as Charlotte Osgood Mason and were published by some of the most reputable publishing companies in New York.

Gwendolyn Bennett was an artist as well as a writer, who contributed to the "renaissance" of the 1920s. (SCHOMBURG CENTER)

Unfortunately, this shining moment was tarnished by an almost total disregard for black women. It has taken 50, 60, sometimes 70 years to establish the value of many of the women who worked and published during the Harlem Renaissance, and many others were denied the opportunities that might have allowed them to pursue their careers.

For decades, lists of Harlem Renaissance writers have usually included the names

Langston Hughes, Countee Cullen, James Weldon Johnson, Arna Bontemps, Jean Toomer, Claude McKay, and (on the more socially aware lists) **Zora Neale Hurston**. Those names, with the exception of Hurston, belong to men.

Writing at the same time were **Jessie Fauset, Nella Larsen, Dorothy West, Marita Bonner, Mercedes Gilbert, Gwendolyn Bennett, Georgia Douglas Johnson, May Miller, Regina Andrews, Anne Spencer**, Helene Johnson, and others. Their names did not make it onto the lists.

While the Harlem Renaissance was in full swing, there were other lists onto which these women did not make it: the A-lists for those parties given by influential white sponsors and the spring and fall lists of those reputable publishers. Unless they were entertainers—blues singers, Broadway dancers—black women were simply not as glamorous as black men. At any rate, that was the judgment of those who made up the lists.

Starting in about 1970, however, these black women began to be rediscovered. A job of excavation and reconstruction—of works and of reputations—has been carried on by literary historians and other women writers. Today, the names of these women are beginning to take on the gleam that has always surrounded the male writers of that special time.

Zora Neale Hurston came closest of all the black women writers to being accepted during the 1920s as the equal of Hughes, Bontemps, and the others, and yet, she was a maverick, a woman who refused to be defined by either race or gender. In her novels, she created worlds in which black people lived and loved and suffered but did not engage in "race relations." There were no people of another race to relate to. Hurston's novels were set almost entirely within the black community.

Hurston's most famous novel, *Their Eyes Were Watching God*, is now on high school reading lists along with George Eliot's *Silas Marner* and Charles Dickens' *A Tale of Two Cities*. In it, Janie, a black woman, is forced to live out other people's ideas of freedom for most of her life. In the end, she finds her own sort of freedom in a life of community, laughter, and love. Her conflicts are with herself and other black people, such as her family and her husband's.

Hurston was sometimes thought of as a novelist who was unconcerned with the black struggle; in fact, she was very much concerned with the struggles of her black characters to find freedom and fulfillment within the constraints of both race and gender. They simply didn't pay much attention to white people while they did it. Today, her work often seems strikingly contemporary.

Nella Larsen, another Harlem Renaissance writer, was the first African American to win a creative writing award from the Guggenheim Foundation. Her novels deal with the black middle class and the severe limitations placed on the women who lived within it. The first, *Quicksand*, published in 1928, was a critical success. The second, *Passing*, published in 1929, was also acclaimed and led to the Guggenheim award. However, because of personal and professional problems, Larsen stopped writing. In 1941, she began to work as a nurse. She died in 1964.

Georgia Douglas Johnson was also a member of the middle class. Her first book of poetry, *The Heart of a Woman*, published in 1918, deals mostly with a young woman's difficulties and frustrations, and she was severely criticized for not addressing racial issues. Her second book, *Bronze: A Book of Verse,* did deal with race and was highly praised by leaders of the black literary community.

Throughout Johnson's writing career, this problem would come up often. When she wrote as she wanted to, she was criticized. When she wrote as the community felt she should, she was praised. Yet, most critics now feel that her finest poetry is in her third volume, *An Autumn Love Cycle,* which does not deal with racial issues. She also wrote a number of plays, most of which deal with black life and race relations.

After the death of her husband in 1925, Johnson had to balance her writing with making a living for herself and her two children. She was unsuccessful in getting grants and fellowships in spite of her excellent record as a writer, but she continued to write. When she died, an eccentric woman of eighty-nine, all of her papers were thrown out.

In the end, the Harlem Renaissance did not lead to a lasting change in the status of black writers in America. It was difficult for these writers to find publication before that remarkable era and, after a decade or two during which the literary establishment opened its doors a crack, it was difficult again.

BEFORE THE EXPLOSION

Did the increasing prejudice and discrimination of the postwar era trigger the civil rights movement of the late 1950s and 1960s, or did the move toward freedom of black Americans in those decades provoke the hatred and oppression that come from fear? Whatever the cause, the 1940s and 1950s were a thin time for African-American writers. But there were black women who broke through the wall of prejudice that descended on the United States after the Second World War. They included three poets, two novelists, and two playwrights.

A poem can be many things: It can be an exploration, a fantasy, or a cry of rage; it can be a landscape or a portrait; it can be a wail. What is almost impossible for it to be, and remain a poem, is propaganda.

Most of the verse by black women that was published during the nineteenth century fell into this last category. It was propaganda in a just cause, and it had the capacity to stir its readers, but it didn't have the spark by which true poetry is recognized. Three black women who began to publish their work in the early 1940s were and are, on the other hand, undeniably poets.

Gwendolyn Brooks, Margaret Walker, and **Margaret Danner** are alike in many ways: all are well educated; they all write poetry that is admired by fellow poets and understood by the average reader; in competition with male and white poets, all have won awards and prizes that reflect the esteem in which they're held by the literary world; and they all write in the authentic voices of black women.

Margaret Walker's first book of poetry, *For My People,* was published in 1942. Its publication has been called one of the most important events in black literary history. It had been fourteen years since a black woman had last published a volume of poetry (Georgia Douglas Johnson's *An Autumn Love Cycle*), and never had a black woman received the critical acclaim that Walker did. She was the first black poet to be chosen for Yale University Press' Younger Poets Series. However, she did not

Gwendolyn Brooks' first book of poetry, A Street in Bronzeville, *was published in 1945 when she was twenty-eight years old.* (NATIONAL ARCHIVES)

publish another book until 1966, twenty-four years later.

In the meantime, Gwendolyn Brooks made her appearance. For her, success as a poet was not a long, hard struggle. Her first book of poetry, *A Street in Bronzeville*, was published in 1945 when she was twenty-eight years old. The response to this book was so positive that, in the next two years, she received two Guggenheim Fellowships and grants from the American Academy of Arts and Letters and the National Institute of Arts and Letters. Her second book, *Annie Allen*, published in 1950, won the Pulitzer Prize for poetry.

Brooks was the first African American ever to win a Pulitzer in any category. She followed that success with a novel, *Maud Martha*, in 1953. It was also enthusiastically

received. Three years later, her first book of children's poetry, *Bronzeville Boys and Girls*, was published.

Almost from the beginning, Brooks had a status that no other black woman had ever enjoyed. She was for many years *the* black woman in literature. Calvin Hernton, in his article "The Sexual Mountain and Black Women Writers," writes, "Except for Gwendolyn Brooks, and perhaps Margaret Walker, the name of not one black woman writer and not one female protagonist was accorded a worthy status in the black literary world prior to the 1970s. Gwendolyn Brooks was *the* exception. Her age, her numerous prizes and awards and honors from the white literary world, the prestige she *already* had, plus her unquestionable genius, made her, *per force*, the acceptable exception."

Great talent might be enough to ensure a white man, or even a black man, a place in the anthologies and the literature textbooks. For a black woman it required, as Hernton put it, "unquestionable genius" and the right moment in history. The quality of Brooks' work and its relevance to history's shifts and changes have guaranteed her a place that is very special indeed.

The third poet of this group is Margaret Danner. Her work first appeared in 1951 in *Poetry: The Magazine of Verse*, for which she was an editorial assistant. *Poetry* was at that time the most impressive poetry magazine in the United States. It was a far cry from abolitionist journals or NAACP publications so far as a young poet was concerned. That first appearance in print won Danner a John Hay Whitney fellowship. Her first book, *Impressions of African Art Forms*, won her the post of poet-in-residence at Wayne State University in Detroit.

Danner's work is not always as accessible as that of Brooks and Walker, but her connection to the black community is strong. In the early 1960s, she founded a community center in Detroit, enlisting the help of other black poets. That center helped make Detroit a focus of the coming black arts movement.

In the 1940s and 1950s, these three poets were joined by two playwrights in keeping the literature of black women alive. They were **Alice Childress** and **Lorraine Hansberry**.

Alice Childress' play *Just a Little Simple* opened at the Club Baron in 1950. It was an adaptation of Langston Hughes's series of newspaper columns entitled "Simple Speaks His Mind"; it was also the first play by a black woman in America to be professionally produced. Childress went on to write the brilliantly funny *Trouble in Mind*, which won an Obie, the off-Broadway theater's equivalent of the motion picture industry's Oscar. She continued to be a force in American theater through the sixties and seventies and into the eighties. Childress also wrote several novels, her best known being *A Hero Ain't Nothin' but a Sandwich*, published in 1973.

A Raisin in the Sun by Lorraine Hansberry, was produced on Broadway in 1959. It was more than an exceptionally fine play; it was a social phenomenon. It shows an ordinary family with ordinary feelings and relationships. They are black, and their blackness affects their lives, but their struggle is universal, and their appeal was universal. The play broke through the wall of hatred and fear and said, very simply and clearly, "Black people are *people*." The message would seem mild a decade later, but the play would continue to be a moving work of dramatic art.

Alice Walker published her first book of poetry in 1968 when she was just out of college. Her subsequent novel The Color Purple *would win a Pulitzer Prize.* (SCHOMBURG CENTER)

The two African-American women-novelists who made their mark during this time were **Ann Petry** and **Paule Marshall**. They were the early strike force for the coming invasion.

Ann Petry's first novel, *The Street*, burst on the scene in 1946 and sold one and a half million copies. Drawn from her experiences as a newspaper reporter in Harlem, it was a stark picture of the life of a young black woman who is abused and tormented by both white and black men. She is finally driven to murder.

Petry follows in the tradition of Zora Neale Hurston, rather than the earlier black women writers who explored the life of what came to be called the "tragic mulatto." Her characters are of the urban North rather than the rural South, but they are poor and unquestionably black. Current author Terry McMillan names Petry as one of her strongest influences because "Ann Petry wrote about the street in her day, in her language, in her voice—our voice. . . ."

Paule Marshall's *Brown Girl, Brownstones* came out in 1959. It, too, has a young black woman in an urban setting as the main character. It does not reverberate with rage, however, as Petry's novel does. Marshall uses the speech of her parents from Barbados to create a very specific ethnic world in which tradition is always a force and the obvious is seldom the reality. In a review of Marshall's 1991 novel *Daughters*, Shirley Jordan writes, "When you read a Paule Marshall text, be prepared to enter a world in which contradictions are as inherent to living as breathing. Solutions are always available, but they do not come easily and without a price."

There were other black women writing during this time, but these seven women managed to make their voices heard, and one of them would spark the explosive phenomenon that is the literature of black women today.

JUBILEE AND AFTER

In the twenty-four years between Margaret Walker's first book, published in 1942, and her second, *Jubilee*, published in 1966, there had been a half-dozen novels of significance by black women and about the same number of notable books of poetry. The *five* years that followed the publication of *Jubilee* saw the following:

In 1967, Nikki Giovanni's first book of poetry, *Black Feeling, Black Talk*, is published, and Virginia Hamilton's first children's book, *Zeely*, is published.

In 1968, Alice Walker's first book of poetry, *Once*, is published; Audre Lorde's first book of poetry, *The First Cities* is published; and **Kristin Hunter**'s young adult book *The Soul Brothers and Sister Lou* is published and sells a million copies.

In 1969, Sonia Sanchez's first book of poetry, *Homecoming*, is published; **June Jordan**'s first book of poetry, *Who Look at Me* is published; and Lucille Clifton's first book of poetry, *Good Times*, is published and later chosen as one of the *New York Times*' ten best books of the year.

In 1970, Toni Morrison's first novel, *The Bluest Eye*, is published; Maya Angelou's *I Know Why the Caged Bird Sings*, the first volume of her five volume autobiography, is published; **Louise Meriwether**'s *Daddy Was A Numbers Runner*, is published; *The Black Woman: An Anthology*, edited by Toni Cade Bambara, is published; and Audre Lorde's second book of poetry, *Cables to Rage*, is published.

In 1971, Maya Angelou's *Just Give Me a Cool Drink of Water 'fore I Diiie* is published. It will later be nominated for the Pulitzer Prize in poetry. *Gemini: An Extended Autobiographical Statement on My First Twenty-Fives Years of Being a Black Poet* by Nikki Giovanni is published. June Jordan's *His Own Where* is published and chosen by the *New York Times* as one of the outstanding books of the year for young adults.

Clearly, something had changed, and that change went through the fabric of American society like threads of indigo in a pale tapestry. The civil rights movement brought changes in law—school desegregation, affirmative action, the opening of public accommodations. But there was an even more profound change: American culture would never again be white.

Along with a new interest in nationalism and black pride, there came the black arts movement, led by Imamu Amiri Baraka (LeRoi Jones), which fiercely attacked American racism and promoted black independence. In the past, black writers had often written for white audiences, attempting to persuade, horrify, convince, or move them to action. The focus of the black arts movement was black readers. The message was to take control of their own lives. Among the women involved in this movement were Sonia Sanchez and Nikki Giovanni.

There were many others who, though not closely identified with the movement, were part of a new wave of interest in black culture and heritage. For a time, as during the Harlem Renaissance, the doors of the literary establishment opened to black authors, and this time, the women walked in with the men.

There was another difference as well. When the doors started to close again, they didn't close all the way. Toni Morrison, Alice Walker, Lucille Clifton, Nikki Giovanni, Sonia Sanchez, Toni Cade Bambara, and several other black women writers just kept writing and winning awards as well as readers. Indeed, as the women's movement came to life in the seventies, more black women came to public attention than in the sixties. It soon became clear that they had struck a chord—and not only in the black community.

Out of the African-American tradition of storytelling, they filled their books with stories. Out of a desire to create black identities,

they filled their stories with wonderful, varied characters. Out of a sheer joy in language, they wrote prose and poetry that sang. The literary establishment didn't know what hit it.

But in the end, it is not the literary establishment that makes a book a classic. It is the people who read it, the teachers who teach it, the anthologies that excerpt it, the students who remember it long after they leave junior high or high school or college. These women were greatly helped in finding their audiences by a move toward multiculturalism in the schools: When teachers and school boards started to demand that the schools teach authors from different backgrounds and of different genders and ethnicities, the educational publishers *had* to revise their literature anthologies. They went out looking for people who spoke in different voices.

Maya Angelou's *I Know Why the Caged Bird Sings* which came out in 1970, was a best-seller and was nominated for a National Book Award. But its status as a modern classic was guaranteed when it was excerpted in high school literary anthologies that were read by millions of teenagers. Twenty-five years worth of students now remember how a young girl in San Francisco fought to get a job as a trolley conductor.

Lucille Clifton's *Two-Headed Woman* won her a Pulitzer Prize nomination in poetry. Her guarantee of immortality is in the memories of students who read short lyrics about a scissors-sharpener or about kids playing on the furniture that has been set out on the sidewalk after an eviction.

Therefore, the black women writers of the sixties did not disappear as had the black writers of the twenties and thirties. They became the major American writers of the eighties and nineties. Alice Walker's *The Color Purple* won a Pulitzer Prize and became a hit film. Rita Dove won a Pulitzer Prize and became poet laureate. After the publication of her sixth novel, Toni Morrison won the Nobel Prize.

Then there are the new kids on the block.

THE BLACK BOOK BOOM

Since 1967, the number of black families with incomes of more than $50,000 has quadrupled to more than one million. This group reads about fifteen books per year per family member. Publishers are just now figuring out that that's a lot of books. The author who helped them make this discovery was Terry McMillan.

McMillan wrote a book called *Mama*, and it was published in 1987. Then she set about marketing it herself. She sent out thousands of letters to black organizations offering to read from the book and asking them to promote it. When her second book, *Disappearing Acts*, came out, it was even more successful than her first. Her third, *Waiting to Exhale*, was on the *New York Times* best-seller list for thirty-eight weeks.

When it arrived there, two other books by black women—Walker and Morrison—were waiting for it.

Since then, black writers have been finding it considerably easier to get published. Bebe Moore Campbell writes of the experiences of young black professionals in her novels and in her nonfiction. Tina McElroy Ansa lives on the Sea Islands of Georgia and writes of the small, mythical town of Mulberry. Playwright and poet **Pearl Cleage** has branched out into fierce, insightful political essays.

The books of these women and many, many others are finding their way onto shelves in mainstream bookstores as well as the many new black-oriented bookstores. They are also finding their way onto best-seller lists. They are chosen as book-club selections and excerpted in major magazines.

This continuation of the cultural explosion that began thirty years ago is, in another sense, a continuation of a heritage that began with Lucy Terry, Phillis Wheatley, and the storytellers on slave plantations. The opportunity for black women to be heard and appreciated has been a long time coming, but it has come with a vengeance.

[This introduction incorporates material from the following articles in *Black Women in America: An Historical Encyclopedia*: "Abolition Movement," by Brenda E. Stevenson; "Autobiography," by Nellie Y. McKay; "Harlem Renaissance," by Lorraine Elena Roses; and "Slave Narratives," by Mason Lowance.]

A

Angelou, Maya (1928–)

"You're going to be famous," **Billie Holiday** told Maya Angelou in 1958, "but it won't be for singing." Holiday's pronouncement, of course, was accurate. Angelou's fame did not grow from the nightclub singing she was then doing to support herself and her son. Yet, in a sense, Holiday was mistaken. Since she first put pen to paper, Maya Angelou *has* been singing.

Angelou's early life is familiar to anyone who has read the several volumes of her highly acclaimed autobiography. She was born Marguerite Johnson on April 4, 1928, in St. Louis, Missouri. Her father, Bailey Johnson, was a doorman and, later, a dietician for the navy; her mother, Vivian Johnson, was a registered nurse. When Angelou was three years old, her parents were divorced. They sent her and her four-year-old brother, Bailey, Jr., to live with their paternal grandmother, Annie Henderson, in Stamps, Arkansas. Henderson ran a small general store and managed to scrape by. She continued to do so after her grandchildren joined her.

Angelou's grandmother was one of many strong women who trained her, helped her, and provided her with role models. The people of her church also nurtured her and gave her a sense of belonging to a community. For the rest, childhood in the South was a nightmare. Speaking of Stamps to *Ebony* in 1982, Angelou said:

My town was mean. Mean and poor. All its inhabitants, save for a few whites who owned the dying cotton gin and the faded stores along the one-block downtown area, were farmers. On our side of town, called quarters (a lingering term used wistfully by whites), all the men were dirt farmers, and those women who did not work with their husbands in the bottom land, and many who did, took in washing,

Few books have so powerfully communicated the pain and joy of the black experience as has Maya Angelou's classic I Know Why the Caged Bird Sings. (MOORLAND-SPINGARN)

ironing, or actually left their homes to go to care for the houses of women only a little better off than they, economically, but who believed that their white skin gave them the right to have Negro servants. When I was taken to California by my grandmother, who had raised me, I vowed never to return to the grim, humiliating South. Except for a tentative trip to visit when I was eighteen, I didn't break my promise until I was forty years old.

When she was seven and a half, Angelou left Stamps for a visit with her mother. While there, she was raped by her mother's boyfriend. He was tried, found guilty, and kicked to death in prison. The confused little girl felt responsible for his death and withdrew into herself. "I was mute for five years," she said in an interview for *I Dream a World*. "I wasn't cute and I didn't speak." In frustration, her mother sent her back to Stamps. Her emotional withdrawal caused many to dismiss Angelou as backward, but her grandmother did not give up on her. "I don't know what would have happened to me had I been in an integrated school. In another society, I'm sure I would have been ruled out. But my grandma told me all the time, 'Sister, Mama don't care what these people say about you being a moron, being a idiot. Mama don't care. Mama know, Sister, when you and the good Lord get ready, you're gonna be a preacher.'" Angelou was also helped by a woman named Bertha Flowers, who introduced her to literature. By the time of her graduation from eighth grade, she was at the head of her class.

At this point, Angelou and her brother went to live with their mother in San Francisco. Vivian Baxter Johnson was by then a professional gambler. Her milieu was infi-

nitely more sophisticated and somewhat more dangerous than the world Angelou had left behind in Stamps. She began to pick up some of that sophistication, while at the same time attending George Washington High School and taking drama and dance lessons at the California Labor School. One summer, she went to stay with her father, quarreled with his girlfriend, and ran away. For a month, she lived with other runaway or homeless children in an abandoned van. Back at home in San Francisco, the teenager decided she wanted to be a streetcar conductor; she was attracted to the uniform. Although San Francisco had never had a black conductor and was not eager to hire one, she persisted and, with her mother's support, managed to attain her goal.

At sixteen, Angelou gave birth to her son, Guy. She had not planned her pregnancy but has always been deeply grateful that it happened. "The greatest gift I've ever had was the birth of my son," she said in an interview for *Essence* in 1985, and then went on to tell of the ways he changed her life. "Because, when he was small, I knew more than he did, I expected to be his teacher. So because of him I educated myself. When he was four . . . I taught him to read. But then he'd ask questions and I didn't have the answers, so I started my lifelong love affair with libraries. . . . I've learned an awful lot because of him."

Still, Angelou's life at this time was not easy. In addition to teaching her son, she also had to support him. She could not get a job as a telephone operator. The Women's Army Corps Service (WACS) turned her down because the California Labor School where she had taken dance classes was tainted with the rumor of communism. She was a cook and a nightclub waitress and, for a short time, "madam" for two lesbian prostitutes. She began doing drugs but then quit after seeing what drugs had done to her brother.

When she was twenty-two, Angelou married Tosh Angelos, a white former sailor. Two-and-a-half years later, she left him and became a professional dancer. Eventually, she moved to New York to pursue that career and study with **Pearl Primus**. In 1954, she was cast in a production of *Porgy and Bess* that toured Europe and Africa. When she came back to the United States, she wrote, with Godfrey Cambridge, a revue called *Cabaret for Freedom* to raise funds for the Southern Christian Leadership Conference (SCLC). In 1960–61, she was Northern coordinator of SCLC. Of that time, she later told *Ebony*, "I met the heroic men who came North. Martin Luther King, Ralph Abernathy, Wyatt Tee Walker, and Andrew Young. The matter they brought to New York was decidedly national and even international in its concern, but it was particularly southern. That region had formed their speech; they spoke in sugary slow accents and talked of southern atrocities and southern protest to those same atrocities." In spite of her affinity with these black Southerners, however, Angelou stayed resolutely away from the scenes of her childhood.

Also in 1961, she appeared in an acclaimed off-Broadway production of *The Blacks* by Jean Genet. The cast was a remarkable array of talent, including Louis Gossett, Jr., James Earl Jones, and **Cicely Tyson**. The show was highly successful and ran until 1964, but Angelou stayed with it only a short time because the director-producer refused to pay for music she had written for the show with Ethel Ayer.

By this time, Angelou was writing poetry, short stories, and songs. Her reputation was growing. Then, in 1961, she and her son went to Africa with South African freedom fighter Vusumzi Make. They lived for a time in Cairo. However, Make became angry when Angelou applied for a job as editor of the *Arab Observer* and, combined with other problems, the quarrel led to a break-up. Angelou and her son moved to Ghana, where they remained for several years. She worked as a journalist and taught at the University of Ghana, returning to the United States in 1966. Shortly after her return, as she retells it in a 1975 *Writer's Digest* interview:

My friend and brother, James Baldwin, took me to Jules and Judy Feiffer's home one evening, and the four of us sat up and drank and laughed and told stories until about 3:30 or 4:00 in the morning. And the next morning, Judy Feiffer called the man who later became my editor and said "Do you know the poet Maya Angelou? If you can get her to write a book, you might have something." So he asked me, and I said, "No." I came out to California, and he phoned, and about the third phone call he said, "Well, I guess you're very wise not to do it, because autobiography is the most difficult art form." So I said I would do it, and I did. It was like that. He should have told me that first.

In 1970, *I Know Why the Caged Bird Sings* was published. It became a best-seller and an almost instant classic. It was nominated for a National Book Award. In 1971, Angelou's screenplay *Georgia, Georgia* was made into a film, making her the first black woman to have an original screenplay produced. The four other volumes of her autobiography are, to date, *Gather To-gether in My Name* (1974), *Singin' and Swingin' and Gettin' Merry Like Christmas* (1976), *The Heart of a Woman* (1981), and *All God's Children Need Traveling Shoes* (1986). She has also published several volumes of poetry and has been nominated for the Pulitzer Prize in poetry for one of them, *Just Give Me a Cool Drink of Water 'fore I Diiie* (1971). Other volumes include *Oh Pray My Wings are Gonna Fit Me Well*; *And Still I Rise*; *Shaker, Why Don't You Sing?*; and *I Shall Not be Moved.*

Maya Angelou has continued to live the varied life that makes her autobiographies so fascinating. She appeared on Broadway in 1973 in *Look Away* and was nominated for a Tony Award. That same year, she married writer/cartoonist Paul de Feu. She adapted Sophocles' *Ajax* for the Mark Taper Forum in 1974. In 1977, she received an Emmy nomination for her performance in the miniseries *Roots*. She was appointed to the Bicentennial Commission by President Gerald Ford and to the Commission of International Woman's Year by President Jimmy Carter. In 1979, *I Know Why the Caged Bird Sings* became a made-for-television movie.

In 1981, Angelou and de Feu were divorced, and Angelou moved back to the South. She accepted a lifetime appointment as Reynolds Professor of American Studies at Wake Forest University in Winston-Salem, North Carolina, joined a local church, and began to grow back into a Southern community. The community and her place in it are very different, making her return possible, but she seems also to have found something she left behind a long time ago: Perhaps that something is the spirit that once helped a small girl speak again so that the world might someday hear her truly magnificent voice.

President-elect Bill Clinton asked Angelou to write a poem for his inauguration, the first time a poet had taken part in a presidential inauguration since Robert Frost read his work at the ceremony for John F. Kennedy. Her poem, "On the Pulse of Morning," includes these lines: "Lift up your eyes/Upon this day breaking for you./Give birth again/To the dream."

KATHLEEN THOMPSON

Ansa, Tina McElroy (1949–)

Tina McElroy Ansa is an award-winning novelist who has a storyteller's ways and a gift for seeing magic in ordinary life. Her rich, evocative writing captures the feeling of small town black life in the heart of Georgia.

Born in 1949 in Macon, Georgia, Ansa is the daughter of Walter J. McElroy, a businessman, and Nellie McElroy, a teacher's assistant. She grew up and attended school in Macon, which was not an exotic place, but the quality of black life in a middle-Georgia town gave her a lifetime of material for her novels.

In 1978, she married Jonee Ansa and, on her honeymoon, she discovered the Sea Islands of the Georgia coast. She had never been to the Atlantic before. She had never experienced the rich coastal life of the former slave communities that still dot the islands. These islands had been cut off from the mainland for most of this century because there were no bridges. As a result, a rich, deeply African culture developed there. This place called to her. On her first visit, she realized that she had found home.

Six years later, she moved to the islands, and they became the subject of her first major nonfiction work, *Not Soon Forgotten: Cotton Planters and Plantations of the Golden Isles of Georgia*. The book was published by a historical society in 1987.

However, Ansa was to become known for her novels, not her nonfiction.

Calling on her gift for Southern storytelling, she wrote a novel entitled *Baby of the Family*, published in 1989. It told the story of a girl coming of age in a small town in Georgia in the 1950s. While the girl has mystical gifts, this is very much a novel about teenagers everywhere, learning hard lessons about friendships, boys, and fitting in. In the book, Ansa also tackles hard issues such as racism and the dangers of alcohol. Interwoven with the awareness of adolescent life is Ansa's gift for magic. Her heroine possesses special wisdom and talks to ghosts.

The critics appreciated Ansa's style and sense of place. As *The New York Times* reviewer said, "Ms. Ansa's rich descriptive passages are evocative, often poetic. . . . " This novel won Ansa an American Library Association award for literature for young readers.

Her next novel was set in this same fictional small town. *Ugly Ways*, published in 1993, is about three grown daughters who have gathered to bury their mother. Their mother is not a stereotypically loving black matriarch but someone whom her daughters at times feared and hated. Her daughters, however, find much to admire in their mother and come to terms with the gifts of dignity and self-reliance she gave them.

Ansa remains a storyteller who speaks for small-town life. As she says, "I plan to remain in the little fictional middle-Georgia town of Mulberry my entire writing career. It is here, in the heart of the South and the heart of Georgia, where I explore the African-American family and the African-American community of this decade and earlier ones. It is an infinitely fascinating and rich subject."

ANDRA MEDEA

B

Bambara, Toni Cade (1939–1995)

"It's a tremendous responsibility—responsibility and honor—to be a writer, an artist, a cultural worker . . . whatever you call this vocation. One's got to see what the factory worker sees, what the prisoner sees, what the welfare children see, what the scholar sees, got to see what the ruling-class mythmakers see as well, in order to tell the truth and not get trapped." To tell the truth and not get trapped in the maze of prevailing stereotypes of the black community: this is the writer/cultural nationalist Toni Cade Bambara's self-proclaimed mission as she explained it in a 1983 interview with the critic/scholar Claudia Tate.

The statement reflects the political and social commitment to improving the welfare of the African-American community (especially the urban community) that Bambara first exhibited in the 1950s and 1960s. Moreover, the statement explains Bambara's focus on social messages in all of her short stories and in the two anthologies she edited during the 1970s.

Her two short-story collections, *Gorilla, My Love* (1972) and *The Sea Birds Are Still Alive* (1977), cover a wide range of African-American experiences and personalities—those of children and young adults, men and women, the elderly, the political activist, and the blues singer.

One anthology of essays, poetry, and prose entitled *The Black Woman* (1970) was unprecedented in American letters: It was designed to allow black women from a variety of ages, classes, and occupations to speak their minds on issues relevant to their lives that the Civil Rights and women's liberation movements at the time did not address.

The Salt Eaters (1980), Bambara's first and only novel, grew out of a short story intended to expose the division within the African-American community among the political, psychic, and spiritual forces that had sustained it in its earlier history. The novel proposes a fusion among these internal factions and a linking between the African-American community and other ethnic communities in the United States, namely Asian Americans, Hispanic Americans, Native Americans, and Americans of Caribbean descent.

Therefore, Bambara's understanding of the complexities of African-American life informs all of her work.

Named Toni Cade at her birth in 1939 in New York City to Helen Brent Henderson Cade, she adopted the name Bambara in 1970 when she discovered it as part of a signature on a sketchbook she found in her great-grandmother's trunk. Toni and her brother grew up with their mother in New York City (Harlem, Bedford-Stuyvesant, and Queens) and in Jersey City, New Jersey. She attended various public and private schools in New York, New Jersey, and the southeastern United States.

When asked in interviews who encouraged and influenced her writing, Bambara always names her mother. Helen Cade had lived in Harlem during the 1920s when such black writers as Countee Cullen, Langston

Hughes, Claude McKay, and Wallace Thurman were publishing poetry, fiction, and drama. She developed a respect not only for their literature but for all types of reading materials. When her children were young, Helen Cade, according to Bambara, encouraged them to daydream, to get in touch with their imaginations, and to follow their inner voices. She encouraged Toni Cade's early efforts to write fiction.

Cade published her first short story, "Sweet Town," in *Vendome* magazine in January 1959. That same year she received her B.A. in theater arts/English and the John Golden Award for Fiction from Queens College. The *Long Island Star* awarded her its Pauper Press Award for nonfiction that same year. While enrolled as a graduate student of modern American fiction at the City College of New York, Cade worked as a social worker for the Harlem Welfare Center during 1959–60. She published her second story, "Mississippi Ham Rider," in the summer 1960 *Massachusetts Review*.

In 1961, Cade studied at the Commedia del'Arte in Milan, Italy, and worked there as a freelance writer. Between 1962 and 1965, she completed her master's degree and worked both as program director at Colony House in Brooklyn and as the recreational and occupational therapist for Metropolitan Hospital's psychiatric division. During those years, she also took various positions as either coordinator or director of local neighborhood programs, such as the Equivalency Program, the Veteran Reentry Program, the Eighth Street Play program sponsored by the Lower Eastside Tenants Association, and the Tutorial Program at the Hamilton Fish Park Branch Library.

After receiving her master's degree Bambara taught at the City College of New York from 1965 to 1969 and served as director/adviser for the Theater of the Black Experience and as adviser for various publications sponsored by the City College SEEK program, such as *Obsidian*, *Onyx*, and *The Paper*. During this same four-year period, more of her stories began to appear in various journals and magazines such as the *Liberator*, *Prairie Schooner*, and *Redbook*.

Bambara came of age during the 1960s and early 1970s when both the black cultural nationalist and women's liberation movements were gathering momentum in the United States. She participated in both for a while but soon realized that neither fully addressed the concerns of the African-American woman. Acting upon the advice of the black scholar Addison Gayle, to whom she complained about this omission, Cade edited *The Black Woman: An Anthology*.

This anthology was a first of its kind in the United States. The year it was published, 1970, is now recognized as the beginning of the twentieth-century renaissance of black women's literature. **Toni Morrison**'s *The Bluest Eye*, **Alice Walker's** *The Third Life of Grange Copeland*, and **Louise Meriwether**'s *Daddy Was a Numbers Runner*—first novels for these writers—were published in 1970. In addition, the poets **Nikki Giovanni, Sonia Sanchez,** and **Margaret Walker** each published collections of their poetry in 1970. In editing *The Black Woman*, Cade cut across age, class, and occupational barriers to include poetry, short stories, and essays by well-known writers (Nikki Giovanni, Kay Kindsey, **Audre Lorde**, Alice Walker, and **Paule Marshall**) and women students in the City College SEEK program to show the world what various black women were thinking and doing about both the civil rights and the women's movements.

In the preface, Bambara, still writing under the name Toni Cade, states that she envisioned the collection as a response to all the male "experts"—both black and white—who had been publishing articles and conducting sociological studies on black women. Even the leading white feminists at that time, Cade felt, were not equipped to understand, much less to explain, the feelings and the situation of the African-American woman. The items included in the anthology vary in their opinions on this matter. Most share some of the same concerns about interpersonal relationships in the black community (men and women, parents and children), social issues such as quality education and housing for black Americans, and black women's personal development. It is evident, however, that at that time, these black women were sharply divided along political lines: Some argued for a radical departure from every known form of black female behavior, while others cautioned that too many changes would jeopardize a woman's emotional security.

These differences notwithstanding, this anthology provided an arena for black women's opinions to be voiced en masse at a time when it was assumed that all black people were preoccupied with racial equality. For Cade, the struggle for black equality in America was important but was not to be obtained at the black woman's expense.

Toni Cade Bambara taught in the English department at Livingston College in New Jersey in 1969–70. She was promoted to associate professor at Livingston, and in addition to her teaching duties, she worked as the co-adviser for the Harambee dancers,

the Malcolm Players, and Sisters in Consciousness. In 1974, she received a plaque from the Livingston College black community for service.

Bambara edited another anthology in 1971 entitled *Tales and Stories for Black Folks*. The purpose of this anthology, she explains in the introduction, is to teach young African Americans the historical value of telling stories. She urges her young readers to take the folktales seriously as lessons on human behavior and as examples of living history.

The first section of the collection consists of stories by professional African-American writers such as Langston Hughes, Alice Walker, Pear Crayton, and Ernest Gaines. Bambara's own story "Raymond's Run" is included in this section. The second half of the collection includes an English translation of a fable by the Senegalese Birago Diop and one by the Ghanaian James Aggrey, as well as several selections written by students in a freshman composition course that Bambara taught at Livingston College. As with her first anthology, Bambara's decision to include student essays with selections by older professional writers shows her desire to give young writers a chance to make their talents known to a large audience. In addition, such a mixture in *Tales and Stories for Black Folks* helped inspire her intended audience, African-American high school and college students, to read, to think critically, and to write.

Most of the stories Bambara wrote as Toni Cade between 1959 and 1970 were published in October 1972 in what was to become her most widely read collection, *Gorilla, My Love*. Eight of the fifteen stories in the collection center on young children and adolescents as they move through their neighborhood learning about themselves while responding to their environment. The hallmark of all of Bambara's fiction is her preference for settings outside of the home. The sidewalk, a movie house, a park or athletic field, a local bar, and a community center are some of the locations that recur in Bambara's fiction. Bambara's characters, like those in *Gorilla, My Love*, are rarely at odds with these settings: They move through their immediate neighborhoods comfortably familiar with the people and with each building, street lamp, and fire hydrant they pass. Each character in *Gorilla, My Love* exudes a streetwise sophistication, a confidence in "mother wit" that helps him or her to intimidate immediate rivals.

During the five-year span from 1972 to the publication in 1977 of her second collection of short stories, *The Sea Birds Are Still Alive*, major events took place in Bambara's life that were to have an effect on her writing. She visited Cuba in 1973, where she met with the Federation of Cuban Women. She visited Vietnam in the summer of 1975 as a guest of that nation's Women's Union. Both the federation and the union taught Bambara how effective women's organizations and creative endeavors could be in a political movement.

She relocated with her daughter, Karma, to Atlanta, Georgia, in 1974. Concurrent with her teaching duties as writer-in-residence at **Spelman College** from 1974 to 1977, Bambara became a founding member of the Southern Collective of African American Writers and the Neighborhood Cultural Arts Center, Inc. She was also director of the Pomoja Writers Guild, a founding member and officer of the Conference Committee on Black South Literature

and Art, and an associate/aide for the Institute of the Black World.

The effects of Bambara's travels abroad, her relocation to Atlanta, and her work in so many community art groups can be seen in the stories published in *The Sea Birds Are Still Alive* and in *The Salt Eaters*. In both works, Bambara is intent on using her art to convey social and political messages about the welfare of the African-American community. In 1980, Bambara won the American Book Award for *The Salt Eaters*.

During the early 1980s, Toni Cade Bambara and her daughter relocated to Philadelphia, Pennsylvania. Beginning in 1986, she taught script writing at Scribe Video Center in Phildelphia. During the last decade of her life, she collaborated with Louis Massiah on several television documentaries, the last of which was a documentary about the life of W. E. B DuBois.

She died of cancer in Philadelphia on December 9, 1995.

ALICE A. DECK

Bennett, Gwendolyn (1902–1981)

"To all Negro youth known and unknown who have a song to sing, a story to tell, or a vision for the sons of the earth"—Gwendolyn Bennett wrote these words to dedicate her poem "Usward" to the writers who were showcased at New York's Civic Club gathering on March 21, 1924, spearheaded by Charles S. Johnson, the force behind *Opportunity* and entrepreneur of the New Negro Renaissance, commonly known as the Harlem Renaissance. These writers were the *esprit de corps* that defined the sentiments of the new expressions in black literature. The honorees were introduced to white pub-

Among Gwendolyn Bennett's many contributions to black culture during the twentieth century was her column for the Harlem Renaissance magazine Opportunity. (MOORLAND-SPINGARN)

lishers and included Alain Locke, Countee Cullen, **Jessie Fauset**, Walter White, Helene Johnson, Eric Walrond, and Gwendolyn Bennett. On this occasion Bennett made her debut as a poet and joined with others to energize the New Negro movement.

Bennett was born in Giddings, Texas, on July 8, 1902, the only child of native Texans Joshua Robin and Maime Franke Bennett. Her father was a professional man, a teacher and attorney who had attended Prairie View College in Texas. He was from a large middle-class family, the son of a barber who was proprietor of his own establishment. Her father taught on Indian reservations until the family relocated to Washington, D.C., to escape financial troubles or for some unknown rea-

son. Her mother taught locally in the black grade schools in Texas. Little is known of her mother's family other than that Bennett's maternal grandmother may have been a member of the Algonquian Blackfoot tribe. The marriage was unstable, and her parents separated and then divorced when Bennett was five or six years old.

Realizing that she could not support her daughter adequately on an educator's income, Bennett's mother changed professions from teacher to cosmetologist and manicurist and secured a position in a District of Columbia finishing school for young Caucasian women. After the court granted Bennett's mother custody, mother and daughter settled down comfortably as a single-parent family. However, Bennett's father was incensed that the court awarded custody of his daughter to his former wife and granted him only visitation privileges. He abducted his eight-year-old daughter by pretending to take her to visit a historical site. Fleeing to various cities and towns in the mid-Atlantic region, he subsequently settled in Harrisburg, Pennsylvania; married Marshall Neil Briscoll, also a teacher; and supported his family through janitorial work and odd jobs while hiding out from the family law authorities. Bennett's stepmother was childless but settled into the role of mother as best she knew how: She provided a safe and secure home environment for Bennett, gave her a firm code of morals, values, and ethics, and instilled in her a belief in Christian Science. While employed as a typist for the federal government, Bennett's father passed the Pennsylvania bar examination and relocated his family to Brooklyn, New York, where the three of them settled down as a respectable professional family. Her father died there in 1926.

After her parents divorced, Bennett attended a black public elementary school in the district and continued her elementary education in Harrisburg after the abduction. Her secondary education began at Girls' High School in Brooklyn, where she was the first black participant in the literary and drama societies. Though she disliked the rigidity of academics, she wholeheartedly involved herself in extracurricular activities. A poster she designed brought her first prize in a school contest; she wrote lyrics to the class graduation song and wrote the graduation speech. At Girls' High, she began to dabble in poetry and expressed an interest in art. These two interests were to chart the course of her life's work—love of the pen and love of the brush. Her high school English teacher, Cordelia Went, and her art teacher were instrumental influences in fueling her creative powers. Bennett graduated from Girls' High in 1921.

The 1920s were a great time to be alive. The ambience of Harlem exerted a magnetic pull that drew black artists to Harlem's cultural centers. In 1921, Bennett enrolled in Columbia University's Teachers College department of fine arts, but the overt racism discouraged her and after two years she transferred to Pratt Institute, where she studied art and drama. Repeating her performance at Girls' High, she plunged into creative endeavors by writing and playing the lead in the class play. By the time she graduated from Pratt in 1924, she was well on her way to being a recognized artist in Harlem.

Her reputation as a poet and artist helped her to obtain a faculty position at **Howard University** in its year-old department of art. However, teaching limited her, confined her, and stifled her creativity. To add to the gloom, the pretentious Washington, D.C., black cultural society lacked the closeness, genuineness, and love among peers and colleagues that she had embraced in Harlem. Delta Sigma Theta provided a much needed outlet by granting her a $1,000 scholarship to study art abroad. In December 1924, the novelist Dorothy Canfield Fisher presented her with the scholarship award. In June 1925, Bennett went on leave to study art in Paris.

She experienced all that Paris had to offer, the cafes, the Louvre, the art galleries, the museums, the musicians, the expatriates, Gertrude Stein, Ernest Hemingway, James Joyce, Konrad Bercovici. She even introduced Paul Robeson and his wife Eslanda, a sorority sister, to the Paris scene. Still, she did not know many people, and so she plunged into her studies to divert herself from the loneliness. Bennett studied art at the Académie Colarossi, Académie Julien, and Ecole du Panthéon and studied French literature at the Sorbonne. She was proficient in watercolor, pen and ink, and oils, but batik was her forte. She held batik exhibitions in Paris, and the batik collections she shipped to New York to be sold brought her some much needed income. When she was not studying art, she continued to write; yet, she longed for Harlem. At the end of the 1926 spring session, she returned home to Harlem to resume her role as an artist and writer in the New Negro movement.

She became assistant editor of *Opportunity*, the magazine that helped to launch the literary careers of contributors to the Harlem Renaissance. Her literary gossip column, "Ebony Flute," kept readers abreast of the black social scene. Moreover, she served on the editorial board of *Fire!* Though she loved Harlem, she had faculty responsibilities at Howard University; fall came much too quickly and she returned to Washington, D.C., to teach.

Washington, D.C., associates introduced her to Alfred Joseph Jackson, a Morehouse graduate who was an older medical student at Howard. The two fell in love and their romance put Bennett in violation of the school's ethics rule: By fraternizing with a student, Bennett committed the ultimate faux pas. The administration frowned on her behavior but they did not take any action; nevertheless, she willingly offered her resignation, which the president promptly accepted.

While Jackson completed his internship at Freedman's Hospital (now Howard University Hospital), Bennett returned to New York, disguised herself as a Javanese woman, and secured work in a batik factory. She had to be deceptive because white employers had established racist notions about the type of work black employees should do. Jackson and Bennett were married on April 14, 1928, and he returned to his native Eustis, Florida, to open his medical practice. Bennett did not join him in Florida right away; she taught art education and English at Tennessee A & I College in the summer of 1928. Once again, she faced the reality that teaching was not her vocation, and she joined her husband in Eustis.

The marriage was not a blissful one. The couple was plagued by money problems and segregationist attitudes. Bennett tried to supplement their income by working as a Spanish teacher in Eustis' Lake County School for $50 a month, but the meager salary was insufficient. In addition, the absence of the cultural and social scene that Bennett needed to thrive meant that she stopped writing. She encouraged Jackson to take the New York medical examination. He passed and the couple moved to Hempstead, Long Island, where Jackson established a successful medical practice for a short time before he became a victim of the effects of the Great Depression and died.

Bennett's major literary activities begin with the New Negro Renaissance and end in 1941 when she became a target of the "red scare." The 1920s proved to be the best times for Bennett: she practiced her crafts as poet, writer of fiction, journalist, reviewer, and scholarly writer. As an artist she held exhibitions and illustrated the covers of the December 1923 and March 1924 *Crisis* magazine and the January 1926, July 1926, and December 1930 covers of *Opportunity*. During the 1930s, she earned her teaching degree from Columbia University and took graduate courses at New York University.

This period found her dividing her time among teaching, administration, and community activity. Much of her time was devoted to the Works Progress Administration's Federal Art Project. Under this program she became the director of the Harlem Art Center. The community took a sincere interest in its progress, and it became a successful entity under her administration. Renowned black artist Jacob Lawrence was one of her students.

Her tenure as director of the center came to an abrupt halt when she was accused of being a Communist. During the 1940s, she tried to piece together her tattered career by founding the Jefferson School for Democracy and the George Washington Carver School, but the House Un-American Activities Committee targeted these schools, and they subsequently closed.

In 1940, Bennett married Richard Crosscup, a white Harvard graduate and English teacher who had volunteered his time at the Carver School. She moved with him to Kutztown, Pennsylvania, where they opened an antiques store. He died in January 1980.

Bennett's poetry reflects her love for the literary and the visual, a combination that for her was inseparable. She was the renaissance woman of the New Negro movement. She died in May 1981, having given the black art world a great gift for over twenty years—herself.

GERRI BATES

Bonner, Marita (1899–1971)

"On Being Young—a Woman—and Colored," a 1925 essay written by Marita Bonner and published in *Crisis*, embodies her concern for the deplorable conditions that black Americans endure, particularly black women. In this essay, Bonner speaks of the constraints placed on black women, emphasizing that females should seek husbands they can look up to without looking down on themselves. She also suggests that black women are doubly victimized by those who devalue their race and gender. Bonner advises young black women to avoid bitterness and, instead, to quietly outthink their oppressors.

Publishing between world wars from 1925 to 1941 in two leading magazines, *Opportunity* and *Crisis*, essayist, playwright, and short-story writer Marita Bonner treated a host of themes including miscegenation, the tragic mulatto, generational conflicts, European definitions of female respectability, dreams deferred, the destructiveness of the urban environment, racial revolution in America, infidelity, Southern decadence, class bias, and interracial ties.

One of four children, Marita Bonner was born on June 16, 1899, in Boston to Joseph Andrew and Mary Anne (Noel) Bonner. Educated locally, Bonner attended Brookline High School before entering Radcliffe College, where she studied English and comparative literature between 1918 and 1922. While in college, Bonner began to teach at a local high school. After graduation, she taught in Bluefield, West Virginia, and then in Washington, D.C., for eight years, where she became friends with **Georgia Douglas Johnson**, Langston Hughes, **May Miller**, Countee Cullen, Alain Locke, **Jessie Fauset**, S. Randolph Edmonds, Willis Richardson, and Jean Toomer.

Between 1922 and 1930, Bonner linked herself to the "S" Salon, a group of writers who met weekly at Georgia Douglas Johnson's home. She was nurtured and encouraged to write by this cadre of writers who became major figures of the black renaissance that occurred in such urban areas as Harlem, Chicago, and Washington, D.C. It was during this period that she published two essays that captured the spirit of the black renaissance: In addition to "On Being Young—a Woman—and Colored," which won first place in the *Crisis* literary contest of 1925, Bonner published "The Young Blood Hungers," which resonates with the warning of violence to come as a result of poor race relations in America.

Bonner wrote several noteworthy experimental plays during her years in Washington, D.C., including *The Pot Maker*, which levels an indictment against infidelity; *The Purple Flower*, which calls for a bloody revolution to temper racism; and *Exit—An Illusion*, which deals with the complications of mixed ancestry.

After marrying Rhode Island native and Brown University graduate William Almy Occomy in 1930, she moved to Chicago, where she raised three children, William Almy, Jr., Warwick Gale Noel, and Marita Joyce, who helped to recover her mother's texts in *Frye Street and Environs: The Collected Works of Marita Bonner Occomy* (1987).

Bonner concentrated exclusively on developing her craft in fiction in the 1930s, a choice that led to her winning several first- and second-place literary prizes offered by *Crisis* and *Opportunity*. The fictitious, multiethnic Frye Street of Chicago is the setting of her short stories. Preoccupied with the destructiveness of the urban environment, her Chicago stories deal with class and color demarcations, poverty, and poor housing. Some of Bonner's stories written in the early 1930s may have influenced Richard Wright, who knew Bonner and her work. Bonner's "Tin Can" resembles in its plot Wright's *Native Son* (1940).

Although Bonner rarely wrote after 1941, she continued to teach periodically during the forty-one years she lived in Chicago, including working with mentally handicapped persons. She died on December 6, 1971, of injuries sustained in a fire in her Chicago apartment.

Marita Bonner's major literary contribution is her characterization of the urban environment as a corrupting force. Her portraits of elite black Chicagoans and their poor counterparts reflect the negative impact of the urban environment on human dignity. Her characters belong to a lost world that cramps people in substandard housing, turns middle-class African Americans against recently immigrated, uneducated Southerners, and allows homeless and other poor people to die unattended. Bonner's mark is no small one, considering that she frequently captured literary prizes and served as a role model to aspiring writers who looked to her innovative craft. Educated at one of the most prestigious universities in America, Bonner rejected prescriptive roles. By balancing a writing career with family responsibilities and teaching, Marita Bonner exemplified the lessons of her first published work, "On Being Young—a Woman—and Colored."

ELIZABETH BROWN-GUILLORY

Brooks, Gwendolyn (1917–)

A poem is a search for understanding, and a poet is a seeker of understanding. In that sense, and in every other, Gwendolyn Brooks is one of the finest contemporary poets. At a time when the American poetry establishment is looking for a voice, Brooks' finely tuned but thoroughly accessible poetry seems every year more valuable.

Gwendolyn Elizabeth Brooks was born on June 7, 1917, in Topeka, Kansas, to David Anderson Brooks and Keziah Corinne Wims Brooks. Her mother's family lived in Topeka, to which her mother returned for a few weeks to give birth, but Brooks is a Chicago poet: As a child, she went to Chicago schools and played in Chicago streets. She began to compose poetry when she was seven and recorded it in notebooks when she was eleven, nurtured by loving parents who imbued her with a love of songs, stories, and learning.

During her otherwise isolating adolescence (she attended predominantly white high schools), Brooks found a connection with other poets. That T. S. Eliot, Ezra Pound, and Wallace Stevens were white men was of much less importance than that they were poets, that they shared with her this thing that *was* life—writing poems. Then, at sixteen, Brooks met Langston Hughes, who read her poetry and encouraged her. His enthusiasm for her work was of tremendous importance to the young poet.

After graduating from high school, Brooks went to Woodrow Wilson Junior College for two years. Two years after that, she met Henry Lowington Blakely II. They were married not long after they met and are still, though they separated from 1969 to 1973.

In 1941, Brooks' development as a poet received another boost when Inez Cunningham Stark presented a class on modern poetry at the South Side Community Art Center. Brooks experienced the stimulation of talk, criticism, and sharing with other writers. Two years later she received an award at the Midwestern Writers' Conference, an award that led indirectly to the publication of her first book of poetry, *A Street in Bronzeville*. The reviews were highly favorable, and the book brought Brooks to the attention of other black writers. She also received Guggenheim fellowships in 1946 and 1947 and grants from the American Academy of Arts and Letters and the National Institute of Arts and Letters in 1946.

Her next book, *Annie Allen*, won the Pulitzer Prize for poetry in 1950. Brooks was the first black person, man or woman, to receive the award in any category. Her autobiographical novel, *Maud Martha*, was published in 1953, and in 1956, her first book of children's poetry, *Bronzeville Boys and Girls*, appeared.

The Bean Eaters, a collection of poetry that appeared in 1960, speaks in powerful, moving, and sometimes bitterly ironic language of the lives of black people. Its poems are often anthologized in high school and college literature texts and are among the classics of American poetry. In 1968, Brooks was named Poet Laureate of Illinois, succeeding Carl Sandburg. She began to conduct poetry contests for young people with prize money she often provided herself and poetry workshops, including at least one for the Chicago gang, the Blackstone Rangers. She also toured extensively, reading her poetry at schools and prisons, libraries and bookstores.

The first black person to receive the Pulitzer Prize, poet Gwendolyn Brooks speaks with simple eloquence of the human condition. (SCHOMBURG CENTER)

In the late 1960s, a change in black consciousness spread through America, and Gwendolyn Brooks let it carry her further along on her poetic path. Her 1968 book, *In the Mecca*, contains a long narrative poem interrupted by ballads and balladlike interpolations. Set in the old Mecca Building in Chicago, it details a mother's search for a lost child among the crowded, violent, hate-and-anger-filled inhabitants of the building. Hortense Spillers calls the Brooks who wrote *In the Mecca* "Gwendolyn the terrible."

With *Riot*, in 1969, Brooks began to publish exclusively with black presses. She also began, as she put it, to "*clarify* my language. I want these poems to be free. I want them to be direct without sacrificing the kinds of music, the picturemaking I've always been interested in." This focus on clarity and simplifying is, in part, a way of reaching out to an ever larger audience of black readers. It also reflects a maturing that can be seen in the great lyric poets of our language. Simplicity in poetry usually comes late in a poet's life, when confidence is at its height.

In *Family Pictures* (1970), Brooks' natural optimism begins to reemerge. Though never blind to the pain of the black experience, Brooks has only rarely reflected its darkest aspects. A certain belief in the positive possibilities of the human condition can probably be expected in a woman who had a happy childhood, who shares a strong lifelong love relationship, who has found fulfillment as an artist in a lifetime of creative work, and who, in the words of her daughter Nora, "opens places for people—new doorways and mindpaths."

Her recent publications include *The Near-Johannesburg Boy* (1986), *Blacks* (1987), *Gottschalk and the Grand Taran-* *telle* (1988), *Winnie* (a poem honoring Winnie Mandela, 1989), and *Children Coming Home* (1991).

In 1994 the National Book Foundation, which oversees the National Book Awards, awarded Brooks its medal for distinguished contributions to American letters.

KATHLEEN THOMPSON

Brown, Linda Beatrice (1939–)

"Yes, I am an African-American writer. Yes, I am a woman writer. Yes, I am an American writer, but I am also none of these," Linda Beatrice Brown said in a 1989 interview. "[M]y concerns are that the struggle for social equality go forward . . . My concerns are global, and I think we start with what's immediate." The interview concluded with a modest request: "That I might not be put in niches is probably the thing I would like to ask the most."

In fact, it is hard to put Brown in niches. Although she places her fiction writing first, she was first published as a poet, and she acknowledges that her fiction is often like poetry. Her public life has similar intersections. Although she has been a college teacher most of her adult life, has spoken on campuses, and has participated in academic conferences all over the country, she has remained committed to the community beyond the academy, serving, for example, on boards and committees for her church, the North Carolina Writers Network, and the Black Child Development Institute, and speaking in communities throughout the state of North Carolina.

Linda Beatrice Brown was born in Akron, Ohio, on March 14, 1939, to Raymond and Edith Player Brown. In spite of being raised in the North, Brown feels that her life has been greatly influenced by her mother's childhood in Mississippi before her father took the family to Ohio in order to escape Southern racism. Brown went South to Bennett College in Greensboro, North Carolina. There she heard Langston Hughes and Sterling Brown. As a junior, she wrote what would be her first published poem, "Precocious Curiosity," which appeared in the 1962 collection *Beyond the Blues* (edited by Rosey Pool).

Her first book, *A Love Song to Black Men* (1974), which includes poems written over more than a decade, reflects the experimental forms, the celebration of being black, the outrage at injustice and racism, and the vitality and humor—albeit sardonic—associated with the black poets who emerged from the 1960s. Although many of the poems are directed outward, in others the voice is lyrical and quiet. One recognizes the dual impulses of personal spirituality and public responsibility that continue to motivate her life and her art. The appearance of *Love Song* placed Brown within a national community of black writers whose works continue to sustain her. Her poems have since appeared in such publications as *The Black Scholar, Encore, Ebony, Jr.,* and *Cricket, A Magazine for Children.* The 1980s marked Brown's debut as a fiction writer.

Stories that a close friend at Bennett told her about growing up in Greensboro and about a local woman the friend had known became the stimulus for Brown's first novel, *Rainbow Roun Mah Shoulder* (1984). The manuscript of *Rainbow Roun Mah Shoulder* was the unanimous choice for first prize in a literary contest sponsored by the North Carolina Cultural Arts Coalition and Carolina Wren Press. After *Rainbow* was published by Carolina Wren Press in 1984,

Novelist Linda Beatrice Brown, author of Rainbow Roun Mah Shoulder *(1984), is also a poet and a teacher.* (LYNDON C. LLOYD)

the National Endowment for the Arts selected the novel as one of a few titles to represent new American writing in international book exhibits. In 1989, Ballantine issued an edition, essentially the same but with some additions. *Rainbow* tells the story of Rebecca Florice, a woman who must balance mystical healing powers with a complex personal life within the racist Southern setting of Greensboro from the 1920s to the 1950s.

Brown's second novel, *Crossing Over Jordan* (1995), is also set primarily in North Carolina. Each section begins with a short scene in a successive month of 2012, with the ninety-six-year-old Story Temple Greene and her daughter Hermine coping with old age and the apparent tedium of constant contact and issues. What lies behind this "present" is the deep and moving subject of the novel, a novel that draws readers into the consequences of slavery over many generations as it reveals these highly original individuals.

A Woodrow Wilson Teaching Fellow at Case Western Reserve University, Brown received her M.A. in English literature in 1962 and held a teaching fellowship at Kent State University from 1962 to 1964. In 1967 and 1969, she and Harold Bragg, whom she had married in 1962, had their children, Christopher and Willa. From 1970 to 1986, Brown served on the English faculty of the Residential College of the University of North Carolina at Greensboro. She earned a Ph.D., with specialties in creative writing and black literature, from Union Graduate School in Cincinnati in 1980, and during this dissertation year held a fellowship from the National Fellowships Fund. From 1986 to 1992, Brown held a faculty position at Guilford College in Greensboro, where she taught African-American literature and creative writing. In 1992, Brown returned to Bennett College, her alma mater, where she is Distinguished Professor of Humanities and holds the Willa B. Player Chair in the Humanities.

Since the 1989 edition of *Rainbow*, the author has gone by her birth name, Linda Beatrice Brown, rather than Linda Brown Bragg. Brown has done some collaborating with her husband, artist Vandorn Hinnant, most recently in a gallery installment, "Piercing the Fractal," for *Crossing over Jordan*.

MARY HUGHES BROOKHART

Burroughs, Margaret (1917–)

For several decades, writer, artist, educator, museologist, organizer, and social activist Margaret Taylor Goss Burroughs has used a variety of media to describe, teach, preserve, and enhance humane values in general and the black experience in particular. Her feelings are best expressed in these lines from perhaps her most famous poem, "What Shall I Tell My Children Who Are Black?":

I have drunk deeply of late from the fountain
Of my black culture, sat at the knee and learned
From Mother Africa, discovered the truth of my heritage,
The truth, so often obscured and omitted.
And I find I have much to say to my black children.
I will lift up their heads in proud blackness
With the story of their fathers and fathers' Fathers.

Although this multitalented woman has been involved in educational and artistic activities all over the world, a great deal of her efforts have taken place in the city of Chicago, where she has been a decided cultural influence.

Margaret Burroughs taught art in Chicago for several decades at the elementary, secondary, and college levels; her writings include three books for children and two volumes of poetry; her works of art represent several forms, from *Still Life Oil on Canvas*, a painting from the 1940s, to *Black Queen*, a bronze sculpture done in 1968. But many consider her most significant contribution to be the founding, in 1961, of the Ebony Museum of African-American History (later the DuSable

Museum of African-American History and Art). This institution, which was established on Chicago's South Side, was named after the black Haitian trader Jean-Baptiste Point DuSable, the city's first permanent resident. Founding a museum of black culture and naming it after a black man whom several have tried to write out of the history of Chicago is typical of Margaret Burroughs' lifelong mission to restore to black people a greater sense of their culture and heritage.

Born in Saint Rose, Louisiana, on November 1, 1917, Margaret Taylor migrated to Chicago with her family at a young age. Like many other black Southerners of that era, her parents, Alexander and Octavia Taylor, left the South to seek a better life.

Margaret Taylor availed herself of many of the educational opportunities that Chicago had to offer: She graduated from Englewood High School in 1933 and from Chicago Teachers College (now Chicago State University) in 1937; later, she studied at the prestigious Art Institute of Chicago, where she was awarded a bachelor of fine arts in 1944 and a master of fine arts in 1948.

In 1939, she married Bernard Goss, an artist who had graduated from the University of Iowa in 1935 and studied at the Art Institute of Chicago from 1935 to 1937. His painting *Always the Dirty Work* was included in an exhibit at Hull House, along with the work of other black artists. Both Margaret and Bernard were active in the Chicago arts community. The couple had a daughter named Gayle.

During the first half of the 1940s Margaret Taylor Goss taught art in elementary school while developing her own skills as an artist. One of her works during this period was an egg tempera on board entitled *I've*

The DuSable Museum of African-American History, one of Chicago's most distinctive and distinguished cultural institutions, was founded by poet and artist Margaret Burroughs, with her husband, Charles. She is seen here receiving a lithographic portrait of Fannie Lou Hamer. (SCHOMBURG CENTER)

Been in Some Big Towns. She divorced Goss and joined the faculty of DuSable High School, where she would teach art for more than twenty years (1946–69). In 1947, she published her first book, a children's book called *Jasper, the Drummin' Boy.*

On December 23, 1949, she married Charles Gordon Burroughs, who was to be an active and supportive participant in her many endeavors. During the following years, she was extremely productive both as a writer and as an artist. She wrote two more children's books: *Did You Feed My Cow? Rhymes and Games from City Streets and Country Lanes* (1955) and *Whip Me Whop Me Pudding and Other Stories of Riley Rabbit and His Fabulous Friends* (1966).

Burroughs' artwork has covered an impressive range of media. She painted a watercolor, *Ribbon Man, Mexico City Market,* after a year of study at the Institute of

Painting and Sculpture in Mexico. Some of her other works include *Insect,* an oil painting (1963); pen and ink sketches from the march on Washington (1963); *Head,* a marble sculpture (1965); and two bronzes in 1968, *Black Queen* and *Head.* Burroughs' art has been exhibited widely, from the South Side Community Center of Chicago to the Studio Museum in Harlem to the Soviet Union. Her works also have been reproduced in numerous newspapers and magazines, such as *Arts in Society, Connoisseur, Art News,* and the Boston *Globe.* In 1962, *Freedomways* featured four of her prints depicting black historical figures and integrated scenes: *Sojourner Truth, Playground Peace, Riding Together,* and *Crispus Attucks.*

In 1961, with the help of her husband, Charles, Burroughs founded in their South Side Chicago home the Ebony Museum of African American History. The purpose of the museum was to provide a cultural resource that would make the art, history, and literature of the black experience available to the community. Later named the DuSable Museum of African-American History, the institution was eventually relocated to Washington Park, where the City of Chicago had donated property. In early 1991, the museum was awarded a Build Illinois appropriation, and later in the year preparations were made to add a new $3 million wing. Margaret Burroughs served as executive director of the DuSable Museum from its founding in 1961 until 1984 and since then has been director emeritus.

At the end of the 1960s, Burroughs was both an inspiration for and a major participant in the black cultural movement. In 1967, she and Broadside Press publisher Dudley Randall edited *For Malcolm: Poems on the Life and Death of Malcolm X,* an anthology of poems by many celebrated black writers and cultural leaders, including Mari Evans, Robert Hayden, Etheridge Knight, **Margaret Walker,** Amiri Baraka, **Sonia Sanchez,** and Burroughs herself, whose contribution is "Brother Freedom." In 1968, Burroughs published a volume of her own poems, *What Shall I Tell My Children Who Are Black?* The title poem portrays the psychological damage of racism:

> What shall I tell my children who are black
> Of what it means to be a captive in this
>   dark skin.
> What shall I tell my dear one, fruit of my
>   womb,
> Of how beautiful they are when ever-
>   where they turn
> They are faced with abhorrence of every-
>   thing that is black.
> Villains are black with black hearts.
> A black cow gives no milk.
> A black hen lays no eggs.
> Bad news comes bordered in black, black
>   is evil. . . .

Some poems, such as "Lines to Blood Brothers and Sisters," "The Beauty of Black," "Poem on Africa," and "Message to Soul Sisters," carry a black cultural theme. "Open Letter to Black Youth of Alabama and Other Places" continues her message of black pride and addresses an anonymous piece, included in the book's preface, that was written by a student at Alabama Agricultural and Mechanical College during an appearance by Burroughs as a guest lecturer at the Second Negro Writers Conference in 1966:

Dear Black Young People:
Recently, I had the pleasure of being a
  guest on the
Campus of Alabama
A. & M. and your Second Writers Confer-
  rence. On seeing
My "Natural" or
"Afro" hairdo, I noted that some of you
  students
Seemed to go into a state of
shock. Later someone asked the questions:
  "Why
is she wearing her hair
like that? Doesn't she know it looks a
mess? What
is she trying to prove?" . . .

I am wearing my hair like this to let the
world know that I am opposed to
the position of second-class citizenship
  which
black people have been
consigned to in this country. Further, I
  wear
it this way as a reminder to
black people that they should be proud of
  their
own beauty and their heritage
both in Africa and the New World. . . .

Other poems in this volume carry more
personal messages: "Apology to My Little
Daughter for Apparent Neglect," "Lines for
My Mother," and "Memorial for My Father," which reflects folk traditions from
African-American culture as well as renders
a vivid portrait:

My father was good at telling ghost stories.
He told us one about the time when
He was cook for a levee gang and whenever
He went into the cooks' shanty, how the
  skillets

And pots had been moved from the stove
  with
Not a soul around. He had seen many
  spirits
And ghosts, having been born with a veil
  over
His eyes

In 1970, she published a second volume
of poetry, *Africa, My Africa!*, after she had
traveled to that continent. The verses provide emotional and descriptive chronicles of
her visit. The poem, "On My Return Home"
begins as follows:

I am home now
At last I've linked the circle round
For so long homeless
Now my own hearth found
I, who was
So forcibly removed am now returning
To gather parts of me that were left behind
In Africa, my sacred lands
And best beloved ancestral lands.

Other poems in this volume, such as
"From the Portal at Legon," "Elmina," and
"The Women of Ghana," examine many
topics, including the devastation of slavery,
the richness of African history and culture,
the beauty of African women, and African
daily life. Moreover, the ironic intrusion of
Western culture into African life is described
in "Of Mercedes Benzes and the Big Coke"
and "The Fetish Princess," whose business
is so good that she owns the only Mercedes
in town and, following her seances, "She
herself is transformed by the TV magic."
  In 1968, Burroughs taught African and
African-American art history at the Art Institute of Chicago. The following year, she
became a professor of humanities at Ken-

nedy-King Community College, where she was a member of the faculty until 1979.

Margaret Burroughs continues to be a dynamic civic and cultural leader. Since the mid-1980s, for example, she has served on the board of the Chicago Park District. Numerous awards and honors have been issued in recognition of her achievements, including a Doctorate of Humane Letters from Lewis University in Illinois and other honorary degrees from Chicago State University, Columbia College, and the Art Institute of Chicago. Mayor Harold Washington declared February 1, 1986, Dr. Margaret Burroughs Day in Chicago. In 1991, Senator Paul Simon of Illinois, inspired by an article in the *Chicago Sun-Times,* read into the Senate *Congressional Record* "What Shall I Tell My Children Who Are Black?," which concludes as follows:

> I must find the truth of heritage for myself
> And pass it on to them. In years to come I
>   believe
> Because I have armed them with the truth,
> My children.
> And their children's children will venerate
>   me.
> For it is the truth that will make us free!

ROSEMARY STEVENSON

Butler, Octavia E. (1947–)

Octavia E. Butler is the first African-American woman to gain popularity and critical acclaim as a major science fiction writer. The author of ten novels and numerous short stories, she has won two of science fiction's most prestigious awards, the Nebula and the Hugo.

Butler's novels include *Patternmaster* (1976), *Survivor* (1978), *Mind of My Mind*

(1977), *Kindred* (1979), *Wild Seed* (1980), *Clay's Ark* (1984), *Dawn* (1987), *Adulthood Rites* (1988), *Imago* (1989), and *Parable of the Sower* (1993); her other writings include "Speech Sounds," a short story that won a Hugo Award in 1984, and the novelette, *Bloodchild*, which won a 1984 Nebula Award and a 1985 Hugo.

An enthusiastic reader, Butler constantly researches new developments in biology, genetics, and the physical sciences, as well as keeping up with current events; in her stories, however, character development, human relationships, and social concerns predominate over intergalactic hardware. A substantial portion of her writing features black women who find the strength to cope with bigotry, persecution, and pain as well as efforts to keep them in their place.

Born in Pasadena, California, on June 22, 1947, Octavia Estelle Butler was the only child of a maid and a shoeshine man. A sensitive, introspective young girl, she became interested in science fiction after being turned off by the standard reading fare of elementary schools. In an essay entitled "Why I Write," she explains: "When I discovered that my first-grade teacher expected me to be content with Dick and Jane, I asked my mother if I could have a library card. From the day she took me to get one, I was a regular at the fairy tale shelves. I also explored, read anything else that looked interesting, got hooked on horse stories for a while, then discovered science fiction."

Although fascinated by the literature of science fiction, she was somewhat disconcerted by the fact that black characters were rare in the genre. Moreover, she was disturbed by the stereotypical images of women and found that most science fiction writing emphasized ideas and machinery over character development. As early as age thirteen Butler was producing stories that, she later concluded, had been heavily influenced by the white-male-oriented science fiction stories she had read.

As an adult, Butler continued to write. After graduating from Pasadena City College, she attended California State University in Los Angeles, but she credits several nonacademic programs for helping her perfect her craft. Two of the most helpful were the Open Door Program of the Screen Writers Guild of America, West (1969–70) and the Clarion Science Fiction Writers Workshop (1970). With the resolve shown by some of her characters, she continued to write in spite of rejection by publishers, financial hardship, and discouragment from family and friends who advised her to get a "real" job. Her obstinacy was later vindicated, however. In 1971, as a result of her participation in the Clarion workshop, one of her short stories, "Crossover," appeared in the Clarion anthology. Five years later, her first novel was published by Doubleday.

Five of Butler's first six novels (*Patternmaster, Mind of My Mind, Survivor, Wild Seed,* and *Clay's Ark*) were part of her patternist series. A prominent figure in this series is Doro, a 4,000-year-old Nubian whose mentally linked descendants form the "pattern." Doro is a "psychic vampire" who takes over other people's bodies at will and uses terror to control his progeny in the pattern. Butler admits in "Why I Write" that there is a connection between herself and this frightening character: "I have a running character named Doro in my patternist novels. Sometimes I can see all too clearly the part of myself from which he was created. Writers, too, are a species of vampires—happily nonlethal, usually harmless, but constantly acquiring bits and pieces of other people's lives."

Patternmaster, the first novel in the patternist saga, describes the struggle between two brothers to inherit control of the pattern from their dying father, the Patternmaster Royal. Coransee, the elder son, is a brutal man who controls with force; his younger brother, Teray, in contrast, relies more on his mental powers. In his struggle to defeat his brother as well as to prevail against attacks by the bestial Clayarks, Teray obtains essential support from Amber, a black woman with healing powers and a strong sense of her own independence. Set in the future, this novel goes far beyond a struggle between good and evil; it also comments on society's class structure, the struggle between brute force and cerebral powers, and the role of women.

Mind of My Mind takes place in Los Angeles and concerns the devastating struggle between the brutal and powerful Doro and his mentally linked community in the pattern led by his daughter, Mary. Unlike Doro, who is compelled to kill and take over other people's bodies, Mary takes over other people's minds by linking them to hers in the pattern. The author provides the following information about how the development of this character relates to Butler's chilling insight into human behavior: "I deliberately made ... Mary Larkin my opposite. She was small, lighter-skinned, feisty, and eventually very powerful. . . . But Mary Larkin didn't handle power very well. I suspect that most people, given sudden power, would have trouble with it. . . . Their careless public utterances may become policy before they realize it. Their pride can become something other people die for. I let this happen to Mary in *Mind of My Mind* after watching it happen in the real world, in the White House every four years."

Eventually Mary becomes wiser in her use of power and finally is able to summon the collective strength of her telepathic community in order to defeat Doro and free the pattern from his malevolent control. Another interesting character in this novel is Mary's grandmother, Emma, whose past is compellingly revealed in one of Butler's subsequent novels, *Wild Seed*.

The patternist novel following *Mind of My Mind* is *Survivor*, which is set in the future. It describes the efforts of Alanna, an Afro-Asian "wild child," to survive amid many ongoing conflicts, including one on earth between the telepathic Patternists and the diseased inferior creatures, the Clayarks. On another planet, an ongoing struggle is being waged by two rival groups of the furry Kohns. In this novel, which examines prejudice based on caste and color, Alanna is forced to mate with a Kohn creature but is able to overcome many difficult situations by her willingness to adapt to an alien environment.

The fourth patternist novel, *Wild Seed*, is a historical saga that incorporates a great deal of the black experience, including slavery. Set in several centuries in the past in Africa and America, this story chronicles the relationship between Doro, the Nubian psychic vampire in *Mind of My Mind*, and the African healer, Anyanwu, who appeared as Emma in that same story. Doro forces many people under his control to participate in breeding projects in order to produce Patternists who will be under his control. Anyanwu, a powerful healer who has the ability to alter her own form, is Doro's lover and at other times struggles against his terrifying activities.

The final novel in the patternist series is *Clay's Ark,* in which the black astronaut Eli, the sole survivor of a trip into space, returns to Earth infected with, and involuntarily spreads, the clayark disease, which spawns a debased race of mutants called the Clayarks, who have plagued the Patternists throughout several earlier novels.

Butler's 1979 novel, *Kindred,* is a deviation from the patternist theme prevalent in her other novels. Dana, a black woman in twentieth-century Los Angeles, is summoned back in time to an antebellum Maryland plantation in order to save the life of the plantation owner's son. Dana is compelled to save the life of this reckless and obnoxious white boy because he is destined to impregnate a black woman with a child who is to become Dana's ancestor. Her travel back into another era is especially perilous because during much of this time, she must be disguised as a slave and learn firsthand the brutalities of slavery.

Butler's award-winning novelette *Bloodchild* offers an intriguing exploration of a reversal of gender roles. In this story, males are used for pregnancy and reproduction.

Butler's most recent series of novels, *Dawn, Adulthood Rites,* and *Imago,* are part of her Xenogenesis trilogy, a series that examines efforts by the human race to survive both a devastating war on Earth and the gene-swapping activities of extraterrestrials. Much of the story is centered around a black woman, Lilith Iyapo, and her son, Akin, who is the offspring of Lilith, an Asian father, and an extraterrestrial. The alien being who is the third element in the propagation process is one of the Oankali, the race that has captured human survivors of the war on Earth and has forced them to breed and exchange genes with them. As a result, both the humans and the Oankali will undergo genetic transformation.

One of the observations made by the extraterrestrials is that humans have the contradictory characteristics of being both intelligent and hierarchical. The second characteristic, which results in prejudice, class divisions, and conflict, makes it almost inevitable that humankind will eventually destroy itself even without the interference of aliens.

Butler's tenth novel is *Parable of the Sower*, which is set in twenty-first century California. In a society that has been ravaged by lawlessness, violence, and structural decay, Lauren Olamina, a young black woman, struggles to survive, to adapt to change, and to maintain hope.

Octavia Butler resides in Los Angeles where, in addition to writing, she volunteers her time as a literacy instructor. Her intense intellectual and emotional involvement in the human experience, as well as her keen powers of observation, continues to be an integral part of her storytelling. As she reveals in the conclusion to her essay "Why I Write," "I began to write consciously, deliberately, about people who were afraid and who functioned in spite of their fear. People who failed sometimes and were not destroyed. . . . Every story I write adds to me a little, changes me a little, forces me to reexamine an attitude or belief, causes me to research and learn, helps me to understand people and grow. . . . Every story I create creates me. I write to create myself."

ROSEMARY STEVENSON

C

Campbell, Bebe Moore (19??–)

An author of fiction and nonfiction, Bebe Moore Campbell is no stranger to controversy. Whether exploring the sweetness and depth of black fatherhood, the pressures on successful women, or sexual harassment in the work place, Campbell is willing to look at things in ways that make people pay attention.

Bebe Moore Campbell was born to a mother who was a social worker and a father who became a paraplegic after an auto accident. Her parents separated while she was young, and she spent most of the school year with her mother and grandmother in Philadelphia. Summers she spent with her father in his family home in North Carolina. In both places, she found warmth and affection, especially from the men in her father's family. These were experiences she later turned into one of her most successful books.

Campbell began her career as a freelance journalist, selling fiction to *Essence* first and then essays and articles to publications such as the *New York Times* Magazine, the *Washington Post*, and *Black Enterprise*.

In 1978, Campbell was awarded the National Association of Negro Business and Professional Women Award for Body of Work, after she had published, as she put it, "about five things." In 1980, Campbell's short story, "Old Lady Shoes," won a National Endowment for the Arts literary grant. Encouraged, she adapted the story as a radio play and won the Midwest Radio Theatre Workshop Competition.

Later in the 1980s, Campbell wrote an article for *Savvy* on the anger that successful women sometimes face from their men. An unexpectedly powerful response resulted in television appearances on *Oprah* and *Donahue*. Sensing that she had tapped into an important issue, she followed the article with her first nonfiction book, *Successful Women, Angry Men*, published in 1987.

Next came an autobiographical book, *Sweet Summer: Growing Up With and Without My Dad*, published in 1989. In this book, Campbell wrote about her childhood and the importance of growing up surrounded by loving, approving male figures.

Campbell also came to terms with her anger at black men who date white women. She was at Disneyland when she realized she was counting interracial couples instead of having fun with her family. She decided, for her family's sake, that she needed to deal with her anger. The resulting essay was published in the *New York Times* and stirred widespread debate.

Her next book was a novel, *Your Blues Ain't Like Mine*, released in 1992. This work won the 1993 NAACP Image Award for Literature. Next came a controversial novel, *Brothers and Sisters*, published in 1994. It told the story of a black woman, a middle-manager who makes friends with a white woman on her job. Later, the white woman accuses their black male boss of sexual harassment. This novel of conflicting loyalties in corporate America did not present any easy answers, but it stimulated dialogue between whites and blacks and between men and women.

Campbell is also a regular guest and commentator on National Public Radio's *Morning Edition,* a daily news commentary. There, as always, Campbell shows a journalist's insightful eye and the courage not to tiptoe around controversy.

ANDRA MEDEA

Cary, Lorene (1956–)

"I was drawn into Lorene Cary's story," said *New York Times* reviewer Phillip Lopate of her memoir, *Black Ice,* "and sorry that it ended before I could receive the full impact of her life. I would be happy to follow this narrator anywhere, and hope there will be sequels. . . ." Whether they will be autobiographical or not, Cary seems destined to make sure that there will be many sequels.

Lorene Cary born in Philadelphia, Pennsylvania, on November 29, 1956. Because both of her parents were teachers, it was not surprising that education was highly valued within the Cary family. When all-male and once all-white St. Paul's prep school sought out black girl students, Lorene and her family responded, eager for the chance at a quality education. In 1971, Lorene transferred from a public high school in Philadelphia to St. Paul's in Concord, New Hampshire. There was another motive for the move as well. Cary wrote in *Black Ice* that she "had been raised for just this opportunity. . . . Wasn't it time for me to play my part in that mammoth enterprise—the integration, the moral transformation, no less,

of America? I had been waiting for this the way a fairy princess waits for a man."

After leaving St. Paul's, Cary attended the University of Pennsylvania. She graduated in 1978 with a master's degree in English and then journeyed to Sussex University in England. There she studied Victorian literature and religion and earned her second master's degree in 1979.

Cary worked as a reporter and writer for *Time* magazine in 1980; from 1981 to 1982, she wrote for *TV Guide.* Perhaps the most interesting position she held during this period was that of teacher: She returned to her alma mater, St. Paul's, and taught there during the 1982–83 school year. She established herself as a freelance writer in 1983. She also served on St. Paul's School's board of trustees for four years, beginning her term in 1985.

Cary's first attempt to write about her experience at St. Paul's was an article published in 1988 in *American Visions* magazine. When she decided to turn the article into a book, she interviewed other black students, men who attended the school before it went co-ed, but no one wanted to speak on the record. So Cary decided she would have to tell her own story if she wanted the reality to be revealed. The result was what columnist Ellen Goodman called "a cautionary and hopeful story about the journey to belonging."

While *Black Ice* chronicled her coming-of-age experience at St. Paul's, Cary's second book, *The Price of a Child,* published in 1995, makes a leap back into the past to the 1850s. Its main character, a slave named Ginnie, is en route with her master to Nicaragua. She falls in love with Tyree, a free black man, during a stop in Philadelphia, and he helps her to escape. "So much of slavery has been stereotyped and sentimentalized," Cary said in an interview with *Essence* magazine, "but I haven't seen the representation of true love between my ancestors."

Cary is married to freelance writer R. C. Smith and has a stepson, Geoffrey, and a daughter, Laura. A contributing editor to *Newsweek* since 1991 and a member of the Author's Guild, Lorene Cary received an Honorary Doctorate of Letters in 1992 from Colby College. *Black Ice* received the Notable Book Citation from the American Library Association in 1992.

Cary crossed miles and cultures to bring her first book to fruition. In her second, through the voice of Ginnie, Lorene Cary crosses history. Clearly, she has other journeys to make to express once again her perspective on the African-American experience.

ROSE WOODSON

Chase-Riboud, Barbara (1939–)

The name Barbara Chase-Riboud stirs as much controversy as that of Sally Hemings, the protagonist of her first and best-selling novel of the same name. The historical romance *Sally Hemings* (1979) is Chase-Riboud's re-creation of the alleged liaison between the third president of the United States, Thomas Jefferson, and his slave mistress of thirty-eight years, which purports a legacy of seven children. Chase-Riboud found herself as sensationalized in 1979 in such newspapers as the *Chicago Tribune*, the *Washington Post*, and the *New York Times* as Sally Hemings was in 1802, the year the story created such furor in such American publications as the *Richmond Recorder*. Chase-Riboud was caught amid the clamor of an outraged public who found it impossible to digest the idea of a president's intimate involvement in miscegenation and of a legion of Jefferson historians who repudiated the relationship in their own biographies. Yet, besides rekindling the historical controversy, Chase-Riboud created a not only compelling but sensitive account of the widely circulated story, and her novel won the Janet Heidinger Kafka Prize in 1979 for the best novel by an American woman.

The main character of her 1994 novel, *The President's Daughter*, is Harriet Hemings, the daughter of Sally Hemings and Thomas Jefferson who leaves Monticello and flees to Philadelphia, where she changes her name to Harriet Petit and passes for white. Throughout the novel, Harriet struggles with her dual identity, at once a white woman beyond the reach of fugitive slave laws and yet living in constant fear that her past will eventually catch up with her. Harriet is witness to many of the key historical events of her time—a fascinating lens on history.

Chase-Riboud is also the author of two other novels and two books of poetry and has been accorded international acclaim for her sculptures and drawings. The novel *Valide* (1986) is a saga of the 1802 kidnapping and enslavement of an American-Creole girl by Algerian pirates. Paradoxically, the girl, Naksh-i-dil, rises to the pinnacle of power to become the Valide, or Queen Mother, of an ancient harem in the Ottoman Empire, while still a slave to the sultan.

In *Echo of Lions* (1989), Chase-Riboud recasts the story of the African slave Joseph Cinqué (Sengbe Pieh), who was seized in an illegal slave trade, imprisoned for organizing a revolt on the slave ship, and later acquitted after a Supreme Court defense by former President John Quincy Adams.

From Memphis to Peking (1974), Chase-Riboud's first book of poetry, reflects her visits to Egypt as a college student and as the first American woman to visit postrevolutionary Peking. Her second book of poetry, *Portrait of a Nude Woman as Cleopatra* (1987), is a gracefully sensuous rendition of the Antony and Cleopatra story in sonnet form, inspired by a Rembrandt drawing.

The nurturing that ultimately led to Chase-Riboud's reputation as a visual artist began during her early years in Philadelphia. The only child of Charles Edward, a building contractor, and Vivian May West, a medical assistant, Chase-Riboud was deemed artistically gifted and was immersed in such cultural activities as classical piano, poetry writing, dancing, sculpting, and drawing prior to entering high school. She later earned a bachelor of fine arts degree from Temple University's Tyler Art School (1957), a John Hay Whitney Fellowship for study at the American Academy in Rome (1957), and a master of fine arts degree from Yale University (1960).

Her artistic pursuits eventually took her to Paris, where she met and married photojournalist Marc Edward Riboud on December 25, 1961. They had two sons, David and Alexis. The marriage ended in divorce, and Chase-Riboud subsequently married art expert, broker, and historian Sergio Tosi in 1981.

During her early years in Paris, Chase-Riboud began a sculpting career that spans a 25-year period and is replete with honors, awards, and a multitude of art exhibits in Europe. She received a National Endowment for the Arts Fellowship and the first prize in the New York City Subway Compe-

Outrage and controversy greeted the publication of Barbara Chase-Riboud's 1979 historical romance Sally Hemings. *The compelling and sensitive novel is based on the widely accepted story of Thomas Jefferson's thirty-eight-year relationship with his slave mistress.* (SCHOMBURG CENTER)

tition for architecture in 1973 and a U.S. State Department traveling grant in 1975. She was named the Academic of Italy with a gold medal for sculpture and drawing in 1978, and in 1981 she received an honorary doctorate of arts and humanities from Temple University.

B. J. BOLDEN

Cleage, Pearl (1948–)

Playwright, poet, and essayist Pearl Cleage energizes her work with her viewpoint as an African American and a woman. Her style is forthright and political. "We have to be focused," she says, "because we are under siege."

Born in Springfield, Massachusetts, in 1948, Cleage was the daughter of Albert Buford Cleage and Doris Graham Cleage. Her father was a minister, and her mother was a teacher. She attended **Howard University** and then spent one year each at Yale University and the University of the West Indies. Settling in Atlanta, she earned her B.A. at **Spelman College** in 1971 and subsequently did graduate study at Atlanta University.

Cleage began her playwriting career while she was still an undergraduate. Her first works were one-act plays. "Hymn for Rebels" and "Duet for Three Voices" were first produced at Howard. "The Sale" was produced at Spelman College. Also while she was in college, she worked at the Martin Luther King, Jr., Archival Library as a member of the field-collection staff. Still in her early twenties, she became a member of the board of directors for the Atlanta Center for Black Art.

After graduation, Cleage made her mark in communications in and around Atlanta. In 1971 she published her first book of poetry, *We Don't Need No Music*. The next year, she became a writer and associate director at WQXI and later worked as director of communications for the city of Atlanta, writer and interviewer for the radio program *Ebony Beat Journal*, and executive producer at WXIA. Also working in print, Cleage became a columnist for the *Atlanta Gazette* and wrote for the *Atlanta Constitution* and *Atlanta Tribune*. By 1978, Cleage had become an instructor at Emory University.

However, Cleage found her most exciting work at the Just Us Theater Company in Atlanta. She began as the playwright-in-residence, eventually becoming artistic director. Her first plays at Just Us were *Puppetplay* (1983), *Good News* (1984), and *Essentials* (1985).

While at Just Us, Cleage branched out into performance pieces, such as *My Father Has a Son* (1986), *A Little Practice* (1987), and *Live at the Club Zebra!* which was cowritten with Zaron Burnett. Cleage also became playwright-in-residence at Spelman College. Her later plays include *Late Bus to Mecca* and *Chain*.

Cleage's biggest success has been the play *Flyin' West*, which opened the 1994–95 season at the Kennedy Center for the Performing Arts in Washington, D.C. Set in 1898 in a historical all-black town in Kansas, the play depicts a family of black women who joined the black migration of the late 1800s, leaving the Deep South for the promise of the West. Cleage felt that most stories about the West were stories of white males; this play was her chance to tell black women's story as well.

Cleage has also turned her hand to political essays. In 1990 she published *Mad at Miles: A Blackwoman's Guide to Truth*. Some of these essays were later added to her 1994 collection, *Deals With the Devil: And Other Reasons to Riot*. Of these essays, Cleage says, "I wanted to see if I could talk about things black women writers address in our novels in a form that is more direct and invites political analysis and discussion rather than literary criticism."

Forthright, political, and articulate in a variety of art forms, Pearl Cleage has made sure that the black woman's voice was heard.

ANDRA MEDEA

Cliff, Michelle (1946–)

Michelle Cliff, poet, novelist, and essayist, was born on November 2, 1946, in Kingston, Jamaica. From age three to ten, she lived in New York City, where she maintained her American citizenship. Returning to Jamaica, Cliff attended private girls' schools where the severity of intraracial violence with its color/caste system of privilege and condemnation converged with the omnipresent colonial past to mark her indelibly. These lines of light and dark, alienation and acceptance, confinement and escape, retribution and complacency mark all of her writing: characters are often portrayed as ghosts among the living who try to sort out the "Jamaica I" (or spiritual "I") from the "I and I" (or the personal "I"). Cliff left Jamaica to complete her education in London, where she received an A.B. from Wagner College in 1969 and a master's in philosophy from the Warburg Institute in 1974.

Cliff's writing clearly reflects her work as a reporter, researcher, editor, historian, and teacher—jobs she has held in the public sphere. Her writing can be spare and cryptic, intermingling patois and standard English. Although her works contain historical detail, they always return to the autobiographical. Her interest in the British colonial history of Jamaica as well as the American colonial history of slavery can both be considered autobiographical due to her dual citizenship.

Her first novel, *Abeng* (1984), expresses the themes of alienation, colonialism, and color consciousness that inform all her work. The background for the characters Clare and Zoe are first outlined in her autobiographical essay "If I Could Write This in

Fire, I Would Write It in Fire." In that essay, as in the novel, the privileges of class and almost-white skin lead one woman away from Jamaica to education and success, while the other, Zoe, remains on the island, trapped by poverty and her dark skin. *Abeng* also recalls the essay's response to colonialism: "We are here because you were there."

No Telephone to Heaven (1987) is about Clare Savage's return to her grandmother's land. The novel weaves back and forth in time from Clare's first leaving Jamaica with her parents to her return to her grandmother's farm, which has fallen into ruination. This novel pursues the subject of immigration and passing, with its attendant humiliation and conflated images of loss. If one passes for white, black culture is lost; if one passes for black, privilege is lost. First, there is the loss of Jamaica as motherland; next, the loss of the grandmother in Jamaica while the Savage family is exiled in New York; finally, the loss of the mother who, unable to bear American racism, departs for Jamaica where she dies, separated from her husband and their eldest daughter, Clare. When Clare realizes that she has lost her father (ironically named Boy Savage) to assimilation and an Italian-American lover, she departs for London and more education. There she confronts her British colonial past from a different perspective and finally flees to Jamaica.

Cliff's recent novel, *Bodies of Water* (1990), continues the journey motif as characters involve themselves in various kinds of crossings. Having described her writing as "fabulous," "mythic," and "insane," Cliff exposes these tendencies in *Bodies of Water*. Although the novel can be read as a series of individual short stories, characters reappear in different stories, forming networks that tie together the entire work. *Bodies of Water* fictionalizes history, weaving it into myth, legend, and folklore.

The title story brings together ghosts from Jess Dillon's past who serve as guides to help her understand her present aloneness, exile, speechlessness, and silence. Cliff parallels the supposed madness of an old woman bereft of her lover with her memories of her brother's forced treatments for homosexuality. Homosexuality serves as a metaphor for a split consciousness in which a person is colonized by his or her other. In this way, *Bodies of Water* recalls *No Telephone to Heaven* and Harry/Harriet's dictum: "Cyan [can't] live split. Not in this world."

Cliff's other books, *Claiming an Identity They Taught Me to Despise* (1980) and *The Land of Look Behind* (1985), reveal her skill as an essayist and poet. She describes *Claiming an Identity*, a collection of prose and poetry, as an expression of her heritage and status in the world: "halfway between Africa and England, patriot and expatriate, White and Black" ("Journey into Speech"). She sees the book as an "honest self-portrait of who I was at the time. . . . Someone . . . who wrote from a feminist consciousness and a rapidly evolving consciousness of colonialism, and a knowledge of self-hatred." In pursuing her craft, Cliff follows the advice of Clare's mother in *No Telephone to Heaven*: "Make something of yourself, and someday help your people."

YVONNE FONTENEAU

Clifton, Lucille (1936–)

Lucille Clifton says plainly: "I am a woman and I write from that experience. I am a Black woman and I write from that experience. I do not feel inhibited or bound by what I am. That does not mean that I have never had bad scenes relating to being Black and/or a woman; it means that other people's craziness has not managed to make me crazy. At least not in their way because I try very hard not to close my eye to my own craziness nor to my family's, my sex's, nor my race's."

This statement is an apt introduction to Clifton's writing, both for adults and for young people. She is one of the most prolific writers of picture books created out of an African American consciousness and experience and she was nominated for the Pulitzer Prize both in 1980 for *Two-Headed Woman*, one of her poetry collections for adults, and in 1988 for *Next: New Poems*. Always, she writes about the totality of who she is—an African-American woman who is a parent, a teacher, a daughter, a writer, a member of a kin group and a community.

The daughter of Thelma Moore Sayles and Samuel L. Sayles, Sr., Thelma Lucille Sayles was born in Depew, New York, on June 27, 1936. At seventeen, she entered **Howard University**, where she held a full scholarship and majored in drama. Leaving there after two years (1953–55), she attended Fredonia State Teachers College in New York. Clifton met Ishmael Reed in a writers' group, and he showed her poems to Langston Hughes, who included a few pieces in his anthology *Poetry of the Negro*. She met her husband, Fred Clifton, through this group. They were married in 1958.

Lucille Clifton worked as a claims clerk for the New York State Division of Employment in Buffalo (1958–60); from 1969 through 1971, she was a literature assistant for the U.S. Office of Education in Washington, D.C. It was during this period that her writing began to attract attention: In 1969, she was the recipient of the Young Men's and Young Women's Hebrew Association (YM-YWHA) Poetry Center (New York City) Discovery Award, and she won the first of her several National Endowment for the Arts grants (also 1970, 1972). Her first book of poems, *Good Times*, was published in 1969 by Random House and chosen by the *New York Times* as one of the ten best books of the year.

When her first book appeared, Lucille Clifton was thirty-three years old and the mother of six children under the age of ten: Sidney, Fredrica, Channing, Gillian, Graham, and Alexia. During the following year, 1970, she published her first book for children, *Some of the Days of Everett Anderson.* This book was influenced by her experiences with her own family, and when her husband died, she explored the stages of mourning in *Everett Anderson's Goodbye* (1983).

Everett has gone on to be the main character in six more books to date, and he is an important character for a host of reasons: Through him, Clifton explores the meanings of the word/concept *black* as used in our culture and language. At bedtime in *Some of the Days*, she wrote, " 'Afraid of the dark / is afraid of Mom / and Daddy / and Papa / and Cousin Tom. / I'd be a silly / as I could be / afraid of the dark / is afraid of me!' / Says ebony / Everett / Anderson." Through Everett, Clifton depicts a child who clearly has been raised in an African-American household. At age seven, during September in *Everett Anderson's Year* (1974), he asserts frankly: "I already know where Africa is / and I already know how to count to ten and / I went to school every day last year / why do I have to go again?" For Everett and his mother, knowledge of Africa is just as fundamental as the skill of counting. His sense

of self and identity is secure, and this is evident to any reader. This fact, for the young black reader, functions as a stabilizing and assuring force. For the white reader, it should merely accentuate the characterization. In fact, there are white and other nonblack characters in Clifton's children's books, but Everett Anderson's voice is an especially powerful and memorable one.

For her contribution to changing the face of American children's literature, as well as for her poetry and nonfiction, various organizations have honored Lucille Clifton over the years: Between 1972 and 1976, she served as a visiting writer at Columbia University School of the Arts and as poet-in-residence at Coppin State College in Baltimore; from 1979 through 1982, she was Poet Laureate of the State of Maryland and was a visiting writer at George Washington University from 1982 to 1983; in 1980, the same year as her Pulitzer Prize nomination, Clifton won the Juniper Prize. In 1974, Clifton's *Don't You Remember* was named a Coretta Scott King Honor Book by the American Library Association, one of the most prestigious awards given in the world of children's literature, annually honoring the most distinguished books published by African-American writers and illustrators. Clifton, along with other recipients of this honor, deem it their honor—and in many cases their responsibility—to speak to African-American young people.

One of Clifton's main concerns in writing for children is that such work needs to portray and sustain the African-American community. In *The Black BC's* (1970) she says, "B is for Books / where readers find / treasures for the heart / and mind," and then later, "Y is for Youth / if any man / or men can save us / the young folk can." The relationship between black children's literature and the larger African-American literary canon is—in a literary, sociological, and historical sense—that literacy has always been a treasure chest for black Americans.

This concern with writing, with books, with literacy is just one link between Clifton's children's and adult literature. She also explores issues such as physical appearances, religion, and spirituality in the black community.

Clifton's concern with the dialogue between the child and the adult is evident not only within her children's literature, but also between her children's and adult writing. Her girl characters talk about the virtues of good hair as opposed to natural hair and in "Homage to my hair" in *Two-Headed Woman* (1980), her adult voice tells us that her hair has the ability to "jump and dance." By exploring issues such as physical beauty, the significance of names, and the meaning of freedom throughout her children's and adult literature, Clifton creates a dialogue between the young and the mature. She is concerned, always, with continuities within communities and across generations. *Generations: A Memoir* (1976) is one of Clifton's most acclaimed books, and in it she appeals to readers with the power of her own family's history/mythology.

Lucille Clifton has been a member of various organizations: International PEN, Authors' Guild of Authors' League of America, Maryland State Committee for Black Art and Culture, and the Windsor Hills Association. Yet, her most enduring membership is the one she holds in the African-American community, the community whose experience she chronicles, interprets, and celebrates. Knowing the value of all that

is positive, she tells us in *Good Times* (1969) to "think about the good times"; in *Good News about the Earth* (1972), writing of the positive, the negative, and the love, she tells us to "pass it on."

Lucille Clifton lives in California where she is a tenured professor at the University of California, Santa Cruz.

DIANNE JOHNSON-FEELINGS

Cooper, J. California (19??–)

A gifted storyteller and writer who speaks to the lives of small-town black women, J. California Cooper has won praise from critics and the support of such distinguished writers as **Alice Walker**. With her talent for tapping into depths of culture and oral traditions, Cooper makes tradition live in a contemporary context.

Cooper says little about her early life, except that she was born in Berkeley, California, the daughter of Joseph C. and Maxine Rosemary Cooper. She did not like her first name, so she named herself California.

Cooper's tales are not about California, however; they are about small-town black lives, especially women's lives. The narrators in Cooper's novels are often not the central characters; instead, they are sisters or best friends who tell another woman's story. This is "the voice of the sister-witness," as Walker put it, who knows and keeps the memory as though it were her own.

Cooper did not begin as a novelist. She first wrote plays, and they were such powerful pieces of storytelling that Alice Walker asked her to rewrite some of them as short stories. The result was so successful that Walker published them herself in her first publishing venture.

This first volume of stories was *A Piece of Mine*, published in 1984. The twelve stories revolve around man/woman problems, all told by older, clear-sighted black women. One reviewer said, "She writes with a robustness that can express both anger, when women (and men) are abused . . . as well as a generous love for those around her, in their successes and their sufferings. . . ."

Cooper's next work was another collection of short stories, *Homemade Love,* which was brought out in 1986. These were described as modern folktales, cautionary tales, each story carrying a message from the narrator to the listener. Again Cooper was working in the great Southern rural tradition. In telling these stories of the events of ordinary people, she made it clear that her common people are not common at all but possessed of dignity, fire, and lightning. This work won an American Book Award.

Her third collection of stories was *Some Soul to Keep*, published in 1987. These five stories had the fablelike quality of the earlier works. However, her first novel, *Family*, published in 1991, was more formal and subdued. It was a narrative of a family's survival under slavery and of the generation that reached freedom.

A recent Cooper work is another novel, *In Search of Satisfaction*. Published in 1994, it is an intergenerational story of two wealthy white families and their links with a poor black family and emphasizes the corruptions of wealth and power. Cooper's Christian beliefs are strongly evident in this work.

Cooper's works are filled with vivacity. Her phrases have style and flair—"he had a mouth full of 'gimmee' and a hand full of 'reach.'" Her gift is for storytelling and capturing the inner truth of small-town lives.

ANDRA MEDEA

Cortez, Jayne (1936–)

Jayne Cortez is a poet who writes about jazz. She is also a poet who writes *through* jazz, using the rhythms and intonations of black music to make her poems speak. Known also as a performance poet, she has made several recordings of poems with live jazz musicians. Celebrating musicians, warriors, and poets, her poems emerge as works of strength and resistance.

Born in Arizona in 1936, Cortez was raised in the Watts district in Los Angeles. She developed her talent in the Watts writers workshops of the radical sixties. Her first book of poems, *Pisstained Stairs and the Monkey Man's Wares*, was published in 1969. A powerful political poet, she wrote boldly about oppression and crafted odes to survival. Even in her earlier work she showed her trademark contrasts in imagery and symbolism.

Cortez's next book of poetry was *Festivals and Funerals*, published in 1971, followed by *Scarifications* in 1973. She took on many of the ritual roles of black culture in her poetry. Some poems were in the African griot tradition, singing praises of great figures who have died; some were praise poems to such musicians as **Billie Holiday** and Duke Ellington, as well as to heroes and freedom fighters. Cortez also drew on the roles of the African-American preacher, exhorting and inspiring the living.

As a student of black music in all its manifestations, Cortez incorporated blues lines, modern jazz, and African rhythms into the cadence of her poetry. The sounds of her poetry were so essential that she began to record her poems on albums, working with jazz musicians. Her first poem/album was *Celebrations and Solitudes: The Poetry of*

Jayne Cortez, recorded with bassist Richard Davis. Later recordings also featured talented jazz musicians, including her own son, Denardo Coleman.

Cortez has published eight books of poetry and made five poetry recordings. Her later books of poetry include *Mouth on Paper* (1977), *Firespitter* (1982), *Coagulations: New and Selected Poems* (1984), and *Poetic Magnetic* (1991). Additional recordings were *Unsubmissive Blues* (1980), *There It Is* (1982), *Maintain Control* (1986), and *Everywhere Drums* (1990). In 1983, she wrote *Poetry in Motion*, a screenplay involving her poetry and performance art, for Sphinx productions of Toronto.

Cortez has also contributed to many poetry anthologies, including *The Poetry of Black America* (1972), *New Black Voices* (1972), *Giant Talk* (1975), *Black Sister* (1981), and *Early Ripening: American Women's Poetry Now* (1987).

Jayne Cortez has taken her poetry and her performance style to audiences around the world. In 1970, she performed at Carnegie Hall, accompanied by the Clifford Thornton New Art Ensemble; she has read or lectured at Queens College, **Howard University**, Dartmouth College, Wesleyan College, and the University of Ibadan and has traveled to Africa, the Caribbean, and South America to seek out Pan-African musical traditions.

Described as "a high priestess for the human race," Jayne Cortez has made the spiritual the political. As "seer and healer, singer and chastiser," she carries the power of traditional forms to the issues of today.

ANDRA MEDEA

D

Danner, Margaret Essie (1915–)

"I want no more humility," says Margaret Danner in her poem "Passive Resistance." It exemplifies an often-repeated theme in her work—the quiet, reflective strain of protest characteristic of her poetry. Through both her writing and her community work, Danner was a force in the 1960s black arts movement.

Margaret Essie Danner was born on January 12, 1915, in Pryorsburg, Kentucky. Her family moved to Chicago, where she attended Englewood High School; from there she went to Loyola, Roosevelt, and Northwestern universities. Her poet mentors during her school years were Paul Engle and Karl Shapiro. In 1945, she won second place in the poetry workshop of the Midwestern Writers Conference.

In 1951, Danner went to work for *Poetry: The Magazine of Verse* as an editorial assistant. A series of four of her poems was published in the magazine that same year, winning her a John Hay Whitney Fellowship, and in 1955, she became the first black assistant editor of the publication. Danner's first collection of poetry, *Impressions of African Art Forms*, appeared in 1960 and expressed Danner's absorbing interest in African materials. It was well received by critics.

In 1961, Danner went to Detroit to become poet-in-residence at Wayne State University. Her time in Detroit was particularly fulfilling for her, largely because of her work in the community. She persuaded the minister of Detroit's King Solomon Church, Dr. Boone, to allow her to turn an empty parish house into a community arts center, which she named Boone House to honor the minister's contribution; a number of other poets helped Danner, including Dudley Randall, Robert Hayden, and **Naomi Long Madgett**. In a poem called "Boone House," she referred to it as "a sun made of shade" and "a balm to those struggling through creativity's strident, summer, city heat." Danner and the center helped make Detroit a focus of the black arts movement of the 1960s.

In 1963, *To Flower Poems* was published, and in 1966 Danner and Dudley Randall collaborated on a volume called *Poem Counterpoem*. This unusual work contained, on each set of facing pages, one poem by Danner and one by Randall, each pair on a single subject. In the same year, Danner made her first visit to Africa; while there, she read her poetry at the World Exposition of Negro Arts in Dakar, Senegal.

Iron Lace appeared in 1968, and from 1968 to 1969 Danner was poet-in-residence at Virginia Union University in Richmond. While there, she edited two anthologies of student poetry. She was one of 18 black women poets invited to read at the Phillis Wheatley Poetry Festival at Jackson State College in 1973. *The Down of a Thistle* was published in 1976; it is filled with African imagery and contains a strong note of protest.

Margaret Essie Danner is married to Otto Cunningham and has one child, Naomi. Her grandson, Sterling Washington, Jr., inspired what Danner calls the "muffin poems."

KATHLEEN THOMPSON

Davis, Thadious M. (1944–)

There are few writers or scholars who have made greater contributions to our understanding of African Americans in literature than Thadious M. Davis. With dedication, intelligence, and wisdom, she works to preserve and inspire black writers.

Thadious M. Davis was born on May 29, 1944, in New Orleans, Louisiana. She graduated from Southern University with a bachelor's degree in English and history in 1966 and went on to Atlanta University, where she earned a master's degree in British and American literature. Two years later, she received her doctorate in the same field from Boston University.

In the meantime, Davis had begun her career in teaching. In 1974, she became an instructor at the University of Massachusetts where, two years later, she went on to an assistant professorship. After receiving her Ph.D., she moved to the University of North Carolina at Chapel Hill, where she stayed until 1990. In that year, she became a professor at Brown University.

From the earliest years of her career as a scholar and educator, Davis has been committed to the exploration of black images and achievements in literature. Her first book, *Faulkner's Negro: Art and the Southern Context*, dealt with the way African Americans have been portrayed by white writers. However, her work on the *Dictionary of Literary Biography* may have been a greater contribution. As editor of three vol-

umes on African-American writers after 1955, she helped to gather and then present to the public invaluable information about the black voices that have struggled to be heard.

In 1992, Davis returned to her analysis of the black image in white literature when she edited *Satire or Evasion? Black Perspectives on Huckleberry Finn* for Duke University Press. The book was an important contribution to the ongoing discussion about Huck and his relationship to the slave, Jim.

In 1994, Davis presented what is probably her most important work to date when she published *Nella Larsen: Novelist of the Harlem Renaissance: A Woman's Life.* **Nella Larsen** was a major writer of the renaissance, but her life was full of rejection and pain. After two important novels, she stopped writing and virtually disappeared, taking a job as a nurse working the night shift on the East Side of Manhattan.

Davis investigates the hidden facts of Larsen's early and later years with sympathy and insight. *Booklist* called the book "an astute, rigorous, and deeply compassionate biography, a real heartbreaker, and an invaluable chapter in the history of African Americans."

Davis will more than likely continue to write chapters in that history.

KATHLEEN THOMPSON

Davis, Thulani (1949–)

"I'm very interested," Thulani Davis told *Essence* magazine in 1992, "in reclaiming black mythology, history and ritual . . . in writing the many black stories that are out there that have never been written." Davis, who was born in 1949 in Hampton, Virginia, is making her dreams a reality: While attending Barnard College in New York City, she started to write and perform her own poetry with poets such as **Ntozake Shange** and Jessica Hagedorn and created poetry events in a wide variety of settings, including the New York Shakespeare Festival. Her cousin, Anthony Davis, who is a jazz musician, wrote the music that accompanied many of her poetry readings.

Then, in 1985, Thulani and her cousins Anthony and Chris did what few other black Americans in the history of performance have done: They wrote and premiered an opera, *X: The Life and Times of Malcolm X.* (Scott Joplin's folk opera *Treemonisha* is one of the few other authentic African-American operas.) For five years they collaborated, with Chris developing the story, Anthony writing the music, and Thulani, the words.

X premiered at Philadelphia's American Music Theatre Festival before it moved on to the New York City Opera. *Time* magazine called the libretto "fierce, angry and brilliant" and went on to say that "*X* is at once a musical entertainment, a folk epic, a cautionary tale and a cri du coeur."

Thulani Davis published her first novel, *1959*, in 1992 to rave reviews. In 1993, she returned to the subject of Malcolm X when she wrote the text for the pictorial chronology/photo essay book *Malcolm X: The Great Photographs*. In addition to her libretto and novel writing, Thulani has worked as a journalist for the *Village Voice* and has published two books of poetry. Most recently, she has been writing the libretto for another opera, *Armistad*. She lives with her husband Joseph Jarman, who is a composer, in Brooklyn, New York.

Carolyn See wrote in *New York Newsday* that the novel *1959* is "extremely thoughtful and extremely fine." The same can well be said of Thulani Davis herself.

HILARY MAC AUSTIN

Delaney Sisters

SARAH (1886–)
ELIZABETH (1888–1995)
They knew W. E. B. DuBois . . . and Jim Crow. They met a very young Lena Horne . . . and the Ku Klux Klan. They were in Harlem during the Harlem Renaissance, and one of them was James Weldon Johnson's dentist. In 1992, the Delaney sisters captured the imagination of the nation in their best-selling book, *Having Our Say: The Delaney Sisters' First 100 Years,* and three years later their story was on Broadway, enacted by **Mary Alice** and **Gloria Foster**.

Sarah (Sadie) and Elizabeth (Bessie) Delaney were born in 1886 and 1888 respectively. They spent their childhood in Raleigh, North Carolina, surrounded by brothers and sisters. There were ten children in all, each destined for college and a professional career. Their father, Henry Beard Delaney, was the vice-principal of St. Augustine's, an Episcopal school in Raleigh; their mother, Nancy Logan, served as matron at St. Augustine's and was responsible for day-to-day operations. Henry Beard Delaney would one day be the first elected African-American bishop of the Episcopal Church of America.

Sadie graduated from St. Augustine in 1910; her sister, Bessie, graduated in 1911. Their father insisted that they continue their education. "He told us we'd never be anything without a college degree and that we owed it to our nation, our race and ourselves to go," Bessie remembered. The young women worked their way through college as teachers.

In 1923, after graduating from Columbia University's School of Dentistry, Bessie Delaney became the second black woman licensed to practice dentistry in New York City; she charged two dollars for pulling a tooth. Sadie, with a degree from Columbia Teacher's College, became an elementary school teacher and then the first black woman to teach domestic sciences on the high school level in the New York public schools.

The lives of the Delaney sisters span more than a century. Their professional standing alone is an accomplishment, achieved against the unrelenting racism of the early 1900s, but their lives speak even more loudly because they were active participants in history. *Colored* and *Whites Only* were real signs with a direct impact on their daily lives; they joined sit-ins to protest Jim Crow laws. Sadie Delaney knew Booker T. Washington. In addition to James Weldon Johnson, Bessie counted many other black writers and artists among her patients. In their time, the sisters met **Ethel Waters**, Bert Williams, Duke Ellington, and Cab Calloway.

The Delaney sisters have come to stand for much of the best in black middle-class culture: honesty, hard work, intelligence, and commitment to simplicity in their lives. In an age of fast food and convenience stores, the Delaney sisters made their own soap. They lived in the same house in Mount Vernon, New York, for 35 years.

They had opinions about everything, from soul food ("Well, it may be good for the soul, honey, but it ain't good for the heart!") to being average ("When Negroes are average, they fail—unless they're very lucky. But if you're average and *white*, honey, you can go far. Just look at Dan Quayle. If that boy was colored he'd be washing dishes somewhere back in Ohio or Indiana or wherever he's from").

Bessie and Sadie Delaney also possessed that rarest of all commodities in today's increasingly mobile society—a sense of community. From Raleigh, North Carolina, to Harlem to Mount Vernon, they held onto their memories, their trials, and each other. "You know why we're still here?" Bessie Delaney asked "We never had any husbands to worry us to death." One suspects that the reason for their longevity has more to do with heritage, both individual and historical.

Bessie Delaney died at the home the sisters shared in Mt. Vernon, New York, on September 25, 1995. She was 104. The sisters had lived together for more than 100 years. *The New York Times* said that "Sadie . . . seemed to handle her sister's death with the same strength that had carried her through a century. 'I'll just do the best I can. I'll continue right on as if Bessie were here.'"

ROSE WOODSON

DeVeaux, Alexis (1948–)

I'm trying to explore with greater concentration the black woman and her love . . . woman in relation to her eros, her sexuality. Where is she in relation to that? Is it a place of beauty for her, a place of harmony, conflict, change, antagonism? What does it have to do with her sense of herself as a political person? Where is she going? That's where I'm going in my writing.

Love dominates Alexis DeVeaux's writings; expressions of black women's love are her forte. She feels a sense of responsibility to foster positive images of black women in literature. She sees no distinction between herself and her creative craft, for she wants her writings to have unity with the lives of black women globally.

She ideally perceives "herstory" as having sameness with "ourstory" because an incident in one black life is compounded into occurrences in all black lives. DeVeaux comes to the writer's table with a mission; the page and the words are the tools she uses to deliver her message about black women as three-dimensional human beings. Her own words sum up the ethos of this prolific writer: "I want to explore her questions, strengths, concerns, madnesses, love, evils, weaknesses, lack of love, pain, and growth. Her perversities and her moralities." She explores the depths of these inquiries through essays, fiction, drama, poetry, and art.

Reluctant to reveal intimate details of family life, DeVeaux has revealed little information except that she was born to Mae DeVeaux and Richard Hill in New York City on September 24, 1948, and that she has sisters and brothers. Her writing emerged from a desire to improve communication with her mother, whose own mother died when she was very young. DeVeaux participated in an independent study program at Empire State College of the State University of New York (SUNY), from which she received a B.A. in 1976.

DeVeaux's background in Harlem and the South Bronx perhaps prepared her to break barriers, exceed parameters, and soar to new heights in literature. She is streetwise—all too familiar with the anguish, despair, poverty, and pain of a contemporary urban environment. In many ways, she is caught up in a 1960s time warp, still emulating the Broadside Press poets of that time in her application of language. She rebels against standard conventions through her use of Black English, all lowercase letters, choppy syntax, slang, street language, and African cultural ties. The spirit of rebellion reigns within her. She champions the cause of the black underclass, forcing the reader to come to grips with a much neglected and ignored subculture that will never conform to the dictates of a white dominant culture but is determined to define its own black aesthetics.

DeVeaux worked as an assistant instructor in English for the WIN Program of the New York Urban League (1969); a creative writing instructor for New York City's Frederick Douglass Creative Arts Center (1971), as a community worker for the Bronx Office of Probations (1972), and as a reading and creative writing instructor for Project Create (1973). She later commuted north to New Haven's Coeur de l'Unicorne Gallery, where her paintings were exhibited. In the same year that she received her B.A., she became a regular contributor to *Essence* and a freelance writer (1976). She guest-lectured at Livingston College (Rutgers University) in 1975 and also spoke in **Paule Marshall's** graduate seminar in writing at Columbia University. DeVeaux continues to write and teach in the New York City area.

She has been honored with first prize in Black Creation's National Fiction Contest (1972); the Best Production Award, Westchester Community College Drama Festival (1973); and the Art Books for Children Award from the Brooklyn Museum (1974 and 1975).

DeVeaux has numerous publications to her credit: *Na-Ni* (1973) is a juvenile book set in Harlem; *Spirits in the Streets* (1973) is a poetic prose narrative (illustrated by De-Veaux) that captures in microcosm the 1970s Harlem world of raw lives and sensibilities; *Li Chen/Second Daughter First Son* (1975) is a prose poem; *Don't Explain: A Song of Billie Holiday* (1980) is a biographical prose poem on the life of the jazz singer, selections from which appeared in *Essence; Adventures of the Dread Sisters* (1982) is an independently published comic book; its publication was followed by *Blue Heat: A Portfolio of Poems and Drawings* (1985); *An Enchanted Hair Tale* (1987) is a juvenile book about a character named Sudan who must learn to appreciate the enchantment of his strange-looking hair.

DeVeaux continues her penchant for freeing black life and black love from the restrictions of Euro-Western realism through her periodical publications. Her short fiction examines the reality of black life in America's largest city. "Remember Him a Outlaw" (*Black Creation* 1972, *Midnight Birds* 1980) tells the story of Uncle Willie through the eyes of his favorite niece, Lexie. Uncle Willie is a survivor on the streets of Harlem whose life is ultimately snuffed out by the mean streets. To the casual observer, he appears to be an outlaw, but to the knowledgeable and the wise, he is an outcast. "The Riddles of Egypt Brownstone" (*Nimrod* 1977, *Essence* 1978, *Midnight Birds* 1980) deals with the young girl Egypt's handling of two sexual encounters as she matures into womanhood, one initiated by her mother's boyfriend and the other by her lesbian French teacher. The riddle of Egypt, literally and figuratively, engulfs the entire story: What has a mother who is a father who has a Negro female child that the twentieth century has tattooed illegitimate? Egypt's

solving of the riddle points to proud ancient African-Egyptian icons, but her present situation deems the solution a paradox.

DeVeaux's political essays take on a neo-Africanist perspective and exhibit her views of the move toward a black feminism. In "Zimbabwe: Woman Fire," she chronicles the contributions of Zimbabwean women to the struggle for independence and the role they played in the establishment of Mugabe as leader and president of the country. She is disillusioned by the subservient positions that women had to assume in a male-dominated society after the struggle was over. "South Africa: Listening for the News" voices her abhorrence of the system of apartheid in South Africa and the dislike of the U.S. alliance with the white-rule government. "Blood Ties," which was inspired by a trip to Haiti in the summer of 1975 where she witnessed firsthand the enormous poverty that plagues the tiny island, attacks with a vengeance the government of Haiti and its chief demagogues, "Papa Doc" and "Baby Doc" Duvalier.

"Sister Love," a prose poem, is an example of the extremes to which DeVeaux will go to discover the ways women love and to bridge the gaps between women and between their struggles. Through this prose poetry, she brings into the mainstream the theme of black lesbian love and implores the reading public, especially women, to be receptive to lesbians and to her own lesbianism. She envisions a world that is not dominated by race, sex, and class, where one can be free to develop relationships devoid of labels.

Her published poetry includes "The Sisters" (*Conditions* 1979, *Home Girls* 1983); "Poems" (*Hoo-Doo* 1980); "Madeleine's Dreads" (*Iowa Review* 1981, *Extended*

Outlooks 1982); "And do you love me" (*Open Places* 1982); "French Doors: A Vignette" (*Open Places* 1982, *Confirmation* 1983); and "Poems" (*Sunbury* 1984). She also has published in *Encore*, *2 Poetry Magazine*, *Black Box*, and the *New Haven Advocate*.

DeVeaux has made an impact in drama as well. She sees the production of her first play as a turning point in her career. *Circles* (1973) is a one-act play about a young black woman who breaks the chains that bind her to home in order to pursue her professional career and realize her dream. The play was performed by the Frederick Douglass Players at the Frederick Douglass Creative Arts Center and by the same group at Westchester Community College's Drama Festival. It was televised by California's KCET-TV's (1976) *Visions*, a program directed by **Maya Angelou**. Deveaux the playwright explores the sexual needs of black women through art and introduces the theme of gay love. In the two-act play *The Tapestry* (1976), Jet, the young black woman law student, must probe her inner self to determine how much to retain of the baggage accumulated in her upbringing. This play was performed by the West Coast Black Repertory Theater (1976) and New York City's Quaigh Theater (1977). Televised productions were shown on KCET-TV's (1976) *Visions*. Public readings were done by Frank Silvera's Writers' Workshop. *A Season to Unravel* (1979) is a one-act Freudian drama whose setting is within the psyche of the leading character. The Negro Ensemble Company premiered this play at New York City's St. Mark's Playhouse (1979).

The one-act dream fantasy *A Little Play* (1972) and the one-act *Whip Cream* (1973) were performed by the Young People's Workshop of All Soul's Church (1973) in Harlem. *The Fox Street War* (1979) is a full-length drama about black women occupying an apartment complex who use the power of voodoo to persuade the owner to improve living conditions. DeVeaux's drama and poetry also have been performed in Greenhaven Prison, the Brooklyn Academy of Music, Cathedral of Saint John the Divine, Empire State College, and Riverside Church. Her work has been broadcast on radio stations WBAI, WNYC, WRVR, and WVLR and televised on WABC's *Like It Is* and WTTG's *Panorama* in Washington, D.C., and shown at the INPUT Public Television Conference in Milan, Italy, in March 1978.

DeVeaux continues in the tradition of the activist-artist. The artist and the art are one inseparable, seamless fiber. She is a spirit in the street, a true echo of the underrepresented underclass who also have stories to unfold. DeVeaux is the catalyst through which the stories surface; she foregrounds black women's experiences to propel her onward, upward, and usward.

GERRI BATES

Dove, Rita (1952–)

"I think people should be shaken up a bit when they walk through life," Rita Dove told *Time* magazine. "They should stop for a moment and *really* look at ordinary things and catch their breath." Because Dove has the peculiar genius required to make her readers catch their breath with wonder at the beauty of ordinary things, she is a most renowned poet. The literary establishment acknowledged her significance in 1987 with a Pulitzer Prize for poetry; then, in 1993, her country gave her its highest honor by making her Poet Laureate of the United States. At 41, she was the youngest person ever chosen for that position, and she brought to it youthful enthusiasm and joy in the power of language.

Rita Dove was born in Akron, Ohio, in 1952 and earned a B.A. from Miami University in Oxford, Ohio, in 1973 and an M.F.A. from the University of Iowa in 1977. She has taught at Arizona State University and now teaches creative writing at the University of Virginia. Writer-in-residence at Tuskegee Institute in Tuskegee, Alabama, in 1982 and recipient of a Guggenheim Fellowship in 1983, Dove is a Fulbright scholar and holds important editorial positions on journals such as *Callaloo*, *Gettysburg Review*, and *TriQuarterly*. She is married to Fred Viebahn, a German novelist; they have a daughter, Aviva.

Rita Dove says that she tried to "string moments as beads on a necklace" in the making of the Pulitzer Prize–winning poetry

In 1933, Rita Dove was named Poet Laureate of the United States. She writes of black lives with controlled power and delicacy. (SCHOMBURG CENTER)

collection *Thomas and Beulah* (1985). The inspiration for this volume came from a story about her grandfather that was told to Dove by her grandmother. The poems grew over the course of five years, starting with the poem "Dusting," which is one of the key pieces in the "Beulah" section but which appeared in 1983 in the volume entitled *Museum. Thomas and Beulah* is divided into two sections: Part One, "Mandolin," is devoted to the grandfather; Part Two, "Canary in Bloom," is devoted to the grandmother.

Dove gathered background material for *Thomas and Beulah* by talking to her mother, by reading Works Progress Administration texts on the state of Ohio, by exploring the significance of black migration from the agrarian South to the industrial North (especially to Akron, Ohio), and by listening to older blues recordings from Lightnin' Hopkins to **Billie Holiday**. This historical information was distilled into the fictional story of Dove's grandparents' lives. Dove won the Pulitzer Prize for poetry for *Thomas and Beulah*, the first black woman to win this award since **Gwendolyn Brooks** received it in 1950.

In addition to *Thomas and Beulah*, Dove has published three volumes of poetry and a collection of short stories. *The Yellow House on the Corner*, published in 1980, relates the experiences of "The Bird Frau," maddened by war, who "went inside, fed the parakeet, / broke its neck." The judiciousness of tone and feeling in this poem about the German woman is matched in the poem "The Abduction," about "Solomon Northrup / from Saratoga Springs, free papers in my pocket, violin / under arm, my new friends Brown and Hamilton by my side" who, participating with his "friends" in a carnival act, "woke and found [himself] alone, in darkness and in chains."

The poems in *The Yellow House* seem more "domestic" than those in *Museum*, published in 1983. These poems have an exotic flair, retelling ancient myths, religious legends, and stories about faraway lands. One of the loveliest selections, "Tou Wan Speaks to Her Husband, Liu Sheng," describes the tomb Tou Wan constructs for her dead mate: "I will build you a house / of limited chambers / but it shall last / forever: four rooms / hewn in the side of stone / for you, my / only conqueror." Rita Dove's collection of poetry, *Grace Notes*, was published in 1989; her volume of short stories, *Fifth Sunday*, appeared in 1985. Probably the best known of the stories in the collection is "The Spray Paint King," a poignant tale about a mixed-blood black-and-German youth who, with a decidedly contemporary touch, spray-paints the ancient walls of the buildings in the city of Cologne. "The First Suite" (a complex story about a traveling puppeteer who performs for elementary school children), is taken from a novel in progress and was published in the fall 1986 issue of *Black American Literature Forum*. Her sixth book of poems, *Mother Love*, was published in 1995.

When Dove was named Poet Laureate in 1993, she was the first African American to be given that title. However, the position, which until 1986 was called "poetry consultant to the Library of Congress," had previously been held by black poets Robert Hayden (1976–78) and Gwendolyn Brooks (1985), but Dove does not need to rely on either ethnicity or gender for her uniqueness: She immediately set out to destroy the image of the poet as "someone sitting in a garret writing things few understood." She sug-

gested that teachers should stop overtesting poetry in schools and even declared that poems belonged on MTV. In 1994, she was asked to serve another term as the nation's poetry advocate.

CAROLYN MITCHELL

Drumgold, Kate (18??–?)

Kate Drumgold was born into the Old Virginia system of slavery and had blossomed into a young girl by the time of the Civil War. Her date of birth cannot be determined because official birth records were not maintained on most enslaved African Americans, but certainly her childhood was lived out under slavery. Her autobiographical narrative, *A Slave Girl's Story*, published in 1898, indicates that she was one of seventeen daughters in the Drumgold family; her only brother died as a teenager when he was sent by his owner to fight in the Civil War. Both the war and slavery severely fractured the family, separating young Drumgold from her mother, father, and siblings. She wrote: "My dear mother had a dear husband that she was sold from also. . . . he waited a while and then he found him another wife."

After the Civil War, Drumgold was reunited with her mother and sisters, but not with her father and brother. In 1865, the family of women migrated north to Brooklyn, New York, where she wrote her *Story* despite frequent bouts with serious illness. The book begins with a reflection on her life under slavery and then documents her life after emancipation up to 1897. Her prose exhibits a rigorous, almost puritanical self-discipline and is filled with praise and tributes to God as being the source of her religious, educational, and teaching accomplishments:

God be praised for the way he has led me since I was three years old until this day, for it was his hand that taught me to remember all those long years. I have in my mind the time at the old home when they put me on the fine dressing table in front of the large mirror, while the Rev. Mr. Walker baptized me in the name of the Father and the Son and the Holy Ghost.

Drumgold spent many years traveling, spreading the gospel, and converting African Americans to Christianity; she even studied for three years and eight months at Wayland Seminary in Washington, D.C.

Published writing by African Americans was rare in the late 1800s, but many former slaves wrote impassioned autobiographies espousing the abolition of slavery, encouraging the education of African Americans, and exhorting self-disciplined piety among African Americans. Drumgold's text speaks directly to the latter two. On education, she wrote:

> I made up my mind that I would die to see my people taught. I was willing to prepare to die for my people, for I could not rest till my people were educated.

On religion:

> If we should fail to give Him the honor due there would a curse come to us as a race, for remember those of olden times were of the same descent of our people, and some of those that God honored most were of the Ethiopians.

Although Drumgold's discourse on slavery is brief, her reflections on how it severed her family can be viewed as having an antislavery theme. Given that the continuing themes of racism, educational advancement, and a spiritual way of life are evident in the modern autobiographies of African Americans, Drumgold can be viewed as a foremother of this tradition as well as a nineteenth-century African-American literary pioneer.

TOMIKA DePRIEST

DuBois, Shirley Graham (1896–1977)

Playwright and composer Shirley Graham DuBois was also renowned as biographer. Between 1944 and 1976, she wrote thirteen books on the lives of important black Americans, from **Phillis Wheatley** to Booker T. Washington, including her husband, W. E. B. DuBois. She was also a founding editor of *Freedomways*, a journal of black literature and culture. DuBois' biographical entry is in the *Theater Arts and Entertainment* volume of this encyclopedia.

Dunbar-Nelson, Alice (1875–1935)

If Alice Ruth Moore had not married Paul Laurence Dunbar, she probably would not have attracted quite as much historical attention. Yet with or without the Dunbar name, she is a figure worthy of notice. With a life spanning the postbellum South to the Great Depression North, her story is uniquely representative of black women in the United States during this pivotal time. Moreover, she commands consideration for her many-faceted racial activism, clubwoman endeavors, passionate sexuality, vibrant and contradictory personality, and achievements as a multigenre author whose work helped to maintain and extend the tradition of African-American women's writing.

Alice Ruth Moore was born July 19, 1875, in New Orleans, Louisiana. Her mother, Patricia Moore, was an ex-slave turned seamstress and was of black and American Indian ancestry; her father, Joseph Moore (who never lived with the family), was a seaman from whom she received some Caucasian ancestry. Her reddish-auburn hair and light skin helped her in Creole society and allowed her occasionally to pass for white in order to imbibe the high culture of operas, bathing spas, and museums in a segregated country intent on racial exclusion. Because of her appearance, Dunbar-Nelson struggled throughout her life with intraracial color prejudice and her own corresponding ambivalence about dark-skinned black people.

Moore completed a public-school education and the two-year teachers' program at Straight College (now Dillard University) in 1892. In addition to her work as a teacher, she was bookkeeper and stenographer for a large black-owned and -operated printing firm. She also studied art and music (playing the piano and cello); acted in amateur theatricals; wrote the "Woman's Column" for the *Journal of the Lodge,* a fraternal newspaper; served as president of the local literary society; and was active in her Protestant Episcopal church.

In 1895, when she was only twenty years old, she published her first book, *Violets and Other Tales,* a potpourri of short stories, sketches, essays, reviews, and poetry that augured her future success. Modestly presented in a tone of ladylike authorship, its brief and impressionistic pieces about history, books, the city, romantic themes, and the status of women show the youthful

Author and activist Alice Dunbar-Nelson published not only poetry and short stories, but also drama, scholarly literary criticism, and journalism. (SCHOMBURG CENTER)

writer trying out the voices and strategies that she used in later years.

Moore began to teach school in Brooklyn, New York, in 1897 and conducted various academic and manual training classes at Victoria Earle Matthews' White Rose Mission (later White Rose Home for Girls) in Harlem. In her work with what she described as "the toughest, most God-forsaken hoodlums you ever saw," her size (she was six feet tall and had a robust physique) was a great advantage.

On March 8, 1898, she married the celebrated black dialect poet Paul Laurence Dunbar, who had begun an increasingly warm correspondence with her in 1895 after seeing one of her poems and her picture in a Boston magazine. From the beginning, their romance was crossed by familial tension and disapproval, temperamental differences and moodiness, Paul Dunbar's medically induced addiction to alcohol and heroin tablets, Alice Dunbar's controlling tendencies, and their inability to have a child. Still, their correspondence reveals their abiding passion for each other, and for the three years they were together (making their home in Washington, D.C., where he was employed at the Library of Congress), they were a glittering couple. When Paul Dunbar died on February 9, 1906, Alice Dunbar received recognition as his wife, and her lifelong career as his widow was officially launched. This auxiliary identity often eclipsed her own important accomplishments, but it paradoxically gave her much-needed income and visibility.

As the lesser-known, female half of the Dunbar writing duo, Alice Dunbar probably benefited from her professional association with her husband. Shortly after they married, his agent, Paul Reynolds, began to market her short fiction to the leading magazines of the day. In 1899, Paul Dunbar's publisher (Dodd, Mead and Company) brought out her *The Goodness of St. Rocque and Other Stories* as the companion volume to her late husband's *Poems of Cabin and Field*. Her stories, more fully developed than those in *Violets*, are set firmly in New Orleans and fruitfully utilize the Creole history and distinctive culture of the city. The reviewer for the *Pittsburgh Christian Advocate* (December 21, 1899) regarded it as a collection of "delightful Creole stories, all

bright and full of the true Creole air of easy-going . . . brief and pleasing, instinct with the passion and romance of the people who will ever be associated with such names as Bayou Teche and Lake Pontchartrain." However, their superficial brightness is belied by deeper themes of sadness, loss, death, and oppression. In the title story, the tall, dark heroine, Manuela, resorts to a voodoo madam and the Catholic Saint Rocque to vanquish her petite blue-eyed blonde rival for the attentions of Théophile. It is replete with Old World Creole traditions, emphasizing family, formality, and a closed society.

In other stories—which either went unpublished or found outlets in black publications—Alice Dunbar frankly confronted race/racism and the problems of the black Creole, adding the popular turn-of-the-century motifs of "passing" and "the color line" to her equally in vogue local-color regionalism. "The Pearl in the Oyster," published in the *Southern Workman* (August 1902), chronicles the fall of Auguste Picou, a fair Creole with a black grandfather, who rejects his Negro friends and neighbors to pass as a white politician. Another series of tenement stories mined her settlement house experience. Set on New York City's Lower East Side, the protagonists are Irish ghetto youth whose hard lives are sympathetically illuminated. Still other works—such as "Elisabeth" and "Ellen Fenton"—explore the psyche of ordinary (white) post-Victorian women. Alice Dunbar also tried her hand at novels (attempting two during this period and two near the end of her career) and, later, popular pulp fiction, but was not successful in these genres. Cumulatively speaking, in the stories that occupied her during these heyday years with Paul Laurence

Dunbar, Alice Dunbar skirted the prevalent black fictional stereotypes of tragic mulatto and happy slave by a variety of interesting means that can be regarded, in retrospect, as her contribution to the newly developing tradition of the short story, especially among black and black female writers.

By the fall of 1902, Alice Dunbar was established in Wilmington, Delaware (joined there by her mother and her sister—who had separated from her husband and brought with her four small children). Until 1902, when she was in effect fired for her independent behavior and political activities, she worked at the Howard High School as teacher, then head, of English and drawing, supplementing classroom duties with supervisory responsibilities, fund-raising, playwriting, and directing. She furthered her own education with special study of English, education, and psychology at Cornell University, Columbia University, and the University of Pennsylvania, while overseeing seven summer sessions for in-service teachers at State College for Colored Students (now Delaware State College). A portion of her Cornell University master's thesis on the influence of Milton on Wordsworth was published in the respected scholarly journal *Modern Language Notes* in April 1909.

Following relationships with her principal, Edwina B. Kruse, and perhaps others, Dunbar-Nelson was secretly married to Henry Arthur Callis, Jr., on January 19, 1910. Later a medical doctor and founder of Alpha Phi Alpha fraternity, he was a fellow teacher at Howard High School, twelve years her junior. Six years after, on April 20, 1916, she formed a more lasting union with Robert J. Nelson, a journalist from Harrisburg, Pennsylvania, widowed with two young children. Their two households merged into an economic and extended family unit, and calm, practical, race-conscious "Bobbo," as he was called, became a quiet blessing she enjoyed for the rest of her life.

Together, they published the *Wilmington Advocate* newspaper from 1920 to 1922 and actively participated in the tumultuous politics of Delaware. Dunbar-Nelson served on the state Republican Committee and directed campaign activities among black women (1920), was a member of the prestigious delegation that presented black concerns to President Warren G. Harding at the White House (1921), and headed the Delaware Crusaders for the Dyer Anti-Lynching Bill (1922). In World War I–related work, she organized a much-publicized Flag Day parade, formed a local chapter of the Circle for Negro War Relief, and toured the South as field representative of the Woman's Committee of the Council of National Defense (1918). As a noted feminist and clubwoman, she was field organizer for the Middle Atlantic states in the fight for women's suffrage (1915). Together with colleagues from the Federation of Colored Women, she founded the Industrial School for Colored Girls in Marshallton, Delaware, where she functioned as teacher and parole officer from 1924 to 1928.

Just as her personal activities during this period were oriented toward concrete projects, Dunbar-Nelson's writing, too, was nonbelletristic, more utilitarian. She edited *Masterpieces of Negro Eloquence* (1914) and *The Dunbar Speaker and Entertainer* (1920), volumes that reflect both the honored place of oratory in African-American culture and her own extensive experience as a noted platform speaker. She wrote formal speeches and contributed articles on Louisiana, Delaware, and war work to the *Journal of Negro History* (1916–17), the *Messenger* (1924), and Emmett J. Scott's (with whom she had a romantic liaison) *Official History of the American Negro in the World War* (1919), respectively. *Mine Eyes Have Seen* (1918), her one-act war propaganda play, was printed and staged. Until she died, Dunbar-Nelson maintained an interest in drama, occasionally writing various kinds of dramatic pieces and trying her hand at screenplays (she was an avid fan of both movies and the theater).

Though she was forty-five years old in 1920 and clearly not one of the brash young voices, Dunbar-Nelson participated in the literary upsurge of the Harlem Renaissance. She received recognition as an older but still active contemporary; attended the numerous race meetings and conferences, rubbing shoulders with the likes of W. E. B. DuBois, **Bessye Bearden**, Carter G. Woodson, **Mary Church Terrell**, and **Georgia Douglas Johnson**; and wrote and published her poetry, which has served more than any other of her writings to keep her name alive. Her sonnet "Violets," which first appeared in the August 1917 *Crisis* magazine, has become her signature poem. It begins: "I had not thought of violets of late, / The wild, shy kind that springs beneath your feet / In wistful April days, when lovers mate / And wander through the fields in raptures sweet." Though her gifts as a writer were more discursive than poetic, Dunbar-Nelson was a fairly good poet who was particularly competent in rhymed

and metered forms and was at her best when she combined these forms with traditional, yet sincerely felt, lyric subjects.

She made shining contributions, however, in the genre of print journalism. The intellect, wit, protest, sassiness, iconoclasm, racial pride, feminism, and humor—in short, all those qualities which marked her as a personality—that do not appear in her canonical writings and fictional heroines are wonderfully evident in her newspaper columns. A male commentator in the 1927 *Opportunity* magazine declared that "there are few better column conductors of her sex on any newspaper. I should like to see her on some influential daily where her unmistakable talents would be allowed full exercise." Drawing on her lifelong experience as reporter, editor, and publisher, Dunbar-Nelson wrote "From a Woman's Point of View," later "*Une Femme Dit*" for the Pittsburgh *Courier* from February 20 to September 18, 1926; "As in a Looking Glass" for the Washington *Eagle* from 1926 to 1930; and "So It Seems—to Alice Dunbar Nelson" again for the *Courier* from January to May 1930.

Dunbar-Nelson's most singular contribution to the field of black women's literature may ultimately prove to be the diary she kept in 1921 and between 1926 and 1931. Discovered in her papers and published in 1984, it is one of only two existing full-length diaries written by a nineteenth-century African-American woman (the other being **Charlotte Forten**'s journal). Kept with effort and in a sophisticated but not self-consciously artsy style, it illuminates areas of crucial concern, such as work, family, sexuality, health, money, and writing. In its pages, for example, can be found documentation for the existence of an active black lesbian network and for Dunbar-Nelson's own romantic involvement with at least three prominent women.

The 1920s were exciting professionally for Dunbar-Nelson because of her position as executive secretary of the American Inter-Racial Peace Committee from 1928 to 1931. Instituted by the Quakers to further racial understanding and international peace, the committee's work gave her an opportunity to use her fame and skills in unique and largely rewarding public ways, traveling and speaking widely, staging large festivals and programs, and managing the functioning of the committee.

In January 1932, Robert was finally given the political sinecure he had worked hard to gain. After his appointment to the Pennsylvania State Athletic (Boxing) Commission, Dunbar-Nelson was at last able to realize her dreams of owning a well-appointed home (in Philadelphia) and enjoying financial security. Playing the roles of philanthropic society matron, patron of the arts, racial activist, and seasoned politico, she lived her remaining years in a manner that graciously befitted the life that had gone before. She died of coronary complications at the University of Pennsylvania hospital on September 18, 1935.

AKASHA (GLORIA) HULL

Dunlap, Ethel Trew   (??-??)

Ethel Trew Dunlap was a prolific contributor to the "Poetry of the People" column of the *Negro World*. This weekly newspaper was founded in Harlem in 1918 by the Jamaican black nationalist Marcus Garvey (1887–1940). It was the official organ of his **Universal Negro Improvement Association** (UNIA), founded in 1916. Discussing issues affecting black men and women in the United States, glorifying Africa, and commenting on the rise of Islam and political issues in the Muslim world, Ethel Trew Dunlap's poetry contributed to and reflected the UNIA's efforts to create a consciousness of the ties among people of African descent around the world.

Little is known of Dunlap's birth and childhood except that she may have been born in the South and was of mixed parentage. In 1921, when her poetry first appeared in the *Negro World*, she was writing from Chicago. At the end of that year, she wrote a few poems in Danville, Illinois; she had stopped there briefly before continuing on to Los Angeles, California, where she settled until sometime in 1923 and where a relative, Eva Trew, also lived. Dunlap may have been affiliated with the UNIA branch in Los Angeles. In 1925, she sent in her poems from Watts, California. Although information on her life is scarce, her poetry is interesting and captivating and the subjects on which she writes inform us about Dunlap, a Garveyite woman of mixed ethnic descent.

From 1921 to 1925, Dunlap contributed close to one hundred poems to the *Negro World*, most of which were written in 1921 and 1922. During those years, her verses focused primarily on African Americans and issues relating to them. She often wrote about historical events such as the Tulsa Riot (1919), the Tulsa Fire, and the Dyer Bill (1921), and about social practices such as Southern peonage and lynching. Toward the end of 1921, she wrote several pieces that reflect her strong attachment to the Black Belt of Chicago, an area where descendants of Africans were concentrated. Some of her rhyming compositions are tributes to noted bards such as Claude McKay and J. R. Ralph Casimir and to social and political figures, including Garvey, **Henrietta Vinton Davis, J. M. Smith**, who was president of the Los Angeles chapter of the UNIA, and J. D. Gibson, surgeon general of the UNIA. Much of her poetry espouses Garvey's mission to rescue and redeem Africans from the grip of Europe and to lead "four million strong" across the water back to their rightful homeland.

Whatever the subject of her poems, they show Dunlap's clear identification with her African roots. This is apparent in two series of verses: In the earlier series, she speaks in the first person as if she is of African ancestry; in the later one, the biblical character Ephraim figures as a symbol representing the "Negro race." She glorifies Africa and yearns for her return to the continent's bosom. On rare occasions, there is ambivalence: at times she speaks of herself as a child of freedom who loves the slave, and sometimes she speaks as if she herself is a slave.

From 1923 to 1925 Dunlap wrote only thirteen poems, few of which are related to African-American issues. Instead, they reflect an increasingly favorable and positive stance toward Islam and an awareness of events taking place in some parts of the Muslim world. In 1923, in addition to a poem extolling the Nile River, she dedicated "Progress" to a Sheikh Ahmed Din and expressed the notions that Christianity and Islam are at war, that the better of the two is the one that will give "storm-tossed souls" rest, and that Islam is a force of progress. In "Tolerance," she exhorted Christians to revere Muhammad, Zoroas-

ter, and Buddha and to love Muslims. That year, the *Negro World* reported on the spread of Islam in Africa, its benefits to black people in general, and the growing interest among African Americans in Islam.

In 1924, two of Dunlap's four poems dealt with racial matters. Of the remaining two, one is in praise of Zaghlul Pasha, an Egyptian nationalist whose name repeatedly appeared in *Negro World* articles on Egypt's occupation by the British. The other, entitled "Voices from Arabia," is a vision of scenes from the accounts of Moses, Jethro, and Zipporia.

In 1925, the last year in which her poetry appeared in the *Negro World*, three of six poems she contributed show partiality toward Islam and question Christianity and the deeds of Christian conquerors in Muslim lands. In them, she conveys the message that Islam will be triumphant in the world, that humankind will marvel in its splendor, and she urges rapprochement between Christians and Muslims. Her poem "El Islam's Call" questions Christianity and manifests a degree of knowledge about Muslim religious culture and its history that suggests that she contemplated converting or in fact became a Muslim. Whatever the case, the *Negro World* provides no concrete answers.

Her poetry struck a chord in the hearts of several of her readers, and many expressed their satisfaction in rhyming lines addressed to her. She and J. R. Ralph Casimir (a Dominican poet, correspondent for the *Negro World*, and a lifelong Garveyite) were mutual admirers who each composed poetry in praise of the other that was published in the *Negro World* and in Casimir's anthology, *Farewell* (1971). Most important, however, is that Garvey, a believer in art for the people and art for the cause, approved of her verses and invited her to read a few poems at Liberty Hall in Harlem (the date is unknown). Moreover, Garvey wrote her a letter of recommendation to facilitate future sales of a small collection of her poetry, which she intended to compile and for which she was requesting financial contributions. In 1923, she supposedly collected $10 for her book; however, the book was not published because of the controversy surrounding Garvey's impending trial.

Nothing more is known about Ethel Trew Dunlap's life following her contributions to the *Negro World*.

AMAL MUHAMMAD

F

Fauset, Jessie Redmon (1882–1961)

"Nothing . . . has ever been farther from my thought than writing to establish a thesis," Jessie Fauset stated flatly in the foreword to her novel *The Chinaberry Tree* (1931). She was not only introducing her third novel, but also defending her first two novels, *There Is Confusion* (1924) and *Plum Bun* (1929), against the criticism that they presented thesis-ridden, middle-class black characters in the service of racial uplift. Fauset's foreword pointed quite specifically to race as the driving force behind her fiction: "Colored people have been the subjects which I have chosen for my novels partly because they are the ones I know best, partly because of all the other separate groups which constitute the American cosmogony none of them, to me, seems to be naturally endowed with the stuff of which chronicles may be made." Throughout her career the condition of black people in America was to be the subject of her writings.

Fauset's insistence, however, that being "a Negro in America posits a dramatic situation" waiting for a writer "to interpret [the elements] with fidelity" included two terms, *Negro* and *American*, inextricably linked in her own interpretative strategy. Her overt connection of the two terms contributed in part to the negative criticism of her fiction as reactionary that persisted into the second half of the twentieth century with critics such as Robert Bone, who labeled her one of "the Rear Guard," old-fashioned writers of

Jessie Redmon Fauset began to write novels in order to take control of the representation of black characters in fiction; her four novels use passing as white as a metaphor to represent the arbitrariness and destructiveness of racism. As literary editor of the Crisis, *she fostered the work of many young writers prominent in the Harlem Renaissance, including Claude McKay, Jean Toomer, Countee Cullen, Arna Bontemps, and Langston Hughes.* (SCHOMBURG CENTER)

the Harlem Renaissance. The focus on her texts as dated novels of manners obscured her modern treatment of gender roles, female socialization, and sexism, a treatment that recent critics such as Carolyn Sylvander have identified in reevaluating Fauset's woman-centered fiction.

As a committed writer of poetry, essays, reviews, and fiction during the Harlem Renaissance of the 1920s and early 1930s, Fauset did have a thesis influencing her literary production. Her conviction was that in order to combat racism, white Americans had to be educated about the realities, rather than the exoticism, of black American life and that black Americans had to be represented in their home life and personal relations as similar to white Americans. In her foreword to *The Chinaberry Tree*, she discussed her conception of "the colored American who is not being pressed too hard by the Furies of Prejudice, Ignorance and Economic Injustice" as "not so very different from any other American, just distinctive." In establishing "the colored American" as having "wholesome respect for family and education and labor and the fruits of labor," Fauset emphasized the terms of her comparison: "the dark American . . . wears his [or her] joy and rue very much as does the white American. He [or she] may wear it with some differences but it is the same joy and the same rue." Fauset remained faithful to this vision of black Americans throughout her career; yet all of her writings show her keen awareness of the racism and sexism often beneath the surface in the cultural and literary politics of the 1920s and 1930s.

Jessie Redmon Fauset's formative years shaped her specific brand of race consciousness and her awareness of the contradictions often apparent in being both black and American that informed her writing. Born in Camden County, New Jersey, on April 26, 1882, she was the youngest daughter of seven children of Annie Seamon and Reverend Redmon Fauset, an African Methodist Episcopal minister who crusaded for racial justice in his community outside of Philadelphia. Her family was cultured and refined but never financially secure. Placing a high value on education for the upward mobility of black people, her parents inspired Fauset to succeed in the Philadelphia public schools, but they also prepared her for the certain impact of racism upon her achievements. An honors student at the High School for Girls, she applied to Bryn Mawr, a women's college that was not prepared to admit a black woman and instead initiated a scholarship for her at Cornell University. There, as a student of classical languages, Fauset continued her record of academic achievement and was elected to Phi Beta Kappa.

Despite an impressive undergraduate record and a 1905 baccalaureate degree, she did not find the world of work hospitable. Throughout her life, her talents and interests rarely matched the limited employment options available to an African American and a female. Fauset was unable to secure a teaching post with the segregated Philadelphia public schools, but she was both resourceful and determined: After a brief tenure in the Baltimore school system, Fauset moved to Washington, D.C., to teach French and Latin at the M Street High School (later renamed Paul Laurence Dunbar High). While teaching, Fauset completed an M.A. in French at the University of Pennsylvania.

Although a popular and well-respected member of the M Street faculty, she desired a greater use of her talents than teaching allowed, and in 1919 she received an offer for more challenging work from the *Crisis*. Its editor, W. E. B. DuBois, had recognized Fauset as the ideal candidate for the new position of literary editor on the basis of both her educational background and her creative writing, which she had begun to contribute to *Crisis* in 1912.

The position in New York with the *Crisis*, the official publication of the **National Association for the Advancement of Colored People** (NAACP), propelled Fauset into a literary career and into a mentoring role for black writers. At the beginning of her editorial work, Fauset persuaded DuBois that the arts, and creative writing in particular, could be a force in racial uplift. Left to pursue her own direction at the magazine, she placed a greater emphasis on poetry and fiction by cultivating the talents of young writers, such as Claude McKay, Jean Toomer, Countee Cullen, George Schuyler, Arna Bontemps, and Langston Hughes, who later recognized her contribution as an enabling force by calling her a "midwife" to the emerging literary renaissance in New York. From her arrival in 1919 to her departure in 1926, Fauset was the astute guiding spirit behind the *Crisis* and its movement into the forefront of literary and racial modernism. With this cultural work, she secured a significant place for herself in African-American literary history.

Not only did Fauset serve as a literary editor, but she also shaped a cultural agenda for the *Crisis*, an agenda that centrally involved the youth of the race. She envisioned a march of racial progress in which succeeding generations would distance black people from the negative societal constructions of inferiority resulting from enslavement. In 1920 and 1921, she directed her energies toward realizing an NAACP monthly magazine for children, *The Brownies' Book*. Although DuBois was its founder, Fauset was its functional editor, and she stated in the magazine's introduction that she was designing a format to "teach Universal Love and Brotherhood for all the little folks—black and brown, yellow and white." She herself wrote numerous children's articles, stories, poems, biographies, and plays, in addition to soliciting and publishing pieces by a number of aspiring authors, such as **Nella Larsen**, who would become prominent during the Harlem Renaissance.

Fauset turned to writing novels in 1922 when she recognized that black authors should take control of their representation in fiction. Begun in response to white novelist T. S. Stribling's *Birthright* (1922), her first novel, *There Is Confusion*, appeared in 1924, the eve of the most productive period of the Harlem or New Negro Renaissance. Both racial identity and racial heritage were central discourses in the cultural movement that gave rise to a new generation of black artists and intellectuals. Fauset's novel explored both discourses in rendering the lives of three interconnected characters, Joanna Marshall, Peter Bye, and Maggie Ellersley, who survive racial discrimination and transcend class divisions during the early decades of the twentieth century.

Ambitious and industrious, Joanna is the daughter of a successful caterer whose ascent from slavery in Virginia anchors his faith in the American Dream of financial success and class mobility for his children. Shiftless and irresponsible, Peter is the son of a freeborn father who descends the socioeconomic ladder and leaves a legacy of despair. Dependent and opportunistic,

Maggie is the daughter of a poor laundress who attempts to teach the value of an honest, self-supporting existence.

The three youths initially misread their access routes to productive adulthoods and misunderstand the impact of racial barriers on their lives, but all three come to terms with themselves, with racism and sexism in American society, and with their own potential for transforming the future. Their experiences in combating marginality and attaining visibility in a multifaceted urban environment reflect Fauset's faith in motivation, work, and discipline as correctives to stereotypical views of black persons, as well as her recognition of the difficulty of public or personal achievement for people of color, particularly women.

Although praised by critics such as DuBois and William Stanley Braithwaite, anxious for positive representations of black men and women, *There Is Confusion* did not propel Fauset into the forefront of the New Negro movement. But her limited success inspired her to concentrate on writing fiction. After studying in France and traveling in Europe during 1925, she resigned from the *Crisis* in 1926. Unable to break the color bar in the New York publishing industry, she could not obtain a job as a publisher's reader despite her graduate education, fluency in foreign languages, and experience in editing, nor could she secure employment with a New York foundation or as a social secretary ("in a private family, preferably for a woman," as she wrote to Joel Spingarn of the NAACP, whose help she sought in finding positions that would allow her more time to write).

Fauset's second novel, *Plum Bun: A Novel without a Moral,* was published in 1929, two years after she had returned to teaching French at Junior High School No. 136 and later at DeWitt Clinton High School. While full-time teaching slowed her writing, the greater difficulty Fauset faced was finding a publisher. The publisher of her first novel, Boni and Liveright, refused the *Plum Bun* manuscript; following rejections from Alfred A. Knopf and other major New York publishing firms actively seeking New Negro books, Fauset secured an acceptance from a small company, Frederick A. Stokes, who remained committed to publishing Fauset's novels despite the mixed reviews.

Fauset's personal experiences as an independent, educated, and well-traveled woman who because of her race and gender encountered social and cultural forces restricting her personal development and limiting her career choices influenced her themes in *Plum Bun.* In a satiric exposition of seductive fairy tale and romance plots for black women, Fauset creates a racialized female *bildungsroman* divided into five sections: "Home," "Market," "Plum Bun," "Home Again," and "Market Is Done." The five correspond to the parts of a nursery rhyme provided as epigraph ("To Market, to market / To buy a Plum Bun; / Home again, Home again, / Market is done."), and they serve to underscore the destructiveness of adhering to a fairy-tale marriage plot when the social constructions of race and the cultural inequities of gender render the black female a powerless commodity.

Angela Murray, the fair-skinned protagonist, understands the restrictions placed on her ambitions not simply because she is a black person but also because she is a woman. Discerning that "men had a better time of it than women, coloured men than coloured women, white men than white women," Angela decides to emancipate herself from the bottom half of the racial hierarchy. After the death of her parents, she leaves her darker-skinned sister Virginia in Philadelphia and moves to New York, where, as Angela Mory, she passes for white. In her dual efforts to become an artist and to marry a white man, Angela seeks not only "freedom and independence," but also "power and protection." Though she recognizes the arbitrariness of color in racial designations and the irony of racism directed toward a white-skinned black person, she does not recognize that her own romantic idealization of marriage invests color with a substantive reality and allows for the white male's exercise of power over her.

Ultimately, Angela relinquishes subordination to men by empowering herself through her painting and her job as a designer. In realigning her priorities, she achieves self-actualization that contributes to her reclaiming her racial identity and affirming her heritage. Yet, in storybook fashion, she receives the reward of a true love, Anthony Cross, whom she is preparing to marry as the novel ends. Coincidentally, at the age of forty-seven and just as *Plum Bun* appeared, Fauset herself married insurance executive Herbert Hill.

Her third novel, *The Chinaberry Tree: A Novel of American Life*, was introduced in 1931 by white novelist Zona Gale. Gale attempted to alleviate claims that Fauset's black characters were unbelievable: "There is in America a great group of Negroes of education and substance who are living lives of quiet interests and pursuits, quite unconnected with white folk save as these are casually met." Fauset herself stated that as a girl of fifteen, she had actually heard the story that became the basis of first a short story,

"Double Trouble," and then the novel *The Chinaberry Tree.*

The plot centers on the women of the Strange family. Aunt Sal Strange has been excluded from the black community of Red Brook, New Jersey, because of her love relationship with the white Colonel Halloway. Laurentine, the product of Sal's union with the Colonel, grows up well provided for but isolated in the white house bought by her father, after she learns from a playmate that she has bad blood. Judy Strange, Sal's sister, nurtures Laurentine out of her retreat, but she departs Red Brook after an affair with Sylvester Forten. Melissa Paul, Judy's daughter, arrives from Philadelphia to live with her relatives whom she sees as lacking respectability. The tension in the household mounts over issues of legitimacy and conventionality: Melissa feels superior to Laurentine, as well as to Sal, and Laurentine resents reminders of her birth outside of wedlock. Melissa's own origins are revealed dramatically when she discovers that Malory Forten, the Red Brook youth who shares her views and values and whom she plans to marry, is her half-brother.

In examining attitudes within the black community toward miscegenation, class pretensions, extramarital and interracial relationships, Fauset attempted to break new ground in her fiction and to represent a revision of the constructs stratifying black people. She positioned social conventions and communal expectations against the grain of meaningful human relationships. In defiance of arbitrary values and rules, her characters come to accept the integrity of human life and the basic equality of all living people. As Dr. Stephen Denleigh remarks in *The Chinaberry Tree*, "Biology transcends society!" His response is to Laurentine's confession of her illegitimacy, a condition that he dismisses:

"The facts of life, birth, and death are more important than the rules of the living, marriage, law, the sanction of the church or man." Denleigh's dismissal of the relevancy of legitimacy in determining an individual's significance nullifies one of the measures of social status overvalued by the newly emergent black middle class. That Denleigh and Laurentine marry argues for a reintegration of the black community and for a transformation of its restrictive attitudes.

Fauset's last novel, *Comedy: American Style,* was published in 1933 when the more intense activity of the Harlem Renaissance was over, and this text may be her satiric response to the elevation of color among its more vocal participants. Olivia Blanchard Carey, the central figure in the text, is a self-hating, deluded woman who despises black people ostensibly because they are victims, vulnerable to injury, and discriminated against in American society. Unable to accept herself as black, she has an all-consuming need to be herself, though she ultimately achieves her desire to pass for white and to escape the confines of American society. Olivia's psychology is not fully revealed; this failure is especially noticeable in the early section of the text, which focuses primarily on Olivia's mother, Janet Blanchard, and her efforts to survive after the death of her husband Lee, and her subsequent happy marriage to Ralph Blake. While Janet is class conscious, all three are secure in their racial identity and are strong supporters of their race. Olivia completely escapes their influence during her formative years.

Olivia's husband, Christopher Carey, a Harvard-trained physician, does not share her obsession with color. He and their first two children, Teresa and Christopher, are light enough to satisfy Olivia's fantasies, but the third child, Oliver, is brown-skinned like Olivia's own father. While the entire family suffers because of her mania, Oliver commits suicide when he realizes the cause of his mother's aversion to him. Even Teresa, who pleases her mother by marrying outside the race, is miserable in her loveless union to a Frenchman who refuses to acknowledge her mother. Only Christopher, who marries Phebe Grant (blonde, blue-eyed, working-class, and proudly black), manages to survive his mother's obsessions and to build a productive life.

In all four of her novels, Fauset used passing as white as a means of representing the arbitrariness and destructiveness of racial constructions in the United States. Her particular concerns with the impact of race on women and the limitations placed on black women by their own communities were often masked in complicated, unwieldy plots culminating in happy marriages. Because her fictional strategy relied upon the anticipation of change within social institutions, her critiques of race, gender, and class ideologies were circuitous, and her messages of female emancipation, development, autonomy, and empowerment were coded. Fauset died in 1961, before the current decoding and revaluation of her fiction began. Read now with fresh critical tools, her texts reveal the determined effort of a woman writer to tell the stories of black Americans that, while not always successful or popular, demand articulation and attention.

THADIOUS M. DAVIS

G

Giddings, Paula (1947–)

While **Toni Morrison, Alice Walker,** and other important novelists have sought out and reinterpreted the history of black women through their fiction, another writer has chosen to deal more directly with that history. In doing so, she has illuminated the past.

Paula Giddings was born on November 16, 1947, in Yonkers, New York. Her father, Curtis G. Giddings, was a teacher and guidance counselor. He later became the first black firefighter in Yonkers. Her mother, Virginia I. Giddings, was also a guidance counselor.

Giddings knew while she was still at Gorton High School in Yonkers that she wanted to be a writer and had published work in the school literary magazine. At **Howard University,** where she earned her B.A. in English, she was editor of the *Afro-American Review.* After graduating in 1969, she took a job as editorial secretary at the Random House publishing company in New York. She was soon promoted to copyeditor.

During a drive to diversify the Random House staff, Giddings became an editor, along with writer Toni Morrison. She worked on the publications of such black writers as **Angela Davis** and Stokely Carmichael. When her mentor, Charles Harris, left Random House in 1972 to found a university press at Howard, Giddings went with him.

In 1975, Giddings left Howard to work for *Encore America* and *Worldwide News.* She persuaded publisher **Ida Lewis** to open a branch in Paris. From there, she traveled,

Paula Giddings can say she knew Toni Morrison before the rest of us. She was an editorial assistant at Random House and typed Morrison's early fiction. She knows Ida B. Wells in a different way: Giddings has spent the last few years getting "inside" the mind and feelings of the fiery iconoclast to try to capture the spirit of this complicated woman (she was involved in virtually every controversy of her time) in what will have to be a massive biography.

reporting on news of interest to black people from France and Africa. She interviewed Winnie Mandela and President Idi Amin of Uganda. She saw a great deal of the world, but she felt separated from her home in a way that she didn't like. In 1977, she returned to the United States.

From 1977 to 1979, Giddings worked as an associate editor in the New York office of *Encore*. Then something happened that would change her life: She went to work for a research project on black women's history. Funded by the federal government, the project was to produce ten studies, and Giddings was responsible for two of them. Her topics were "Black Women in the Arts" and "Black Women and the Resistance Struggle in America."

The project inspired in Giddings a fascination with the history of black women. She wrote a proposal to the Ford Foundation and was given a grant to work on her own research. The result was her landmark book, *When and Where I Enter: The Impact of Black Women on Race and Sex in America*, focusing on the history of black women since the late nineteenth century.

The book was published in 1984, and soon Giddings was lecturing around the country. The book has sold well and is used in many college courses. In 1988, she published *In Search of Sisterhood: Delta Sigma Theta and the Challenge of the Black Sorority Movement*.

Since the publication of her first book, Paula Giddings has written for a wide range of magazines and newspapers, including *The New York Times* and *Essence*. She has become an important figure in the black intellectual community. She teaches at Duke University and is working on a full-length biography of **Ida B. Wells-Barnett**. Her contribution to the knowledge and understanding of black women's history is immense.

Giovanni, Nikki (1943–)

Nikki Giovanni emerged on the artistic and political scene as one of the new black poets who became popular in the 1960s. The outspokenness of her style and her message earned her extraordinary public acclaim, which she continues to enjoy. Her first poems were militant calls to armed action for all black people who desired freedom from racism and injustice in America. Her writing and her political activities, however, were large, clear reflections of her commitment to end oppression and her allegiance to the emerging civil rights movement.

One of the best examples of Nikki Giovanni's militant poems is "The True Import of Present Dialogue, Black vs. Negro," which appeared in her first collection, a self-published volume entitled *Black Feeling, Black Talk* (1967). The poem begins, "nigger / Can you kill / Can you kill / Can a nigger kill / Can a nigger kill a honkie." The shock value in the opening lines continues as the poem names the enemies of black people and Giovanni writes, "We ain't got to prove we can die / We got to prove we can kill." Of equal importance in the poem is Giovanni's attention to black attitudes of inferiority, which also have to be killed. She writes, "Can you kill the nigger / in you / Can you make your nigger mind / die / Can you kill your nigger mind / And free your Black hands to / strangle." Part of the structural innovativeness of the poem is its repetition of the rhetorical question "can you kill?," which eventually reads not as a question but as an imperative.

Two poems from Nikki Giovanni's early work foreshadow her later thematic focus. One, "Seduction," from *Black Feeling, Black Talk*, pictures the poetic persona taking time out from making revolution for making love. She disrobes her lover, but he is preoccupied with the momentum of the political movement and seems oblivious to

Nikki Giovanni's poetry reflects not only her personal history but also the shifting nature of the black experience in America.
(SCHOMBURG CENTER)

her actions until the last four lines, when the poet writes, "then you'll notice / your state of undress / and knowing you you'll just say / 'Nikki, isn't this counterrevolutionary'?" "Nikki Rosa," probably the most anthologized of Giovanni's poems, is a lovely, accessible poem that reveals the human complexities of traditional black life. Focusing on childhood memories, the verses show the alternate side to Giovanni's militant political consciousness. "Nikki Rosa" first appeared in *Black Judgement*, published by

Broadside Press in 1968. *Black Judgement* was combined with *Black Feeling, Black Talk* and published by William Morrow in 1970.

"Nikki Rosa" and "Seduction" are poems that suggest the nonviolent and personal direction of Giovanni's subsequent work. Her later work rejects the violence, and Eugene Redmond points out that the new poetry charts her "rite of passage toward womanhood." **Paula Giddings** writes that by "the early seventies, the Black movement was in disarray. . . . Giovanni, however, could still maintain an appeal across ideological lines." Giddings suggests that young people who missed the "heroic age of the SNCC (**Student Nonviolent Coordinating Committee**) successes in the South, or the urgency which inspired them" were drawn to the personal qualities in Giovanni's poetry. Giddings astutely observes that older people also like her, finding her "precocious persona . . . more mischievous than 'bad,'" probably getting "vicarious pleasure from her sharp-tongued defense of the race."

Nikki Giovanni (named Yolande Cornelia after her mother) was born in Knoxville, Tennessee, on June 7, 1943, to Gus and Yolande Giovanni. Her parents, who met while students at Knoxville College, relocated to Wyoming, Ohio, a suburb of Cincinnati, when Nikki was very young. The younger of two daughters, Nikki had an independent, assertive, courageous temperament that was apparent early; these qualities also defined the temperament of her maternal grandmother, Louvenia Watson, with whom Nikki lived during her sophomore and junior years of high school. Louvenia Watson probably reinforced these attributes in Nikki, who would manifest them not only in her personal life but also in her poetry and prose.

Giovanni entered Fisk University in September 1960 when she was seventeen years old. Given the political viewpoint in her subsequent writing, it is interesting to note that she supported Barry Goldwater, an extreme right-wing Republican, who was campaigning to be president of the United States. Though Giovanni was conservative and middle class, Fisk (traditionally respected for educating the children of middle-class blacks) did not appeal to her; she did not get along with the dean of women and left the campus without permission to spend Thanksgiving in Knoxville with her grandmother. She was placed on probation upon her return and was later suspended when her "attitude" did not improve.

Nikki Giovanni returned to Fisk University in 1964, graduating magna cum laude in February 1967 with honors in history. She took part in the Fisk Writers Workshop, directed by the distinguished author John O. Killens, who influenced her writing and her politics. Her change in political consciousness is marked by the fact that she was responsible for getting SNCC reinstated on Fisk's campus. In June 1967, Giovanni planned the first Cincinnati Black Arts Festival; she helped show the links between art and culture and became a major figure in the movement to foster black awareness in the city. Giovanni's political activities caused concern in her parents, who saw no professional future in her organizational work. Her response was to enroll in graduate school. She received a Ford Foundation grant and attended the University of Pennsylvania School of Social Work but later entered the School of Fine Arts at Columbia

University. As an assistant professor of English, she taught in the SEEK Program at Queens College of the City University of New York.

Nikki Giovanni's work has been criticized as unpredictable and uneven; similar critiques are often also leveled against her as a person. Eugene Redmond's observation that the range of her work represents her rite of passage into womanhood is very important because life is fluid and because Giovanni's poetry and prose reflect normal personal and intellectual change. In an interview with Claudia Tate, the editor of *Black Women Writers at Work* (1983), Giovanni says that she does not reread her prose because she does not want to be trapped by what she has previously said. The comment provides partial insight into Giovanni's aesthetic philosophy because she does not believe that "life is inherently coherent." She continues, "If I never contradict myself then I'm either not thinking or I'm conciliating positions and, therefore, not growing." These thoughts are important clues to the often controversial positions that Giovanni has taken since she first emerged on the literary scene.

Nikki Giovanni's poetic transition from militant revolutionary to a more "balanced" perspective is evident in the poem "Revolutionary Dreams" from her 1970 collection *Re-Creation*, published by Broadside Press. She writes, "i used to dream militant / dreams of taking / over america . . . / i even used to think i'd be the one / to stop the riot and negotiate the peace / then i awoke and dug / that if i dreamed natural / dreams of being a natural / woman doing what a woman / does when she's natural / i would have a revolution." The poem echoes **Aretha Franklin**'s version of the song "Natural

Woman," and the sexual implications of Giovanni's words are obvious; yet, there is something to be said for the latent political interpretation of the poem: "revolutionizing" oneself before attempting to change the world. Her subsequent volumes of poetry, *My House* (1972), *The Women and the Men* (1972), *Cotton Candy on a Rainy Day* (1978), and *Those Who Ride the Night Winds* (1983), continue the introspective personal tone that began in *Re-Creation*.

Giovanni's volumes of children's poetry are delightful, and her prose works are scrappy, thought-provoking texts that present brilliant observations of the social, cultural, and political scene in contemporary America. *Spin a Soft Black Song: Poems for Children* (1971), *Ego-Tripping and Other Poems for Young People* (1973), and *Vacation Time: Poems for Children* (1980) are collections written by Nikki Giovanni for children. One of the best and most widely known of Giovanni's verses, the title poem in the volume *Ego-Tripping*, begins, "I was born in the congo / I walked to the fertile crescent and built / the sphinx / I designed a pyramid so tough that a star / that only glows every one hundred years falls / into the center giving divine perfect light / I am bad." The poem continues by celebrating and mythologizing the power of ancient black people whose civilizations have been misrepresented in history. It ends with these lines: "I am so hip even my errors are correct / I sailed west to reach east and had to round off / the earth as I went. . . . I am so perfect so divine so ethereal so surreal / I cannot be comprehended / except by my permission / I mean . . . I . . . can fly / like a bird in the sky." The theme of flying back to Africa is central to black folklore, but Giovanni gives it a contemporary spin by telling of African

magnificence at a time when blacks were struggling to know themselves in the context of their African past.

Gemini: An Extended Autobiographical Statement on My First Twenty-five Years at Being a Black Poet (1971), composed of autobiographical essays—some previously published—contains much of Giovanni's earliest prose. It provides selective glimpses of the feisty Nikki, including the four year old "protecting" her older sister, Gary, and the young woman giving birth to Tommy. Though the publication of essays on the first twenty-five years of one's life might seem presumptuous, the collection is refreshingly opinionated and honest and was nominated for a National Book Award. Giovanni's importance as a young writer is underscored by two texts that record her conversations with her black literary foreparents: *A Poetic Equation: Conversations between Nikki Giovanni and Margaret Walker* (1974) and *A Dialogue: James Baldwin and Nikki Giovanni* (1973) are especially valuable not only because of the collaboration with the older writers but also for the extraordinary documentation of the evolution of black artistic and aesthetic thinking from one generation to another. Nikki Giovanni's collection of essays, *Sacred Cows and Other Edibles* (1988), is full of comfortable, casual observations as well as insightful commentary on the seemingly unchanging nature of social and political conditions in America.

Most interesting, given her life as a writer, Giovanni says, "There will never be a poem that will free mankind." Her belief is that writers preach to the saved, rarely changing people's minds. Giovanni's early writings make excellent sense if we accept her idea that art is potentially dangerous because it is egalitarian. Though her personal and political decisions might not be those of others, she has moved beyond the rhetoric of the 1960s, understanding that militant words are not sufficient to make lasting political change. She reiterates her point: "Writing is not who I am, it's what I do." If readers allow Nikki Giovanni her right to change, given her belief that life itself is fluid and incoherent, they will find her current work an accurate measure of American and black American life in the last years of the twentieth century.

CAROLYN MITCHELL

Golden, Marita (1950–)

When the literary establishment began to open its doors in the 1970s to black writers, the number and quality of women who boldly walked in was staggering. Among those women was journalist and novelist Marita Golden.

Marita Golden was born April 28, 1950, in Washington, D.C., the daughter of Francis Sherman and Beatrice Reid Golden. Her father was a taxi driver and her mother a landlord. She received her bachelor's degree from American University in 1971 and her masters from Columbia University in 1973.

After graduating from Columbia, Golden went to work as an associate producer for WNET-Channel 13 in New York City. The next year, in 1975, she took a job as assistant professor of mass communications at Roxbury Community College; four years later, she became assistant professor of English at the same college. In 1981, she moved to Emerson College in Boston, where she was assistant professor of journalism for two years.

In 1983, Golden published her first book; although she was only twenty-nine years old, it was an autobiography, *Migrations of the Heart*. She explained to the *Washington Post* that "I wanted to meditate on what it meant to grow up in the '60s, what it meant to go to Africa the first time, what it meant to be a modern black woman living in that milieu. I had to bring order to the chaos of memory." This first book received good reviews, and some critics recognized a remarkable new voice. Her second book, *A Woman's Place*, was a novel about the lives of three black women. Again, Golden was praised for her prose style and her honest approach to complex issues.

By the time her second novel was published in 1989, Golden was an established writer, exploring diverse parts of black society. *Long Distance Life* tells the story of a young woman in the 1920s who grows up on a farm in the South and then moves North. It then follows the generations of her family through the civil rights movement and the deadly struggle of one child with drugs.

Golden's third novel, *And Do Remember Me*, again deals with the affect of civil rights struggles on the lives of ordinary people. With grace and insight, Golden moves between the personal and the political in this story of two black women living in different worlds.

Marita Golden is part of the group of black women writers who have emerged in the last three decades in the United States. She summed up the drive behind this important literary movement when she told *Contemporary Authors*, "I write essentially to complete myself and to give my vision a significance that the world generally seeks to destroy."

KATHLEEN THOMPSON

Greenfield, Eloise (1929–)

Says Eloise Greenfield: "When I'm carrying a story around in my head, I feel as if I'm holding my head funny. Sometimes I want to explain to people on the street that I'm just trying to keep the words from spilling out until I get to a quiet place with pen and paper." As a child Greenfield did not like to write, so she carried stories around in her head for many years before she actually began to write them down.

Eloise Greenfield was born on May 17, 1929, in Parmele, North Carolina, to Weston W. Little and Lessie Jones Little. They moved to Washington, D.C., when Little was only a few months old, and she was educated at Miner Teachers College (1946–49). One of her first jobs was as a clerk-typist for the U.S. Patent Office (1949–56); it was partly because of her boredom with this job that she first began to write short stories. She continued at the Patent Office until 1960 as a supervisory patent assistant; then from 1963 to 1964, she was a staff member of the Unemployment Compensation Board. She subsequently went to work as a secretary, a case-control technician, and an administrative assistant for various employers from 1964 to 1968.

In the early 1970s, Greenfield began to work for the District of Columbia Black Writers' Workshop: She served as director of adult fiction (1971–73) and as director of children's literature (1973-74). In 1973, and again from 1985 to 1986, she was a writer-in-residence for the District of Columbia Commission on the Arts. It was during the 1970s that her love of reading and of words developed into a love of writing. *Bubbles*, her first book, was published in 1972; *Sister* appeared in 1974; her first book of poems, *Honey, I Love and Other Love Poems*, was published in 1978 and was recorded with music in 1982.

Greenfield's writing, therefore, takes many forms: poetry, picture books, recordings, and biographies, and she has collaborated with all of the most celebrated African-American illustrators, including Tom Feelings, Leo and Diane Dillon, Carole Byard, and John Steptoe, and she writes about some of the most inspirational African-American historical figures: Paul Robeson, **Rosa Parks**, and **Mary McLeod Bethune**. Her commitment stems from her belief that "a true history must be the concern of every black writer. It is necessary for black children to have a true knowledge of their past and present, in order that they may develop an informed sense of direction for their future."

Reviewers of children's literature have sometimes disagreed on the quality of Greenfield's writing. For example, *Childtimes: A Three-Generation Memoir* (the first of two books written with her mother) received almost universal acclaim; in contrast, some sharply criticized *She Come Bringing Me That Little Baby Girl* as propagating socially taught sexist behavior. More often than not, however, the world of children's literature has recognized the excellence of Eloise Greenfield's writing. She received the Carter G. Woodson Award for *Rosa Parks* in 1974. Despite the controversy it generated, *She Come Bringing Me That Little Baby Girl* won the Irma Simonton Black Award in 1974. *Me and Neesie* was named an American Library Association Notable Book of 1975; the same honor was given to *Honey, I Love* in 1978. In 1976, *Paul Robeson* was recognized with the Jane

Addams Children's Book Award. Green-field's entire body of work has been celebrated formally, too, by the Council on Interracial Books for Children (1975), the District of Columbia Association of School Librarians (1977), and Celebrations in Learning (1977).

African-American children's literature is an important subcategory of children's literature in general. One of the most prestigious annual honors bestowed upon a black writer and black illustrator is the Coretta Scott King Award (awarded by the American Library Association). Greenfield has garnered this honor twice, for *Africa Dream* in 1978 and for *Nathaniel Talking* in 1990. *Nathaniel* is most notable because it is written largely in the form of "rap" lyrics, demonstrating Greenfield's concern with interpreting for children not only the past but also the present.

Eloise Greenfield married Robert Greenfield in 1950. They have one son, Steve, and one daughter, Monica. Greenfield has stated that her family and her efforts against racism are the two most important concerns in her life; yet, in a very tangible way, she has adopted all black children as her family by choosing to address racism through writing books especially for them. She is arguably the foremost African-American children's poet and has secured her place in the history of African-American children's literature by writing consistently and truthfully about history, about social issues, and, perhaps most important, about family.

DIANNE JOHNSON-FEELINGS

Grimké, Charlotte (1837–1914)

Antislavery activist Charlotte Grimké was also a poet of some note. Most of her work appeared in antislavery periodicals such as the *Liberator*, *National Anti-Slavery Standard*, and *Anglo African*. Most of these poems had an antislavery theme, but there were others. One of her most famous, "Red, White, and Blue" was written in memory of black Revolutionary War hero Crispus Attucks. Set to music, it was performed by a choir at a Boston memorial service to the heroes of the Boston Massacre in 1858.

Grimké also wrote essays about her experiences teaching newly freed black citizens on South Carolina's Sea Islands. These essays were published in *Atlantic Monthly* in 1864. Charlotte Grimké's biographical entry is in the first volume of this encyclopedia, *The Early Years, 1619–1899*.

Guy, Rosa (c. 1925–)

Neighborhood children hurled insults and objects as Rosa Cuthbert Guy walked to school in New York City during the 1930s. Perhaps those children resented her Trinidadian accent, or maybe they considered her an outsider even though they shared the same skin colors and many of the same experiences. Today, young adult readers shower her with praise and accolades for her novels. Some of the honors bestowed upon her novels include the American Library Association Notable Book Award for *The Friends* (1974) and the American Library Association's Best Books for Young Adults Award for *Ruby* (1976), *Edith Jackson* (1978), and *The Disappearance* (1979).

Rosa Cuthbert was born on September 1, 1925 or 1928 (the year is disputed and Guy has not resolved the discrepancy), in Trinidad, West Indies, to Henry and Audrey Gonzales Cuthbert. Her parents immigrated to the United States through Ellis Island in the early 1930s; like many immigrants, Henry and Audrey Cuthbert came first and then sent for their children, Rosa and younger sister Ameze, in 1932.

Audrey Cuthbert died when Rosa was nine years old. For a few years, she and Ameze lived with a cousin who was a follower of Marcus Garvey, an early advocate of Pan-African unity among the African diaspora. Her father remarried but then died in 1937. Thereafter, Rosa was shuttled back and forth among institutions and foster homes.

She quit high school at age 14 to help support her sister, taking a job in a brassiere factory. She married Warner Guy (now deceased) in 1941 and bore a son, Warner, in 1942. They moved to Connecticut in 1945, but Rosa Guy returned to New York City in 1950 after the dissolution of their marriage. In the early 1940s, she began to study acting and eventually wrote a one-act play, *Venetian Blinds* (1954), that was staged off-Broadway.

Guy attended New York University to study writing and the theater and then became involved in the creation of the Harlem Writers' Guild. The guild has proven to be an important source of support for African-American writers, among them John O. Killens and **Maya Angelou**.

Guy speaks the Creole of her native Trinidad, as well as French and English. She travels extensively throughout the Caribbean and Africa. Currently, she resides off-and-on in New York City, gives readings of works, and occasionally teaches.

Few writers blend the literary, personal, and political in their novels as successfully as Guy. She avoids propaganda, overt didacticism, and strident tones, preferring instead to emphasize respect, pride, and knowledge

about Africa, African Americans, and Afro-Caribbeans. Guy maintains that the time she spent in her cousin's home profoundly affected her intellectual and political development. For Guy, that early exposure to the teachings of Marcus Garvey led her to seeing Malcolm X as a hero who symbolizes the "gold" (individuals) unsalvaged in America's ghettos.

Rosa Guy considers herself a storyteller. The stories she weaves are characterized by meticulous attention to the craft of writing. Guy explores a variety of themes, such as the conflicts that develop among people of color, the survival of children in hostile environments, love, coming of age, quests for identity and purpose in life, the relationships among family members and strangers, friendship, and many others. Her settings are vivid: the reader smells the stench of Harlem tenements or the fresh, fragrant air of middle-class enclaves. Her characters are complex and fully developed; she does not resort to stereotypes or one-dimensional figures to advance her plots. She captures the nuances of West Indian and African-American social dialects. Two novels, *The Friends* (1974), an exploration of the complicated and painful relationship between West Indian Phyllisia and African-American Edith, and *My Love, My Love* (1985), a retelling of *The Little Mermaid* set on a fictional Caribbean island, capture Guy's writing at its best. Her more-recent books include *Billy the Great* and *The Music of Summer*, both published in 1992.

Critics praise the naturalistic qualities of her work and the sensitivity with which she addresses complex issues such as defining the family and familial responsibilities, love and caring among family and friends, and the consequences of "coming of age" in an era when innocence is no longer a hallmark of childhood or adolescence.

Rosa Guy's legacy so far, in addition to the canon of quality literature she has produced, is a body of work that takes artistic risks. Guy respects the ability of young adult readers to understand, analyze, and judge the themes, characters, and issues she incorporates into her novels. She trusts her readers and does not compel them to learn a lesson. Equally important, her personal political philosophy, commitment to justice, beliefs in freedom from oppression and in caring for those unlike oneself are not compromised. Her philosophy can be summed up in these words: "A novel to me is an emotional history of a people in time and place. If I have proven to be popular with young people, it is because when they have finished one of my books, they not only have a satisfying experience—they have also had an education."

VIOLET J. HARRIS

H

Hamilton, Virginia Esther (1936–)

Poised in gauzy pink, velvet, or taffeta dresses, five-year-old Virginia Esther Hamilton mesmerized family and friends with her singing voice. She thoroughly enjoyed performing at family gatherings and church socials. Now she astounds readers with the unique literary voices woven from what she remembers, knows, and imagines.

Her literary career began at age nine or ten when she began to write stories for her pleasure. Her first published novel, *Zeely* (1967), helped alter the image of Africans in children's literature. Other novels followed: *The House of Dies Drear* (1968), a mystery that explored slavery, interrelationships, and the Underground Railroad through the experiences of a contemporary African-American family; *The Time-Ago Tales of Jadhu* (1969), an example of storytelling; *The Planet of Junior Brown* (1971), an exploration of genius, contemporary social problems, and survival; *W. E. B. DuBois* (1972), a biography of a childhood hero; *Time-Ago Lost: More Tales of Jadhu* (1973); and the exceptional *M. C. Higgins, the Great* (1974).

Hamilton was born March 12, 1936, the fifth and youngest child of Kenneth James Hamilton and Etta Belle Perry Hamilton. Virginia adored her father and talks about him in many of her essays: Intelligent, well-read, and a musician, Kenneth Hamilton could not pursue the business career for which he trained (at Iowa State Business College) because of racism, but he shared with his daughter a love of reading, music, travel, storytelling, and two personal heroes—Paul Robeson and W. E. B. DuBois.

Her maternal relatives, the Perrys, settled in Yellow Springs, Ohio. Family lore related that an ancestress of the family, a leader in the Underground Railroad, guided her son out of slavery and into freedom in Ohio. This great grandfather married into one of the other families in the area and settled into farming. Future Perrys purchased land, became farmers, and raised children. Hamilton's early life in this circle of family love appears in vignettes in her work; she characterized her childhood as a "fine one" because of her experiences growing up in an extended family.

Few racial strictures penetrated this seemingly ideal existence. Hamilton's formal schooling included little of the contributions of African Americans to culture and history, but she received what she labeled "the Knowledge" from home. The Knowledge supplanted what she received at school about African Americans; her father recounted the lives of famous African Americans—especially DuBois and Robeson, as well as entertainers **Florence Mills** and Blind Lemon Jefferson.

Hamilton attended a rural elementary school and high school, performing well enough in school to receive a scholarship to attend Antioch College (1952–55), for her B.A. degree. She later enrolled at Ohio State

University (1957–58) and the New School for Social Research.

Visiting and living in New York City were lifelong dreams for Hamilton, and during her college years she worked summers in New York City as a bookkeeper. She moved there in the late 1950s and remained for fifteen years, working at a variety of occupations from bookkeeper to singer, all the while writing and enjoying community life in the East Village. During this time, Hamilton met and married Arnold Adoff, a Jewish teacher in Harlem, poet, graduate student, and manager of jazz musicians. Adoff won critical praise in children's literature for his stories about biracial families, the poetry anthologies he edited, and the volumes of poetry he created. He received the prestigious National Council of Teachers of English poetry award for his work. Adoff also serves as Hamilton's manager. They are the parents of a daughter, Leigh, and a son, Jamie. Hamilton and Adoff currently reside in Ohio.

M. C. Higgins, the Great (1974) secured Hamilton's literary reputation. This exceptional novel depicts a young male's concern for his family's safety (they live on a mountain ravaged by strip mining), his dreams of a singing career for his mother that will enable the family to leave the mountain, first love, relationships, and the quest to fulfill one's dreams. The book is filled with the sweet anguish of the family's love, music, and cultural traditions; it also contains a very gentle love relationship between parents. The novel garnered several major literary awards: Hamilton is the only author to receive the Newbery Medal (given by the American Library Association for the "most distinguished contribution to literature for children published in the United States dur-

ing the preceding year"), the *Boston Globe-Horn Book Magazine* Award, the National Book Award, the Lewis Carroll Shelf Award, and the International Board on Books for Young People Award for the same book. Some of the original manuscripts of her books are housed in the Kerlan Collection at the University of Minnesota.

Hamilton considers herself a storyteller who carries on the tradition that enabled many African Americans to survive slavery and postslavery experiences. The stories she weaves do not signify an ignoble people beaten down by poverty and racism; instead, her stories reflect the myriad experiences of African Americans, the bittersweet along with the triumphant. High John De Conqueror is a favorite image. This folklore character appears when needed most by his people. He is a trickster-hero who gives strength, courage, and laughter that sustains his people. She contends that he has emerged as a symbol of a new ethnic literature and that he represents the hunger for humor in African-American literature. Proponents of any single authentic literary depiction of African Americans raise Hamilton's ire—she writes that she is "weary and wary" of cultural arbiters; instead, she supports an artistic vision that enables her to write about the particulars of her "dreams, lies, myths, and disasters," in order to see and understand universal values and experiences.

Hamilton believes that the writer must grow and change, that it is the experience of living and partly living that illuminates the writer's art. This view prevents her from writing the same novel or repeating a set of characters in her novels. She has no desire to write about her family or her heritage indefinitely unless doing so enables her to explore new ideas, experiment with new forms or styles, or transform the source of an image. Hamilton chooses not to refer to African Americans and other people of color as minorities; rather, she uses the term *parallel culture* to connote the belief that people of color share in "American" culture as well as their own. The concept does not allow for presumed superiority or inferiority. The dreams, visions, myths, and ideas of a culture across the North American continent are referred to as being a component of the hopescape. *Hopescape* implies both the promise achieved and the promise unfulfilled.

Hamilton writes to entertain: The sharp humor and images in *Willie Bea and the Time the Martians Landed* (1983) provoke roll-in-the-aisles laughter. Though she always writes with humor, Hamilton has worked in a range of genres: contemporary realistic fiction, historical fiction, science fiction/fantasy, folk tales, and biographies. She has explored several themes in her books: the experiences and culture of African Americans, surviving and survivors in a variety of milieus, quests of various types, coming of age, the struggles of famous African Americans, first love, parent love, conflict between parent and child, attachment to one's homestead, environmental concerns, outsiders, and many others.

Folk tales have a significant presence in children's literature; Hamilton's contributions, *The People Could Fly* (1985), *In the Beginning* (1988), and *The Dark Way* (1990), found favor with readers and critics. The latter two were world tales about creation and the more malevolent elements of humans. *The People Could Fly*, a best-seller for Hamilton, recreates the language and beliefs of African Americans in a manner that contrasts sharply with the traditional depictions of Joel Chandler Harris or the contemporary renditions of Julius Lester. Actor James Earl Jones joined with Hamilton to record some of the tales; their voices, along with music, create haunting, vibrant, and memorable storytelling. *Many Thousand Gone* (1993) is a companion volume to *The People Could Fly*.

Biographies about great men have long been a staple of children's literature. Hamilton's offerings—*W. E. B. DuBois: A Biography* (1972) and *Paul Robeson: The Life and Times of a Free Black Man* (1975)—are remarkable because of the extensive research Hamilton conducted, the choice of controversial subjects, and the candor apparent in the books' content. These biographies provide an excellent introduction to the lives of two phenomenal men.

Hamilton remains the only African American who has written science fiction/fantasy for young readers. The Justice Trilogy books—*Justice and Her Brothers* (1978), *Dustland* (1980), and *The Gathering* (1981)—explore concepts such as good versus evil, psychic powers, the origin and development of various life forms, and the power unleashed when those of varying psychic abilities meld their talents.

Hamilton continually surprises her readers. *Plain City* (1993) examines racial identity and the complex, sometimes contradictory factors that influence it. Buhlaire, the main character, is multiracial, a loner, and distinguished by her carrot-colored dreadlocks. Escaping north to freedom is a common literary theme. Hamilton subverts the usual interpretations about "underground railroads" in *Jaguarundi* (1994) by focusing on endangered animal species in Central and South America. *Her Stories* (1995) is a unique contribution to literature:

her retelling of a group of folk, supernatural, and fairy tales, animal stories, legends, and "true narratives" about African-American girls and women.

Critics of Hamilton's work focus on content, style, and treatment. First, some argue that her subject matter is too complex for most children and that only the most gifted of readers enjoy her works. Second, some critics feel that some of the stylistic devices she uses—stream of consciousness, incomplete sentences, invented languages, and shifting settings and times—are distracting for many readers. Third, other critics suggest that her plots ramble occasionally, some plot twists seem contrived or forced, and some events are implausible or inappropriate for a particular setting. Few, however, criticize her characterizations or her vision.

Her critics aside, Hamilton has created an impressive and accomplished body of literature about African-American life and culture in all their complexities. Her many honors include the Hans Christian Andersen Award and the Laura Ingalls Wilder Award. In 1995 she became the first children's book author to receive a "genius" fellowship from the MacArthur Foundation.

She has helped to forge new standards of creative and literary excellence that inspire children and adults. Yet, Hamilton has remained true to her initial reasons for writing: to entertain and to tell a good story while providing readers with new visions of the world.

VIOLET J. HARRIS

Harper, Frances Ellen (1825–1911)

In "Sowing and Reaping" (1876–77), Frances Ellen Watkins Harper describes one of her characters as "a firm believer in the utility of beauty." Had she been talking about herself, she could not have chosen a more apt phrase. For sixty-eight years, Frances Ellen Watkins Harper wrote, recited, and published poetry and fiction, essays, and letters, all designed to delight and to teach people how to live lives of high moral purpose and dedicated social service. She became an internationally recognized journalist, the nineteenth century's most prolific African-American novelist, and its best loved African-American poet.

Frances Harper was known as the "bronze muse," but the publication of over a dozen books and innumerable poems, essays, and stories was but a part of her efforts to work for what she called "a brighter coming day." Harper was an active member of the Underground Railroad, one of the first African-American women to be hired as an abolitionist lecturer, a founder of the American Woman Suffrage Association, a member of the national board of the Women's Christian Temperance Union, and an executive officer of the Universal Peace Union. She was a founding member of the **National Association of Colored Women**, the director of the American Association of Educators of Colored Youth, and a tireless worker for the African Methodist Episcopal Church and the National Colored Women's Congress.

By word and by deed, she became such a symbol of empowering and empowered womanhood that women across the nation organized F. E. W. Harper Leagues or, like the many Frances E. Harper Women's Christian Temperance Unions, named local chapters of national organizations after her. She was judged a "Woman of Our Race Most Worthy of Imitation," listed in *Daughters of America; or, Women of the Century*, and included in *Patriots of the American Revolution*. In his memorial tribute, the president of the Universal Peace Union, Alfred H. Love, reports that she had "acquired the title of 'Empress of Peace and Poet Laureate.'"

Frances Ellen Watkins was born to free parents in the slave city of Baltimore, Maryland, on September 24, 1825, but by the age of three, she was an orphan; it was a loss to

Frances Ellen Watkins Harper was an internationally recognized journalist, the nineteenth century's most prolific black novelist, and its best-loved black poet. Her novel Iola Leroy *was written to correct the record on slavery and Reconstruction, to inspire African Americans to be proud of their past and diligent in their work toward a greater future, and to persuade all Americans that a stronger sense of justice was essential to the peace and prosperity of the country.* (MOORLAND-SPINGARN)

which she was never reconciled. In a letter to a friend many years later, she wrote: "Have I yearned for a mother's love? The grave was my robber. Before three years had scattered their blight around my path, death had won my mother from me. Would the strong arm of a brother have been welcome? I was my mother's only child." In comparison with the majority of black Americans of that time, however, Frances Ellen Watkins lived a privileged life. She was reared by relatives and attended the prestigious William Watkins Academy for Negro Youth, an institution founded by her uncle and noted for its emphasis upon biblical studies, the classics, and elocution as well as for the political leadership and social service of its graduates. As a young woman, Watkins was noted for her industry and intelligence. By the age of fourteen she had acquired an education superior to that of most nineteenth-century women of any color or class in the United States. She had gained a reputation locally as a writer and a scholar, but when she left the academy, the best employment she could obtain was as a seamstress and baby-sitter for the owners of the local bookstore.

The slave city of Baltimore was never a comfortable place for free black people to live, but by 1850, it had become perilous indeed. When her uncle closed his school and moved his family to Canada, Frances Watkins decided to leave also. She moved to Ohio and became the first female faculty person at the newly established Union Seminary, the precursor to what is now Wilberforce University. In his annual report, principal John M. Brown noted that "Miss Watkins . . . has been faithful to her trust, and has manifested in every effort a commendable zeal for the cause of education;

and a sacrificing spirit, so that it may be promoted." After Union Seminary, she taught in Little York, Pennsylvania; then in 1853, she moved to Philadelphia in order to devote herself entirely to the abolitionist cause. The exact nature of her involvement there is not known, but we do know that she lived with the William Still family whose home was the main depot of the Philadelphia Underground Railroad. She frequented the local antislavery offices where she learned both the theory and practice of that organization, and she published several poems and essays in Frederick Douglass' paper the *Liberator*, the *Christian Recorder*, and other periodicals.

By 1854, Watkins was in New Bedford, Massachusetts, lecturing on antislavery and equal-rights topics, and shortly thereafter she was employed by the Maine Anti-Slavery Society as a traveling lecturer. Watkins's travels took her throughout the New England area and southern Canada, as far west as Detroit, Michigan, and Cincinnati, Ohio. She became a highly popular speaker and earned accolades from journalists who applauded her highly articulate and "fiery" speeches; yet, they reported, her delivery as "marked by dignity and composure" and "without the slightest violation of good taste." Watkins often incorporated her own poetry into her lectures. This, combined with her regular publication in various newspapers and magazines, helped to create her national reputation as a poet. Thus, when *Poems on Miscellaneous Subjects* was published in 1854, it was printed in both Boston and Philadelphia, sold more than 10,000 copies in three years, and was enlarged and reissued in 1857. Most likely, it was her considerable contribution to the antislavery efforts that

has made many scholars refer to her as an abolitionist poet, but this volume and all of her subsequent collections contained poems on a variety of subjects. In addition to well-known antislavery poems such as "The Slave Mother," "The Fugitive's Wife," and "The Slave Auction," the majority of the poems in *Poems on Miscellaneous Subjects* deal with issues such as religion, heroism, women's rights, black achievement, and temperance. Some of the poems are responses to contemporary writers such as Harriet Beecher Stowe and Charles Dickens. Some are reinterpretations of Bible stories; others comment on events such as the murder of Elijah Lovejoy in 1837, the Methodist Church's expulsion of one of its ministers because of his antislavery stance, and the news report about a slave in Tennessee who was beaten to death because he would not testify about an escape attempt by other slaves.

The major themes of Harper's early writing and lectures are those that she expounded throughout her career: personal integrity, Christian service, and social equality. Far from repeating homilies and slogans, however, the full corpus of her work reveals a unique blend of idealism and pragmatism, faith and philosophy. Though she consistently wrote of being "Saved by Faith," of looking for "Light in Darkness," and of believing that "The Pure in Heart Shall See God," she also spoke crisply, even stridently, about the need for mass political action, the virtues of civil disobedience and economic boycotts, and the occasional necessity for physical confrontation. She argued that it was not enough to express sympathy without taking action. According to the Philadelphia press, she was one of the most liberal and able advocates of her day for the Underground Railroad and the slave. She was a longtime friend and colleague to activists such as **Sojourner Truth**, Susan B. Anthony, Frederick Douglass, and Henry Highland Garnet, and she remained a staunch and public supporter of John Brown after the failure of the Harpers Ferry raid. Her personal hero was Moses. "I like the character of Moses," she said, because "he is the first disunionist we read about in the Jewish scriptures."

Hers was not an assimilationist or a separationist creed; Harper preferred education over violence. She believed, as one of her early essays declared, "We Are All Bound Up Together." The burdens of one group were "The Burdens of All" and as the poem of that name makes clear, without interracial cooperation, no group will be spared: "The burdens will always be heavy, / The sunshine fade into night, / Till mercy and justice shall cement / The black, the brown and the white."

Yet, Harper recognized the contradictions and complexities of issues and was not afraid to take controversial stands or to compromise when necessary. For example, she worked assiduously with the American Equal Rights Association but when the racism of Elizabeth Cady Stanton, Susan B. Anthony, and other white feminists became apparent in their disparaging remarks about black men, she sided against them, urged the passage of the Fifteenth Amendment allowing blacks to vote even though it excluded women, and ultimately contributed to the dissolution of that group and the formation of the American Woman Suffrage Association. Harper made her position widely known. She believed in equal rights for all, but if there had to be a choice between rights for black Americans and rights for women,

then she would not encourage any black woman to put a single straw in the way to prevent the progress of black men. She took this stance even though she also argued that her own close observation had shown that women are the movers in social reform, that while men talk about changes, the women are implementing them.

In 1860, Watkins married Fenton Harper, a widower with three children. They moved to a farm outside Columbus, Ohio, and they had a daughter, Mary. Marriage and family responsibilities left her little time to lecture or to write, but during the Civil War years, Harper did continue to speak out and to publish occasionally. Fenton Harper died in 1864, and that same year Harper returned to full-time lecturing. For the next several years, she traveled continuously throughout the North and in every southern state except Texas and Arkansas, lecturing and working for the Reconstruction effort. Papers throughout the nation advertised her appearances, reported on her travels, and published her letters about her experiences. Despite her hectic schedule, Harper did some of her most experimental writing in the postbellum years.

In 1869, she published a serialized novel, *Minnie's Sacrifice*, in the *Christian Recorder* and *Moses: A Story of the Nile*, a long dramatic poem that retells the Old Testament version of the Hebrews' Egyptian captivity and exodus. *Sketches of Southern Life* (1872), a pioneering effort in African-American dialect and folk characters that tells the story of slavery and Reconstruction through a series of poems by "Aunt Chloe," is considered by many critics to be her most innovative and best literary contribution. In 1873, Harper began writing for the *Christian Recorder* a series of fictionalized essays called "Fancy Etchings." Using a cast of characters whose conversations upon current events and social mores served to expose the issues and propose solutions, Harper pioneered the journalistic genre that others such as Langston Hughes were to make popular a half-century later.

Her experimentation with literary technique supplemented but did not replace her preference for lyrical ballads nor did her writing detract from her social involvement. In 1871, Harper arranged for the publication of the twentieth edition of *Poems on Miscellaneous Subjects* and of the first collection of her published poetry since 1857, a volume simply titled *Poems*. About that time, she also bought a house, and 1006 Bainbridge, Philadelphia, Pennsylvania, became her address until she died. She had become a homeowner, but Frances Harper was rarely at home. She was in great demand as a speaker for lecture series and as a delegate to numerous conventions. She helped develop Sunday schools and Young Men's Christian Association groups in the black community and she worked for the rehabilitation of juvenile delinquents and the security of the aged and infirm.

In 1873, she became superintendent of the Colored Section of the Philadelphia and Pennsylvania Women's Christian Temperance Union and in 1883 she became national superintendent of work among people of color. In this capacity, she tried to help those who wished to join the white groups to do so and those who preferred to organize themselves separately to do that. For Harper, it was a matter of coalition building: She recognized and did not apologize for racism among some of the individuals with whom they might need to affiliate but declared this a "relic . . . from the dead past." Her comments in "The Woman's Christian Temperance Union and the Colored Woman" (1888) are typical of her stance on this issue. In writing about the Southern white women who would not work in harmony with black women, Harper satirizes their pretentiousness and makes it clear that in failing to acknowledge their common interests these women are not only risking their political future but also their Christian rewards. "Let them remember," she writes, "that the most ignorant, vicious and degraded voter outranks, politically, the purest, best and most cultured woman in the South, and learn to look at the question of Christian affiliation on this subject, not in the shadow of the fashion of this world that fadeth away, but in the light of the face of Jesus Christ. And can any one despise the least of Christ's brethren without despising Him?"

On issues of joint concern, Frances Harper believed in and worked with coalitions, but her priorities were always with the progress and elevation of African Americans. Two of her serials, "Sowing and Reaping: A Temperance Story" (1876–77), whose title says it all, and "Trial and Triumph" (1888–89), a story about the black middle class during the post-Reconstruction period, were written to that end. It was the 1892 novel, *Iola Leroy, Or, Shadows Uplifted*, a work that the *African Methodist Episcopal Church Review* called the crowning effort of her life, that became her best-known novel. Weaving her story from threads of fact and fiction, Harper wrote to correct the record on slavery and Reconstruction, to inspire African Americans to be proud of their past and diligent in their work toward a greater future, and to persuade all Americans that a stronger sense of justice and a more Christlike humanity was essential to the peace and prosperity of the United States. Incorporating the patterns of antebellum slave narratives and of novels such as *Clotel, The Garies and Their Friends, The Royal Gentleman*, and *Bricks without Straw*—while refuting the themes of works such as *In Ole Virginia* and *Birth of a Nation*—Harper hoped to demonstrate yet again the utility of beauty.

Iola Leroy appears to have been Harper's last long literary project. After that work, she published at least five collections of poetry: *The Sparrow's Fall and Other Poems* (c.1894), *Atlanta Offering: Poems* (1895), *Martyr of Alabama and Other Poems* (c. 1895), *Poems* (1900), and *Light beyond the Darkness* (n.d.). However, these are generally rearrangements of previously published volumes supplemented by previously uncollected works.

At the beginning of the twentieth century, Harper declared the beginning of a "woman's era" and clearly intended to be a part of that brighter coming day. She traveled less and published infrequently, but her counsel and her concern continued to be eagerly sought. During her last years, Harper was often sick. Believing that because of her failing health and her old age, she would not be able to support herself, many people offered her a place to live and continuing care. Always, Harper gently but firmly declined, saying that she had always been independent, that she loved her liberty, and that she would support herself without charity, as she had always done.

Frances Ellen Watkins Harper died February 20, 1911. Her funeral was held at the First Unitarian Church in Philadelphia, and she is buried in Eden Cemetery. A firm believer in the utility of beauty, she was independent, loved liberty, and was self-supporting. Her record stands as a testimony to the strength, courage, and vision of African-American women who wrote and worked for a brighter day to come.

FRANCES SMITH FOSTER

hooks, bell (1952–)

Essayist, poet, professor, feminist analyst, and prolific writer, bell hooks has been on the forefront of feminist and black intellectual thought. As one reviewer said, her "theoretical rigor, intellectual integrity, breadth of knowledge and passion" have made her presence felt.

Born Gloria Jean Watkins, hooks was raised in Hopkinsville, Kentucky, a small, segregated town. Her father, Veodis Watkins, was a janitor; her mother, Rosa Bell Watkins, was a maid. She had one brother and five sisters. Her entire family shared a love of poetry and, during power failures, when the family would hold an impromptu talent show, Gloria Jean would recite their favorite poetry.

Raised in a tightly knit black community, hooks named herself after an ancestor, a Native-American woman who was known for her strong will and her sharp tongue. Once, a local storekeeper reprimanded the young girl, saying, "You must be kin of Bell Hooks;" hooks decided that that was good and later published her books under that name.

Hooks left small-town Hopkinsville for Stanford University in the late 1960s. California was a shock. She had never before flown on an airplane or ridden on an escalator. But she survived the transition and graduated with a B.A. in English in 1973.

Three years later, she earned her M.A. from the University of Wisconsin at Madison and began to teach English and, later, ethnic studies at UCLA. During the 1980s, she taught a variety of courses at the University of California at Santa Cruz and at San Francisco State University. She received her doctorate from UC Santa Cruz in 1983.

Meanwhile, hooks had begun her writing career: First was a chapbook of poems, *And There We Wept*, in 1978; next was a landmark work in feminist nonfiction, *Ain't I a Woman: Black Women and Feminism* in 1981. Eleven years later, *Publishers Weekly* ranked the work among the twenty most influential women's books of the last twenty years.

Her next books expanded her thoughts on black feminism: *Feminist Theory: From Margin to Center* in 1984 and then *Talking Back: Thinking Feminist, Thinking Black* in 1989. *Yearning: Race, Gender, and Cultural Politics*, published in 1990, was a collection of essays; *Breaking Bread: Insurgent Black Intellectual Life*, in 1991, was a dialogue of essays with Cornel West.

Hooks' seventh book was *Black Looks: Race and Representation* in 1993, followed by *Sisters of the Yam: Black Women and Self-Recovery* in 1993, a particularly popular book about healing from the hardships of oppression. Hooks published two books in 1994 alone: *Teaching to Transgress: Education as the Practice of Freedom* and *Outlaw Culture: Resisting Representations*.

Aside from her prolific writing, hooks taught at Yale and later at **Oberlin College**. In 1994, she was named distinguished professor of English at the City College of New York; that same year, she received the $105,000 Writer's Award from the Lila Wallace-Reader's Digest Fund.

An intellectual, hooks has always been proud of her roots among working-class black women and has described the encouragement she received from other black women at the telephone company while she was struggling to make ends meet and write *Ain't I a Woman*: "They provided support and affirmation of the project, the kind of support I had not found in a university setting. They were not concerned about credentials, about my writing skills, about degrees. They, like me, wanted someone to say the kinds of things about our lives that would bring change or further understanding."

That goal seems to be bell hooks' in everything she writes.

ANDRA MEDEA

Hopkins, Pauline Elizabeth   (1859–1930)

"The true romance of American life and customs is to be found in the history of the Negro upon this continent," Pauline Elizabeth Hopkins asserted in 1901. This sentiment reverberates throughout Hopkins' novels, short stories, plays, and nonfiction, all of which capture the heroism, the drama, and the struggles against evil and racial oppression that are implicit in her term, *romance*. A remarkably prolific, talented, and pioneering writer, Hopkins sharpened awareness both of blacks' accomplishments and of racial issues with her lively, compelling fiction, drama, and essays that were aimed at a wide audience.

Born in Portland, Maine, in 1859 to William A. and Sarah Allen Hopkins, Hopkins was the great-grandniece of poet James Whitfield. Her mother was a descendant of Nathaniel and Thomas Paul, who founded Baptist churches in Boston. When Pauline was a child, the Hopkins family moved to Boston, where Pauline attended elementary and secondary school, graduating from Girls High School.

Pauline's writing talents emerged when she was only fifteen: she entered a writing contest sponsored by Boston's Congregational Publishing Society and supported by William Wells Brown, an escaped slave who wrote one of the first black novels, *Clotel* (1853). Brown wished to promote temperance, believing it to be a virtue that would enhance the black community. Pauline's essay, an eloquent if moralistic response to the contest theme, "The Evils of Intemperance and Their Remedy," won the first prize of ten dollars.

Hopkins was twenty years old when she completed her first play, *Slaves' Escape: or The Underground Railroad*. Just one year later, on July 5, 1880, *Slaves' Escape* was produced at Boston's Oakland Garden by the Hopkins Colored Troubadours. The play is a musical comedy that celebrates the bravery and ingenuity of such slaves as **Harriet Tubman** and Frederick Douglass who escaped bondage. The cast included Hopkins' mother, stepfather, and Pauline herself, who later achieved fame being billed as "Boston's Favorite Colored Soprano."

For twelve years, Hopkins performed with the Colored Troubadours, during which time she wrote another play entitled *One Scene from the Drama of Early Days* in which she dramatized the Biblical story of Daniel in the lion's den. At this point, she decided to leave the stage and train herself as a stenographer to better support her writing. In the 1890s, she worked at the Bureau of Statistics and developed a career as a public lecturer.

At the turn of the century, Hopkins became instrumental in the development of a new publication, *The Colored American Magazine*. Aimed at predominantly black audiences, *The Colored American* contained short stories, articles, and serialized novels, all designed to entertain and educate simultaneously. The magazine was a medium for black writers to demonstrate their talents. Hopkins was not only a founding member and editor of *The Colored American*, but she also published three novels, seven short stories, and numerous biographical and political sketches there. The sketches, which reflect her skill as a dramatist, flesh out the positive images that appear in her fiction by applauding the achievements of luminaries such as William Wells Brown, **Sojourner Truth**, Harriet Tubman, and Frederick Douglass. The sketches also combine her scholarly and literary talents.

In May 1900, the first issue of *The Colored American* carried her short story "The Mystery within Us." At the same time, the Colored Co-operative Publishing Company, a Boston firm that produced the magazine, brought out Hopkins' *Contending Forces: A Romance Illustrative of Negro Life North and South*.

Contending Forces showcases the themes and techniques that inform all of Pauline Hopkins' fiction. In her effort to present "the true romance of American life . . . the history of the Negro," Hopkins employs strategies used in popular historical romances of her day. Suspenseful, complicated plots involving superhuman heroes, imperiled heroines, and incomparable villains inform the audience about black history and about social issues and concerns. *Contending Forces* is an ambitious story about several generations of a black family from their pre–Civil War Caribbean and North Carolina origins to their later life in the North. The main plot involves Will and

Dora Smith, brother and sister, and their friend Sappho Clark, with whom Will falls in love. In addition to the formula plot of boy meets girl, boy loses girl, boy marries girl, the narrative dramatizes essential American historical realities: slavery, lynching, hidden interracial blood lines, post-Reconstruction voting disfranchisement, and job discrimination against blacks.

Underlying these themes and techniques is Hopkins' announced purpose in the preface to *Contending Forces* "to raise the stigma of degradation from my race." To that end, her black characters are admirable and intelligent, and many are educated. Writing at a time when black writers struggled with the nearly inescapable color prejudice that exalted an ideal of beauty based on Anglo-Saxon features, skin, and hair, Hopkins invariably described her heroines as light-skinned, sometimes so much so that they themselves were unaware of their racial origins. Sappho Clark, and the characters in much of Hopkins' fiction, exemplified the cultural contradictions in which black writers were often caught in their efforts to recast black cultural identity.

Hopkins' three other novels, all of which were serialized in *The Colored American*, employ additional romance techniques. Cliff hangers, episodes concluding with an unresolved question, such as who the murderer really was, enticed the reader to anticipate the next issue of the magazine. Mistaken identities and disguise typify these novels, as do outrageous coincidences, supernatural occurrences, and evil schemes.

Hagar's Daughter: A Story of Southern Caste Prejudice (serialized in 1901–2) is a generational novel like *Contending Forces*. The characters in *Hagar's Daughter* are, however, mostly white. Anticipating today's romance novels and soap operas, *Hagar's Daughter* concerns a glamorous leisure class that is preoccupied with clothes, gambling, and intrigue; in each generation, an adored, beautiful woman, fully entrenched in a white, wealthy culture, discovers herself to be black, forcing her to cope with racism and rejection. *Hagar's Daughter* strongly implies that wealth and status do not equate with ethics. Moreover, the novel concludes with a bitter indictment of American racism, even among the white Americans who are supposedly sensitive to racial issues.

Winona: A Tale of Negro Life in the South and Southwest (serialized during 1902) is a historical romance set during slavery. Hopkins weaves into the love story about a black woman and an antiracist white Englishman dramatic incidents involving slave traders, the Underground Railroad, and John Brown's Free Soilers. Judah, a militant black man who is described as "a living statue of a mighty Vulcan" stands proudly at the center of the novel, telegraphing blacks' positive historical roles during slavery. Judah not only embodies resistance against slavery, he also transmits Hopkins' notion that blacks should always resist oppression.

Of One Blood: or The Hidden Self (serialized in 1902–3) explores Hopkins' belief that blacks should revere their African origins. Reuel, who has never identified himself as black, visits Africa. There he becomes aware of the superiority of African civilization and culture and begins to embrace his heritage. Reuel's emergence as a descendent of African kings underscores Hopkins' belief that black Americans should ignore racist messages of inferiority. *Of One Blood* not only encourages racial pride for black Americans; it also voices a Pan-African vision, unifying and celebrating black people all over the world.

During the time that Hopkins serialized her novels in *The Colored American*, she published seven short stories in the magazine. The stories echo many themes and techniques found in her novels. The unmasking of black characters passing for white, such as those in "As the Lord Lives, He Is One of Our Mother's Children" and "A Test of Manhood," reiterates Hopkins' insistence that racial barriers are irrational. Black characters are extraordinary and ethical, contributing to Hopkins' urge to create positive images of African Americans. The stories contain the devices of romance and popular fiction, such as coincidence and the supernatural. Hopkins' stories, like her sketches, complement the aims and tactics of her novels to form a coherent body of work.

Hopkins' contributions to *The Colored American* thus included her voluminous fiction and nonfiction, her editorial talents, and her business skills. Hopkins promoted the magazine through Boston's Colored American League, which she founded. She also went on tour in 1904 to promote the magazine. In fact, the extent to which she wielded power over *The Colored American* was significantly underestimated until the 1980s. As a woman, Hopkins struggled against many odds, including the discrediting and suppression of her work by scholars.

When Booker T. Washington bought *The Colored American* in 1903, Hopkins' influence began to fade. By September 1904, her dissatisfaction with this situation, combined with her poor health, led her to resign. During the next fifteen years, Hopkins published several other pieces, including "The Dark Races of the Twentieth Century" (1905) and the novella "Topsy Templeton" (1916). At the time of her death, she was a stenographer for the Massachusetts Institute of Technology.

Hopkins died on August 3, 1930, "when the liniment-saturated red flannel bandages she was wearing to relieve the neuritis she suffered were ignited by an oil stove in her room," writes **Ann Allen Shockley**. Equally as tragic as Hopkins' death is the critical neglect she suffered afterward: Despite her impressive career as a poet, playwright, novelist, essayist, lecturer, editor, and actor, Hopkins was virtually forgotten until Shockley rediscovered her work in 1972. Since then, Hopkins' reputation has gradually reemerged. A feminist and Pan-Africanist dedicated to celebrating and preserving her racial history, Hopkins prefigured such writers as **Jessie Fauset**, **Zora Neale Hurston**, and **Alice Walker**. Moreover, her work is as serious, timely, and accessible today as it was nearly a century ago.

JANE CAMPBELL

Hunter, Kristin (1931–)

Kristin Hunter began her professional writing career at the age of fourteen as a columnist and feature writer for the Philadelphia edition of the *Pittsburgh Courier*. She had been writing poetry and articles for school publications, having learned how to read by the age of four. She has won critical acclaim for her short stories, novels for adults and young adults, and documentaries.

Kristin Eggleston was born in Philadelphia on September 12, 1931, to George Lorenzo and Mabel Eggleston. The only child of parents who were both schoolteach-

Kristin Hunter's children's book The Soul Brothers and Sister Lou *sold more than a million copies and won the Council on Interracial Books Children's Award in 1968.* (SCHOMBURG CENTER)

ers, when her father insisted that she also become a teacher, she acquiesced and received her B.S. in education from the University of Pennsylvania in 1951. She accepted a position as a third-grade teacher but resigned before the school year had ended to pursue her dream of writing. She accepted a position at the Lavenson Bureau of Advertising, where she worked as a copywriter, and later worked as an information officer for the city of Philadelphia and as director of comprehensive health services at Temple University.

In 1955, Hunter entered her television documentary, *Minority of One*, in a competition sponsored by CBS and won first place. This award attracted a great deal of attention, and Hunter continued to combine copywriting and freelance writing until 1964, when she published her first novel, *God Bless the Child*. Perhaps her most critically acclaimed work, *God Bless the Child* is the tragic story of the rise and fall of Rosalie Fleming as she works untiringly to escape the slum into which she is born.

In her second novel, *The Landlord*, Hunter portrays Elgar Enders, a wealthy white misfit who purchases a dilapidated tenement in the ghetto. Gradually his interactions with the black tenants transform Enders into a humanitarian who finds acceptance and a niche in the most unlikely of worlds. In 1970, United Artists released the movie adaptation of the novel, for which Hunter wrote the screenplay.

Hunter has also written at least four works for young adults. One million copies were sold of her first young adult book, *The Soul Brothers and Sister Lou*, written in 1968; the novel, which won the Council on Interracial Books Children's Award in 1968 and been translated into several languages, chronicles the emergence of a group of young, aspiring black musicians who sing their way out of the ghetto. In a 1981 sequel, *Lou in the Limelight*, Hunter examines the entanglements that often beset pop artists in their struggle to maintain success.

A member of the Philadelphia Art Alliance, Hunter has been the recipient of numerous awards: In 1955 she received the Fund for the Republic Prize for her television documentary, *Minority of One*; in 1964, she won the Philadelphia Athenaeum Award; the 1968 publication of *The Soul Brothers and Sister Lou* brought several important awards in addition to those mentioned above—the Mass Media Brotherhood Award from the National Conference of Christians and Jews in 1969 and the Lewis Carroll Shelf Award in 1971; finally, Hunter's young adult novel *Guests in the Promised Land* was a National Book Award finalist in 1974, winner of the Christopher Award in 1975, and recipient of the Chicago Tribune Book World Prize in 1973.

Hunter also has written several critically acclaimed short stories and articles. Her article "Pray for Barbara's Baby," first printed in *Philadelphia Magazine*, received the Sigma Delta Chi Best Magazine Reporting Award in 1969.

As a journalist and creative writer, Kristin Hunter has produced works in many genres. In addition, she continues to teach creative writing at the University of Pennsylvania, where she has taught since 1968. Married to a photojournalist, John Lattany, Sr., she is the mother of one stepson, John, Jr.

SHIRLEY JORDAN

Hurston, Zora Neale (1891–1960)

Zora Neale Hurston was a colorful and flamboyant figure in the 1920s and 1930s who created controversy whenever and wherever she appeared. She also created a remarkable body of writings— folklore, anthropological studies, plays, short stories, essays, novels, and an autobiography.

Born on January 7, 1891, in the all-black town of Eatonville, Florida, she was the fifth of eight children of John Hurston and Lucy Potts Hurston. In her autobiography, Hurston described her childhood as a safe and secure world where her imagination was unencumbered by the restrictions of race or gender and where she had the opportunity to develop her own individuality. This idyllic childhood was shattered by the death of her mother around 1904 and the disintegration of her family. Her father, Reverend John Hurston, sent her off to boarding school, and her sisters and brothers scattered into marriages, schools, and journeys of their own. Her father's remarriage several months after her mother's death destroyed her family life and some educational opportunities and catapulted her out of the safe world of Eatonville. This was a major experience in Hurston's life, marking the beginning of her wanderings in search of freedom from the constraints of race and gender that the larger world imposed upon African Americans.

For several years, Hurston wandered from job to job and lived in the homes of family members and strangers. She worked as a maid in a traveling Gilbert and Sullivan theater company. While working as a maid and a manicurist, she finished her high school education at Morgan Academy in Baltimore, Maryland, and her college education at **Howard University** in Washington, D.C., and she earned a graduate degree from Barnard College in New York City. With the assistance of such luminaries as Charles S. Johnson and Alain Locke, she began her career by publishing several short stories in *Opportunity* magazine, including "Drenched in Light" in December 1924, "Spunk" in June 1925, and "Muttsy" in August 1926. In collaboration with other writers, including Langston Hughes and Wallace Thurman, Hurston edited the short-lived magazine *Fire!* in which her short story "Sweat" appeared in November 1926. In 1930, in collaboration with Langston Hughes, she wrote a play entitled *Mule Bone*, a comedy about African-American life; it was never performed during her lifetime. After developing her skills as an anthropologist, she wrote a volume of folklore, *Mules and Men*, which was not published until 1935, and a second volume of Caribbean folklore, *Tell My Horse*, published in 1938. Hurston then turned her attention to the novel.

In 1934, she published her first novel, *Jonah's Gourd Vine*, loosely based on the life of her parents, particularly her father. Her masterpiece, *Their Eyes Were Watching God*, was published in 1937; *Moses, Man of the Mountain* in 1939; and *Seraph on the Suwanee*, the least successful of her writings, in 1948. Equally important in Hurston's canon is her autobiography, *Dust Tracks on a Road*, published in 1942.

In these novels, set within an all-black or mostly black background, Hurston rejects color and race identity as important to her situation, although the implications of these factors are woven skillfully into her work. It is in the response to the reality of race and racism that this all-black community comes into existence. Yet, within this world, Hurston brings forward gender as critical in influencing African-American women's and men's ability to come to self-realization. She creates characters who deal with gender in an African-American, rural, middle-class world. Poverty is not at the core of their problem, as it is for the majority of African Americans; rather their struggle is for an internal sense of freedom—of spirit and body. In her novels, this struggle of African Americans for both spiritual and physical freedom is carried out behind the walls of segregation.

Although Hurston presents gender as central to identity, her works also reveal the construction of race and its relationship to class behind the walls of segregation. The tension among color, class, and gender is revealed further in her autobiography, *Dust Tracks on a Road*. Shaping and molding these meditations on gender, race, color, and class is Hurston's search and struggle for freedom—freedom as an artist, as a woman, as an African American, freedom as a space to be enlarged upon. How to be black without being limited by that reality; how to be a woman without the constraints of womanhood; and how to remain true to both of these identities and still be an educated artist plagued Hurston all her life.

Hurston's work, coupled with the details of her life, suggests that she accepted the legitimacy of African-American culture and by doing so established the authenticity of this cultural formation. For Hurston, this culture had its own internal logic and moral code. She did not challenge the ideology of racism by attempting to prove the humanity of African Americans, but rather she challenged the hegemonic power of the dominant culture to represent African-American people negatively. Her literary works particularly establish Hurston as a keen observer of African Americans and the world in which they lived.

Hurston challenged and contested the notion that the integrity of the African-American race needed defending and that the responsibility for this defense must be borne by each individual black person. She believed that such a burden originated from essentially the same racist ideology: that is, that black people were deficient and had to be uplifted for approval by the dominant society and that each representative Negro must assume the burden of both uplifting and defending the race even at the cost of personal wishes and needs.

These views were developed and shaped to a considerable extent by her anthropological training at Barnard College under the direction of the renowned anthropologist Franz Boas. Boas believed in the value and legitimacy of all cultures and trained his students to discover the internal logic of the cultures they studied. Hurston, one of his most devoted students, was strongly influenced by this perspective, which led her to reject the prevailing notion of black culture as inferior and immoral. For Hurston, the race needed no improvement or justification.

Hurston also contested the gender conventions that required a ladylike image for women, confining them to both the private sphere of marriage and motherhood and the public sphere of nurturing roles as teachers, nurses, and other homespun heroines uplifting the African-American race. She refused, in other words, to be a female "race man," at least in her public persona, and this defiance is embedded in both her artistic and autobiographical writings. Unlike characters in the novels of two of her contemporaries, Richard Wright and **Jessie Fauset,** Hurston's characters are not engaged in race relations; they seek instead to build, quite deliberately, worlds where African-American people concern themselves with life issues outside the control and purview of white hegemonic structures. Race moves from an all-controlling factor to one that influences but does not wholly determine day-to-day existence. Instead, Hurston's characters struggle through life in spite of race, drawing on their own communities and culture for strength and direction. They focus on gender, family, and community relationships in an effort to find space for the individual. This view of race is in sharp contrast to the reality of her life, where white patrons required demeaning behavior of her before granting the financial support she needed to complete her work. Yet, she looked to her own strengths in her private struggle in gender, family, and community relationships where she sacrificed marriage, family connections, motherhood, and community acceptance in order to be a scholar and artist.

Hurston was a rural, Southern, black woman attempting to be an artist in a world controlled by white people and men. Her struggle, as evidenced by her artistic, ethnographic, and autobiographical writings, dealt with how love is possible, how color can liberate and imprison at the same time, how ambiguous an identity it is to be an American, how genius can or cannot be borne, and how womanhood can both adorn and strangle a life. Hurston refused to be confined by gender and racial roles. Her critics misunderstood her public behavior and also missed the meaning of her scholarly and artistic production. It is in her novels that one finds the key to her understanding and confusion surrounding the realities of gender, race, and class.

In the introduction to her folklore collection, *Mules and Men,* Hurston provides insight into the mind of black rural people: Black people "are most reluctant at times to reveal that which the soul lives by and the Negro, in spite of his open-faced laughter, his seeming acquiescence, is particularly evasive. . . . The Negro offers a feather-bed resistance. That is, we let the probe enter, but it never comes out. It gets smothered under a lot of laughter and pleasantries." Hurston suggests that this "onstage" consciousness of African Americans was distinctly different from their "offstage" consciousness. She argues for a deliberate deception constructed by African Americans that establishes mental protection from the intrusion of the outside world. If African Americans could not protect themselves totally from physical and economic exploitation, they could resist intrusion into their inner lives, into their soul: "I'll set something outside the door of my mind for him to play with and handle. He can read my writing but he sho' can't read my mind."

Mules and Men and Hurston's other folklore writings are humorous and informative collections of the conversations, sermons, and joke-telling as well as the cultural behavior, religious customs, and local characters in Florida and Louisiana. The humor and seeming triviality of the stories conceal important discussions on gender and race in community life. The discourse on race is far different from the one found in the dominant culture. In this discourse, race is not a badge of inferiority; instead it is a trick to be played on the arrogant, a way of referencing race and class, and a way of protecting the inner lives of black people. Gender tensions rest uneasily beneath an apparent male dominance in these tales, and a sensitivity to color is also evident. These folktales establish Hurston's understanding and respect for African-American culture and her acute awareness of racial and gender constructions in rural culture.

Hurston's most famous and popular novel is *Their Eyes Were Watching God*, published in 1937 and set in the all-black world of Eatonville, Florida. The central character is a woman, Janie, who struggles to realize her true self in a world where self-definition is filtered through race and gender. It is an African-American world to

be sure, but within that world there are those who seek their identity and therefore their freedom in models drawn from the white, male-dominated world outside of Eatonville. The idioms and foundation for their freedom are sought in that external world and are then interpreted within a black context. Janie's grandmother, her first two husbands, and some members of the community seek to impose lifestyles and definitions of self on Janie that restrict and confine her. Hurston explores and unpacks the basis of spiritual and physical freedom in this story.

Freedom in this work is intimately tied to the question of land and how land is a symbol for freedom; yet, land must be shared in common. Janie (and through her Zora) saw the world through community eyes, and that structured how she conceived love, ownership of property, justice, and labor. For Janie, freedom remains an elusive quest as long as she is outside or above the black community; only when she is part of a whole community, one in which men and women work in concert with the human needs of each other, can she be free to be herself.

Throughout the narrative, freedom for Nanny Crawford, Logan Killicks, and Jody Starks, people central to Janie's life, is defined in material terms. For Janie, freedom means love and fulfillment, and she first witnesses both in the pollination of the pear tree. For Nanny, who has only known the horrors of slavery and the meaning of women's oppression, the major concern and fear is that Janie will live a similar life of despair and deprivation. She knows that women have often been a "spit cup" for men and white folks. Marriage and security represent freedom for Nanny and escape for

Janie. Deprived of material security, Nanny knows that property and class offer protection in the white world and position in the black world. It is not that she wants to make Janie literally "like white folks"; she wants what white represents. She forces Janie, therefore, to marry the aged but wealthy (as defined by the black community) Logan Killicks.

Killicks takes Janie to a lonely and isolated existence, away from people, unconnected to anyone; she is simply another piece of property. She is not free to be a person, and neither is he. Killicks stifles Janie, and the environment robs her of any lifegiving force. She runs away with the handsome Jody Starks, hoping to find her freedom in his promise of love. Jody plans to be a big man with a big voice. He buys land, builds a town, installs himself as the head official, and puts Janie on a pedestal. She sits on the pedestal that Nanny envisioned for her; but she is just as alone and unsatisfied as she was on Killicks' farm. Janie is not permitted to take part in the stories that the local folk participate in because she serves as a showpiece for Jody.

Slowly, the marriage dies from a lack of connectedness. Jody's deathbed scene after twenty years reveals the price he paid to be a "big man with a big voice." Janie insists that he know the mistake he made before he dies. With skillful use of black dialect, Hurston captures the rhythm and texture of the African-American cultural spirit as Janie forces Jody to witness their life together: "You wouldn't listen. You done lived wid me for twenty years and you don't half know me atall. And you could have but you was so busy worshippin' de works of yo' own hands, and cuffin folks around in their minds till you didn't see uh whole heap uh

things you could have had." In spite of Jody's anguish and wish for silence, Janie insists on having her say: "you wasn't satisfied wid me the way Ah was. Naw! Mah own mind had tuh be squeezed and crowded out tuh make room for yours in me."

Jody dies as "the icy sword of the square-toed one had cut off his breath and left his hands in a pose of agonizing protest." Janie ponders their life together and the price Jody paid for his power and success: "'Dis sittin in the rulin chair is been hard on Jody,' she muttered out loud. She was full of pity for the first time in years. Jody had been hard on her and others, but life had mishandled him too." Starks had bought land and set himself above the people; he was not a part of them. He had not labored with or loved with them. His model of freedom and leadership had been drawn from outside the community.

After Jody dies, leaving Janie materially secure, she enters into a relationship with Teacake, a penniless younger "ne'er-do-well," and with him she finds her freedom. Her freedom comes not as a possessor of land but as part of a community connected to the land and laboring on the land. It is a self-actualized community. The home that Teacake and Janie share on the "muck" is always alive with people. They come to gamble, tell stories, and listen to music. Janie is a part of the life there, and she wonders what Eatonville would think of her in "her blue denim overalls and heavy shoes? The crowd of people around her and a dice game on her floor!" Here she can listen and laugh and tell her own stories. Life on the "muck" shows people in motion—singing, talking, playing—with peripheral vision. It is a community where negative conflict occurs only when idioms based on color and class enter and are filtered through gender.

A careful reading of her texts reveals that, for Hurston, real freedom can only occur in a whole, self-actualized community. She explores this discussion of the meaning of freedom in texts constructed within the black world. The white world encases this world to be sure, intruding at times with its values and definitions, but Hurston locates her focus squarely in the black world, and this shapes her understanding of freedom, gender, and race. It is an idealized world, one where Hurston works out her views of race, class, and gender. By using this approach, Hurston addresses how gender relations are constructed in this world, the role that class plays in gender identity, and how the ways of talking about these issues are embedded in folk material. What she discovers is that while many sought their identity in the values of white society, others struggled for self-realization in the "muck" of the African-American world.

Further, Hurston's discussion of these issues connects with the larger discussion going on in the world inhabited by African Americans: How should women manage their encounters with men and other women? How should men and women deal with Jim Crow in the North and South? How can one move up in social class and deal with the jagged edges of social mobility? How should one think about humble origins? Writers and activists such as **Anna Julia Cooper**, W. E. B. DuBois, **Ida B. Wells-Barnett**, James Weldon Johnson, Langston Hughes, and others pondered these concerns in their writings. Massive numbers of Southern peasants and Northern workers were also pondering these concerns as they moved to urban communities in the North and South and struggled to define freedom in spiritual and material terms. These questions, too, are taken up in Hurston's autobiography, *Dust Tracks on a Road*.

When J. B. Lippincott approached Hurston in 1941 with the idea of writing her autobiography, her response was less than enthusiastic; she was uncomfortable exposing her inner self to the world and initially resisted the idea. The request came in the middle of her career, she protested, and her career was hardly over. Two books of folklore, two novels, and a series of articles and short stories had established her as a major literary figure; despite her success, however, Hurston was still very dependent on patronage for her writing and artistic endeavors. Financial stability continued to be elusive: Her only means of earning additional money was to comply with Lippincott's request for the autobiography.

Katherine Mershon, a wealthy friend in California, offered her a place to live and work on the autobiography, so Hurston moved there from New York in the spring of 1941. She completed a draft of the manuscript by mid-July; however, rewriting took more than half a year, which was unusual for Hurston. Her biographer, Robert Hemenway, has suggested that much rewriting became necessary after the bombing of Pearl Harbor because Hurston disliked the colonial and imperialist implications of World War II; her dislike of war is evident in her satirical comments about American marines who "consider machine gun bullets good laxatives for heathens who get constipated with toxic ideas about a country of their own" and Americans who sang "Praise the Lord and Pass the Ammunition" (*Dust Tracks on a Road*, 1942). Lippincott deleted such passages from the final version of her autobiography. What remained and was finally published in November 1942 was a document that some have argued is the most problematic piece in Hurston's canon.

Dust Tracks on a Road is a simulated story of Hurston's life. Facts are often missing or distorted in this text; for example, she portrays herself as younger than she actually was when her mother died—she states that she was nine years old, but census records establish her age as probably thirteen. *Dust Tracks on a Road* is her life played out in full view of the white world, the world that defined images and determined which works received acceptance. It was a world in which only primitive black people were authentic. It is the life of a woman resisting the confinement of rigid gender conventions that required the appearance of submission by women to male and white authority. In this work, she attempted to discuss an idyllic childhood where neither race nor poverty was central; a disrupted family caused by the death of her mother that sent her wandering in search of education and self; the creation of a woman scholar and artist aided by patrons; and a Southern individual who would not be contained or transformed. She attempts to do this in a manner acceptable to a white audience that was a necessary part of the story. What emerges from this autobiography is what her former employer, writer Fannie Hurst, called a "woman half in shadow."

Navigating between the black and white worlds was not an easy task: If she exposed the pain and anger that black women invariably felt when trying to enter doors blocked by racism and sexism, no admittance would ever have been possible. Her entrance into the privileged world of academic degrees would have been forever denied. Her di-

lemma was to unblock that passageway and at the same time retain the essence of herself that included her Southern identity and her intellectual independence. In commenting on her years at Barnard, she referred to herself as Barnard's sacred black cow. She once stated, "I feel most colored when I am thrown against a sharp white background." Her essays, "How It Feels to Be Colored Me" (1928), "The Pet Negro System" (1943), and "My Most Humiliating Jim Crow Experience" (1944), are testimony to her understanding that racism confined and restricted and that the struggle for a healthy existence is a lifelong engagement for African Americans.

The decades of the 1940s and 1950s were not easy for Hurston. After the publication of *Seraph on the Suwanee* in 1948, she struggled to write a novel about Herod the Great, which she never completed. She left the literary world of New York and returned to Florida, where she continued to write articles for various newspapers and magazines. Her finances were low, and by the mid-1950s, her health began to deteriorate.

Hurston spent some of the last years of her life responding to the U.S. Supreme Court's 1954 decision to desegregate public schools. On August 11, 1955, the *Orlando Sentinel* in Orlando, Florida, published a letter Hurston had written to express her disapproval of the court decision. For most African Americans and Euro-Americans alike, the decision represented the culmination of more than fifty years of struggle to end segregation by law. For Hurston, the decision was deplorable and an insult to her people. Hurston defended the job done by African-American teachers, arguing that unless there was some quality or facility in white schools that could not be duplicated in black schools, there was simply no reason to desegregate. She contested, "I can see no tragedy in being too dark to be invited to a white school social affair. The Supreme Court would have pleased me more if they had concerned themselves about enforcing the compulsory education provisions for Negroes in the South as is done for white children." Embedded in these comments was the fierce racial pride that others had thought was missing from her consciousness. Recognizing that her comments would not be well received by the civil-rights leadership, Hurston defended her views and made clear the basis for her opposition. She stated, "Them's my sentiments and I am sticking by them. Ethical and cultural deseg-regation. It is a contradiction in terms to scream race pride and equality while at the same time spurning Negro teachers and self-association."

During the last decade of her life, Hurston fell into obscurity—she was poor, ill, alone, but still proud. She remained virtually unknown for two decades after her death in 1960. Her burial in an unmarked commoner's grave belied the genius of a gifted and rich life that had once captured the hearts and minds of thousands. Her life and work yield a mosaic of gender, racial, and class images that reveals much about the mental state, social realities, and political tensions of African-American life.

TIFFANY R. L. PATTERSON

J

Jacobs, Harriet Ann (1813–1897)

The most important slave narrative written by a black woman is almost certainly *Incidents in the Life of a Slave Girl: Written by Herself*. This remarkable book was written by Harriet Ann Jacobs in 1861, but, for most of the twentieth century, it was believed to be a piece of fiction by a white writer. In 1987, *Incidents* was published in an annotated edition that cleared up the question of Jacobs' authorship.

The story Jacobs tells in the book is one of slavery, sexual harassment, and deception; it is also, however, a story of tremendous courage and endurance. At one point in her life, in order to be with her children and escape capture, Jacobs lives for seven years in a crawl space seven feet wide, nine feet long, and no more than three feet high. Jacobs finally escaped and, with her children, lived in New York for many years. One of her white employers, without her knowledge, "purchased" her and her children from her former master and then freed them.

It was then that Jacobs decided to write her story. With the help of African-American abolitionist William C. Nell and white abolitionist Lydia Maria Child, she published it herself. Harriet Ann Jacobs' biographical entry is in the first volume of this encyclopedia, *The Early Years, 1619–1899*.

Johnson, Georgia Douglas (1877–1966)

In 1927, **Alice Dunbar-Nelson** described her friend Georgia Douglas Johnson as having "as many talents as she has aliases. . . . One is always stumbling upon another nom de plume of hers." Johnson did sometimes publish under various pseudonyms, but the merit of Dunbar-Nelson's comment lies in her recognition of Johnson's many gifts as musician, poet, playwright, columnist, short-story writer, wife, mother, and friend.

This multitalented woman began her life as Georgia Blanche Douglas Camp on September 10, 1877, in Atlanta, Georgia. She grew up in Rome, Georgia. Her mother was Laura Jackson, of Indian and black ancestry, and her father was George Camp, whose wealthy and musical father had moved to Marietta, Georgia, from England. Her mixed ancestry prompted Georgia's lifelong preoccupation with miscegenation.

Georgia Camp attended elementary schools in Atlanta and then entered Atlanta University's Normal School, from which she graduated in 1893. During these years, she was particular about her friends and chose to remain primarily alone, teaching herself to play the violin. Her interest in music took her to Oberlin, Ohio, to train at the Oberlin Conservatory (1902–3).

On September 28, 1903, Georgia Camp married Henry Lincoln Johnson. "Link" was born to ex-slaves in 1870 and became a prominent attorney and member of the Republican Party. The couple had two children, Henry Lincoln, Jr., and Peter Douglas. In 1910, the family moved from Atlanta to Washington, D.C., where Link not only established a law practice but also, in 1912, accepted President William Howard Taft's appointment to serve as recorder of deeds for the District of Columbia.

Moving to Washington was the stimulus that Johnson needed to begin her literary career. In 1916, three of her poems appeared in *Crisis*, and in 1918, her first book of poetry, *The Heart of a Woman*, was published. In the introduction, William Stanley Braithwaite praised the work for "lifting the veil" from women. Johnson's musical gifts are evident in the lyrical quality of poems that reveal the difficulties and frustrations faced by women and that echo Johnson's youthful isolation.

Johnson's first book did not explore racial themes, a choice for which she was criticized. During this time of the "New Negro," black writers were expected to address racial issues to expose and overturn prejudice. In 1922, Johnson responded to her critics with a book of poetry titled *Bronze: A Book of Verse*, which addresses miscegenation as well as mothering in a racist world. She was praised by W. E. B. DuBois and **Jessie Redmon Fauset** for this work, but Johnson herself admitted in a letter to Arna Bontemps that she preferred not to write on racial themes, saying that "if one can soar, he should soar, leaving his chains behind."

The home of poet, playwright, and novelist Georgia Douglas Johnson served as a salon to Harlem Renaissance writers such as Jean Toomer, Langston Hughes, Angelina Grimké, and Alice Dunbar-Nelson. (SCHOMBURG CENTER)

During this productive period, Johnson struggled to balance her roles as housewife and writer. She was an unconventional wife and mother, preferring reading to cooking, and her husband was not always sympathetic to her creative efforts, though he did financially support her in them. After the death of Henry Lincoln Johnson, Sr., on September 10, 1925, her difficulties intensified as she divided her day between earning a living and writing, a struggle that would follow her to her death. She put Peter through Williston Seminary, Dartmouth College, and **Howard University**'s medical school, while Henry Lincoln, Jr., went to Asburnham Academy, Bowdoin College, and Howard University's law school.

During this difficult period, Johnson accepted an appointment by President Calvin Coolidge in 1925 to work for the U.S. Department of Labor as Commissioner of Conciliation, requiring her to investigate the living conditions of laborers. Working full-time caused her to feel that she never had enough time to write. However, she did produce a third book of poetry in 1928, *An Autumn Love Cycle*, considered to be her finest. She again avoided racial themes, returning instead to the theme of a woman in love. The best-known poem in this volume is "I Want to Die While You Love Me."

While Johnson refused to limit her poetry to racial themes, she greatly contributed to the New Negro Renaissance by opening her home at 1461 S Street Northwest, Washington, D.C., as a salon. Every week, writers such as Jean Toomer, Langston Hughes, **Angelina Grimké**, and Alice Dunbar-Nelson gathered for a meeting of the Saturday Nighters' Club. She also invited prisoners with whom she had corresponded to the weekly gatherings, once they were released. In fact, Johnson named her home "Half-Way Home," in part because she saw herself as halfway between everybody and everything and trying to bring them together and also because she wanted to make her home a place where anyone who would fight halfway to survive could do so.

Zona Gale—a white writer to whom *An Autumn Love Cycle* was dedicated—encouraged Johnson to try writing plays, which she did with success. In 1926, Johnson received an honorable mention in the *Opportunity* play contest for *Blue Blood*, a drama about miscegenation

through rape in the South. Her most famous play, *Plumes*, was awarded *Opportunity*'s first prize in 1927. This drama is a folk tragedy that pits modern medicine against folk customs. Other published plays include *A Sunday Morning in the South* (1974), which was a "lynching play," and the historical dramas *Frederick Douglass* (1935) and *William and Ellen Craft* (1935). While these are the only plays published, Johnson did produce many more dramas about "average Negro life," "brotherhood" between the races, and the intermixture of races. One of her great contributions to drama is the representation of authentic folk speech rather than stereotypical mutilated English.

Life, of course, grew harder for Johnson after the Harlem Renaissance with the onset of the Great Depression. She tried ceaselessly to obtain fellowship money, but with the exception of an honorable mention from the Harmon Foundation in 1928, she never succeeded. Nevertheless, she continued to be productive: She wrote a weekly newspaper column from 1926 to 1932 titled "Homely Philosophy" that was syndicated to twenty newspapers. Though it was somewhat clichéd, Johnson tried to bring cheer into the homes of Americans during economic devastation, with such columns as "A Smile on the Lips" or "Find Pleasure in Common Things."

Johnson was listed in the 1932 edition of *Who's Who of Colored America* and was asked to join the D.C. Women's Party, Poets League of Washington, and Poet Laureate League. Losing her position with the U.S. Department of Labor in 1934, Johnson was forced to turn to temporary work, but she continued to write, winning third prize in 1934 in a poetry contest sponsored by the D.C. Federation of Women's Clubs.

Johnson was also a member of several literary social clubs and organizations, such as the American Society of African Culture and the League of American Writers.

During World War II, she continued to publish poetry as well as to read her poems over the radio, returned to music, and tried her hand at short story writing. Her three extant stories are "Free," "Gesture," and "Tramp"; the last two were published under the pseudonym "Paul Tremaine" and are derived in large part from the life of Gypsy Drago, a man who did not discover that he was black until the age of thirty. These stories predominantly focus on relationships and not on racial themes, however. Johnson tried in vain to locate a publisher for the biography of her late husband, *The Black Cabinet*, and for her novel, *White Men's Children*. Her last book of poetry, *Share My World*, was published in 1962.

One year before her death, in 1965, she was awarded an honorary doctorate from Atlanta University. During these later years, she developed into a local institution, widely known as "the old woman with the headband and the tablet around her neck." The tablet was for her to write down any idea that came to her.

When Georgia Douglas Johnson died of a stroke on May 14, 1966, she left a multitude of papers that were literally thrown out. Much of what she wrote is lost, but she lived a remarkable and unselfish life.

JOCELYN HAZELWOOD DONLON

Jones, Gayl (1949–)

For Gayl Jones, fiction and storytelling are different. "I say I'm a fiction writer if I'm asked, but I really think of myself as a storyteller. When I say fiction, it evokes a lot of

Calling herself a storyteller, poet, and novelist Gayl Jones used the blues as a thematic undercurrent in her novels Eva's Man *and* Corregidora. (SCHOMBURG CENTER)

different kinds of abstractions, but when I say storyteller, it always has its human connections." Those human connections were made for Jones when as a child her mother, grandmother, and other adults introduced her to the art of telling stories.

Gayl Jones was born in Lexington, Kentucky, on November 23, 1949, to Lucille and Franklin Jones. In her childhood, Jones "first knew stories as things that were heard." Her mother wrote stories to be read aloud to Gayl and her brother Franklin. Gayl's favorite was called "Esapher and the Wizard," but all of them contrasted greatly with some of the "really unfortunate kinds of books . . . children learned to read out of" when she was growing up.

Jones' mother and grandmother were important early influences, but teachers and educational institutions also provided encouragement. Jones began to write her own stories in the second or third grade, but she gives credit to her fifth-grade teacher, Mrs.

Hodges, for encouraging her efforts to write. As a student at Connecticut College, she won an award for writing the best original poem and became one of four undergraduate poets who toured the Connecticut poetry circuit. After earning a B.A. at Connecticut College, she continued her education at Brown University in Providence, Rhode Island, where she earned an M.A. (1973) and a D.A. (1975).

Although Jones is best known for her two novels, *Corregidora* (1975) and *Eva's Man* (1976), she has also written short stories, poetry, and plays. While still a student at Brown, she began to explore the themes and experiment with the techniques that later bore fruit in her novels. In short stories such as "The Welfare Check" (1970), "The Roundhouse" (1971), and "The Return: A Fantasy" (1971), Jones assumes the story-teller's voice and writes in the first person. The technique of writing in the first person allows Jones to minimize authorial intrusion while achieving the directness of the story-teller's relationship to her audience. *Chile Woman*, Jones' first play, was produced at Brown in 1973 by Rites and Reason, a university/community arts project. In *Chile Woman*, Jones explores the legacy of slavery and examines the devastation it wreaked on human relationships. Her use of blues music as a means of voicing and structuring the themes of the play is a device to which she returned in her first novel, *Corregidora*.

Corregidora is a challenging book to read. Its central character, blues singer Ursa Corregidora, is the last in a line of women fathered and debauched by the Portuguese slavemaster Simon Corregidora. Stories about the incest and prostitution that are her heritage have been handed down from mother to daughter for four generations. An accidental fall makes it impossible for Ursa to bear children and triggers her search for a means of coming to terms with her past. Jones uses blues as the means by which Ursa gives voice to her pain, and it becomes the means of her transcendence as well.

Reviewers of *Eva's Man*, Jones' second novel, tended to see it as too similar in tone and subject matter to *Corregidora*. In *Eva's Man*, however, Jones merely shows herself to be the kind of musician who can play endless variations on a central group of themes. As a blues singer, Ursa Corregidora is able to use language as an instrument of regeneration, whereas Eva, the central character of *Eva's Man*, is imprisoned within her own silence. Eva listens to blues music but does not speak of her own pain. As a result, the sexual violence that is transcended in *Corregidora* results in murder and madness in *Eva's Man*.

Gayl Jones returns to Brazil as a setting for other stories in her two book-length poems, *Song for Anninho* (1981) and *Xarque* (1985). The background of *Song* is the story of a Portuguese attack on Palmares, a settlement founded by African slaves who had escaped from their masters, but at the forefront is the story of two lovers who affirm their love in spite of the brutality that they cannot escape. In *Xarque*, the remarkable spiritual energy that is present in *Song* is now dissipated by intergroup disharmony. Thus, in this pair of story-poems, as in her pair of novels, Jones concentrates on theme and variation.

In addition to her prolific career as novelist, playwright, and poet, Jones is also an academic. She was a professor of English at the University of Michigan, Ann Arbor, 1975–81. *Liberating Voices* (1991) is a scholarly work about the use of the oral tradition in the work of African-American writers.

CYNTHIA J. SMITH

Jordan, June (1936–)

In addition to her successful career as a college professor, June Jordan is famous for her writing, particularly her poetry, her children's and young people's fiction, and her essays. Her social and political awareness, combined with her prodigious literary skill, have earned Jordan both critical praise and popular acceptance.

Born in Harlem, New York, on July 9, 1936, June Jordan is the only child of Granville Ivanhoe Jordan and Mildred Maud (Fisher) Jordan, who came to America from Jamaica. Jordan grew up in the Bedford-Stuyvesant section of Brooklyn, but as a teenager she traveled to Midwood High School in southeast Brooklyn, where she was the only black student. After one year at Midwood, her parents enrolled her in the Northfield School for Girls, a preparatory school now part of Mount Hermon, in Massachusetts.

After graduating from high school in 1953, Jordan entered Barnard College in New York City. While there, she met Michael Meyer, a white Columbia University student, whom she married in 1955. Later that year, when Meyer left New York to attend the University of Chicago, Jordan went too and also enrolled in the university. In 1956, Jordan returned to Barnard for one more semester before finally leaving in February 1957. In 1958, the couple's only child was born, Christopher David Meyer. Jordan and Michael Meyer divorced in 1963, the year that Jordan became employed as production assistant on the crew of Shirley Clarke's film about Harlem, *The Cool World*.

In 1966, Jordan began her academic career, teaching English at the City University of New York; two years later, she moved to New London, Connecticut, to teach English at Connecticut College as well as to direct the Search for Education, Elevation, and Knowledge (SEEK) program. Later that year, she joined the writing faculty of Sarah Lawrence College in Bronxville, New York, where she remained until 1974. A visiting professor at Yale University in 1974–75, she later became assistant professor of English at City College of New York. In 1976, she took a faculty position at the State University of New York and was promoted to a full professorship in 1982; in 1989, Jordan be-

Versatile writer June Jordan began to attract wide attention with her first book of poetry, Who Look at Me, *which explores black-white relations and a black person's process of self-definition in a white-dominated society.* (SCHOMBURG CENTER)

came professor of Afro-American Studies and Women's Studies at the University of California, Berkeley.

Jordan established her writing career with the publication of her stories and poems (under the name June Meyer) in magazines such as *Esquire,* the *Nation,* and the *New York Times Magazine.* Her writing began to attract national attention in 1969 when Crowell published her first book of poetry, *Who Look at Me,* a collection of works that portrays black-white relations and a black person's process of self-definition in a white-dominated society. In 1970, she edited *Soulscript: Afro-American Poetry,* a collection of poems by young people aged twelve to eighteen. Jordan has published nineteen works to date, including poetry, books for children and young people, and collected essays, articles, and lectures. Among these are the award-winning *His Own Where,* a novel for young adults (1971); *Some Changes,* poems (1971); *Fannie Lou Hamer,* a biography (1972); *New Room: New Life,* a book for children (1975); *Living Room: New Poems, 1980–1984* (1985); and *On Call: New Political Essays, 1981–1985* (1985). Jordan also is the author of several plays, including *The Spirit of Sojourner Truth,* staged at the Public Theater in New York City in 1979, and *For the Arrow That Flies by Day,* performed during 1981 by the New York Shakespeare Festival.

Taking her place among the radical poets who emerged during the 1960s, Jordan is esteemed for her political and aesthetically black stance as well as for her technical control. Much of her poetry grapples with the issue of black self-identity as well as the powerful and often problematic influence that parents have on their children. In her works for children, Jordan displays a commitment to the use of Black English and the promotion of what she describes as "Black-survivor consciousness." In her work, Jordan also has examined such biographical topics as her mother's suicide in 1966 and her father's death in 1974.

June Jordan has received many prizes, grants, and fellowships for her writing, including a Rockefeller grant for creative writing in 1969. She also received a fellowship in poetry from the National Endowment for the Arts in 1982 and a fellowship award in poetry from the New York Foundation for the Arts in 1985. *His Own Where* was selected by *The New York Times* as one of 1971's most outstanding works for young adults and was nominated for the National Book Award. Jordan is an executive board member of the American Writers Congress, a board member of both the Center for Constitutional Rights and the Nicaraguan Culture Alliance, and a member of the International Association of Poets, Playwrights, Editors, Essayists, and Novelists (PEN). She also is a regular political columnist for the *Progressive* magazine.

FENELLA MACFARLANE

K

Kincaid, Jamaica (1949–)

Bring together the West Indies and the *New Yorker*, and you have Jamaica Kincaid, one of the Caribbean-American writers who have emerged in the last few decades.

Born Elaine Potter Richardson on May 25, 1949, in St. Johns, Antigua, Kincaid was the daughter of Annie Richards. She did not know of or meet her biological father until later in her life and was brought up thinking that her mother's husband, a carpenter, was her father. When she was nine years old, her mother gave birth to the first of three sons, whom Kincaid seems to have experienced as intruders. When she was sixteen, Kincaid left Antigua. She went to New York to try to establish herself as a writer. Her entrée into the New York literary scene was the *New Yorker*, to which she sent clever descriptions of African-American and Caribbean plant life, which were published regularly between 1974 and 1976.

In 1976, Kincaid became a *New Yorker* staff writer. In 1983, a collection of her short stories and other short pieces, most of which had been published in the *New Yorker*, was published under the title *At the Bottom of the River*; it received generally positive reviews. In 1985, Kincaid's first novel, the autobiographical *Annie John*, a lyrical recreation of her childhood with her mother, was published; five years later, *Lucy* was published, a sequel in many ways to the earlier book, though the protagonist has a different name. In the meantime, Kincaid also wrote and published *A Small Place*, a political analysis of Antigua that is highly critical of European and American exploitation of the island. The emotional content of her books deals almost entirely and intensely with relationships between women.

Kincaid is married to Allen Shawn, son of William Shawn—the legendary editor of the *New Yorker*. They have two children, a son, Harold, and a daughter, Annie.

Kincaid's novel *The Autobiography of My Mother* was published early in 1996 and was hailed by critics as brilliant. Her writing has been compared to that of **Toni Morrison** and V. S. Naipaul. She has broken with the *New Yorker,* now lives in Bennington, Vermont, and teaches creative writing part time at Harvard University.

The critic Henry Louis Gates, Jr., has said that one of Kincaid's most important contributions is that she never feels the necessity of claiming the existence of a black world or a female sensibility; she assumes them both. "I'm not writing for anyone at all," Kincaid says, "I'm writing out of desperation. I felt compelled to write to make sense of it to myself—so I don't end up saying peculiar things like 'I'm black and I'm proud.' I write so I don't end up as a set of slogans and clichés."

KATHLEEN THOMPSON

L

Larsen, Nella (1891–1964)

Novelist and short-story writer Nella Larsen created images of black women that dispelled the myth of the typical and simplistically caricatured tragic mulatto of American literature. Like her heroines,

Nella Larsen was the first black women to win a creative writing award from the Guggenheim Foundation. Herself the product of a mixed marriage, she wrote two novels that broke ground in exploring the alienation of people of mixed ancestry. (SCHOMBURG CENTER)

Larsen felt out of place and was in search of a firm foothold in a world that seemed not to understand the inner conflicts associated with mixed ancestry. Literary critics and authors who were acquaintances of Larsen praised her for adeptly portraying the life of bourgeois African Americans of mixed ancestry, a class for which a paucity of literature is extant.

Nella Larsen was born in Chicago on April 13, 1891, to a West Indian father and a Danish mother. Larsen's father died when she was two years old, and her mother later married a white man with whom she had a second daughter. Growing up among a family of European descent was uncomfortable for Larsen, who rarely spoke of her family except to recall that she attended a private school in Chicago with her white half-sister.

After attending high school in Chicago, Larsen studied science from 1909 to 1910 at Fisk University in Nashville, Tennessee; from the all-black world of Fisk, Larsen moved to Copenhagen, where her relatives lived and where she studied at the University of Copenhagen between 1910 and 1912. Larsen's odyssey next found her in New York City, where she studied nursing at Lincoln Hospital from 1912 to 1915 before serving as assistant superintendent of nurses at Tuskegee Institute in Alabama from 1915 to 1916. Returning to New York City, Larsen worked at Lincoln Hospital from

1916 to 1918 and for the New York City Department of Health from 1918 to 1921.

Never feeling connected to her mother, her half-sister, and a stepfather who viewed her as an embarrassment, Larsen found solace in her relationship with physicist Elmer S. Imes, whom she married on May 3, 1919. She worked as a library assistant and children's librarian from 1921 to 1926, a career that inspired her to read omnivorously and to write. Her favorite authors included James Joyce, John Galsworthy, eighteenth-century playwright Carlo Goldoni, Marmaduke Pickthall, Taylor Gordon, Rudolph Fisher, Walter White, and Carl Van Vechten, who was instrumental in securing a contract for Larsen's novels from Alfred A. Knopf.

As a socialite wife, Larsen became acquainted with a cadre of black authors in New York City who encouraged her to write, including James Weldon Johnson, **Jessie Fauset**, Jean Toomer, and Langston Hughes. With strong support from black author Walter White and the leading white patron of New Negro authors, Carl Van Vechten, Larsen published her first novel, *Quicksand*, in 1928.

Substantially autobiographical, *Quicksand* focuses on a mulatto of Danish and West African parentage named Helga Crane, whose quest in search of self takes her from Naxos, a southern black college, to Chicago to seek white relatives, to Harlem to mingle with African Americans, to Copenhagen to live with white relatives, to Harlem again, and finally to rural Alabama, where she marries the arrogant, despicable, and unkempt Reverend Pleasant Green. Her husband minimally fulfills her spiritual as well as sexual needs, which she has repressed because of Victorian notions of woman-hood. The novel concludes with Helga, still weak and bedridden from the birth of her fourth child, preparing to give birth to a fifth.

Larsen's novel skillfully captures the lives of many Northern middle-class African Americans at the turn of the century who, because they were formally educated, cultured, and of mixed parentage, found themselves alienated from white Americans and from the masses of black Americans, many of whom had rural Southern roots. In addition to exploring race and class-related conflicts, Larsen also treats gender issues in *Quicksand*. The delicate, fickle, and passionate Helga seems not only to be running from her divided racial self but also from her own sexuality. When Helga has an opportunity to take a lover on several occasions, she bolts. Larsen's novel shows the limitations of black bourgeois women in the 1920s who were forced to choose marriage at any cost as the only way to express their sexuality. The ending of *Quicksand* is less than satisfying because Helga, who has become progressively stronger and more self-assured, reverts to self-doubt: She becomes a pathetically helpless woman whose destiny will be determined by a man she does not love and with whom she has very little in common.

With the publication of Larsen's second novel, *Passing*, in 1929, just thirteen months after the national acclaim of *Quicksand*, the thirty-eight-year-old novelist was hailed as a major New Negro author. *Passing* centers on women's friendship, women's sexuality, mixed ancestry, and preoccupation with respectability and materiality and illustrates that African Americans who pass for white often yearn to be part of the black community. Born in poverty and raised by her white aunts, Clare Kendry risks losing her wealthy white husband, daughter, and social standing for the chance to socialize with her Harlem friends. Irene Redfield, Clare's friend who passes for white when it is expedient, ruins her own marriage because she fears change and because of her obsession with maintaining middle-class standing. Like *Quicksand*, *Passing* has a weak ending: Larsen leaves unresolved whether Clare has fallen, jumped, or been pushed out of the window by Irene, who suspects her friend of having had an affair with her husband. In spite of the less-than-satisfying ending, *Passing* depicts the dilemmas and complexities of a growing black middle class.

Following the success of her two novels, Nella Larsen in 1930 became the first black woman to win a creative writing award from the prestigious Guggenheim Foundation. Shortly before Larsen was to leave for Europe to do research in Spain and France for her third novel, she was accused of plagiarism in one of her short stories published in *Forum*. Though she responded to the attack with an essay in *Forum* and was supported by her editor, Larsen's public humiliation stifled her writing, and she never completed another novel. A marriage that had begun to show signs of deterioration in 1930 ended in divorce in 1933 when rumors spread that Larsen's husband was having an affair with a white woman and that Larsen had tried to kill herself by jumping out of a window. This second public humiliation apparently weakened Larsen's self-confidence and diminished her productivity as a writer.

From 1941, Larsen worked as a nurse at several hospitals on the East Side of Manhattan. She died in New York City on March 30, 1964.

Larsen made a significant contribution to black history and culture by capturing in impressive detail the mannerisms, values, concerns, and emotional conflicts of the black bourgeoisie, underscoring that even members of this class were victimized by racism. Especially important is Larsen's exploration of black women's lives of her time. Her legacy is a map of the complex lives of America's black nouveau riche during the New Negro movement.

ELIZABETH BROWN-GUILLORY

Lorde, Audre (1934–1992)

Among contemporary writers, there are few who so completely challenge the categorization and consequent repudiation of individuals as does Audre Lorde. Her challenge takes the interesting and powerful form of embracing all the categories into which she herself fits or can be squeezed. "I am a Black lesbian feminist poet," she says and demands recognition of the fact that she has not uttered a paradox. "I am a Black Lesbian," she says and then goes on, "and I *am* your sister." To those who would deny familial connection with her, metaphorical though it might be, she presents an infuriating and usually sensitizing determination to define herself and, by so doing, to define the world around her.

Audre Lorde was born in Harlem on February 18, 1934. From the beginning, her sense of her identity was unusually complex. Her parents had come to New York from their home country of Grenada and for many years firmly believed that they would one day go home. When, during the Great Depression, they realized that they would probably never go back, a permanent sorrow entered their household. Their nostalgia for the country of their birth provided the background of Lorde's childhood. For this young New York girl, there was an island in the West Indies—an island she had never seen—that she was expected to think of as home.

One of Lorde's books, *Zami: A New Spelling of My Name*, presents a clear picture of her early life. A fictionalized biography—or biomythography, as she calls it—the work graphically retells racist incidents that the author suffered as a child. It also describes with wonder her discovery of language and its power: At an early age, she began to use the latter as a tool to exclude, resist, and even manipulate racist attitudes.

The strictness of her parents' home along with her own sense of herself as an outsider led Lorde into rebellion as a teenager. She began to seek out others who felt as she did, and she found them at Hunter College High School. One companion misfit was poet Diane Di Prima.

After graduation from high school, Lorde moved to her own apartment and began to support herself. The jobs she was able to find were low paying and unsatisfying. She endured great loneliness because of her inability to find a world in which she felt at home. It was during this time that she had her first lesbian affair, in Connecticut, while she was working in a factory.

Another affair with a woman, one that occurred while she was in Mexico in 1954, led Lorde wholeheartedly into the Greenwich Village "gay-girl" scene. It was the closest she had yet come to a sense of belonging, and she found it in a sea of almost entirely white faces. This irony and the conflict it aroused in her provoked years of thinking, writing, and feeling. At this time,

"I am a Black lesbian feminist poet," declared Audre Lorde with deliberation. She created a world of eroticism, sensuality, and symbolism in her work, which defies categorization. (SCHOMBURG CENTER)

she also went to college and began to work as a librarian, and she wrote her poetry.

The poetry led her, for a time, to involvement with the Harlem Writers Guild. Its members, including Langston Hughes, were the vanguard of a growing movement in African-American literature. Here was another possible home for the aspiring young writer. Hughes himself showed an interest in her work. Yet, according to Lorde, the homophobia of the guild members alienated her once again.

In 1959, Lorde received her B.A. from Hunter College; in 1960, she was awarded an M.L.S. from Columbia University's School of Library Service. For a number of years, Lorde wrote poetry and worked as a librarian, ending up as head librarian at the Town School in New York. She also was married and had two children; the marriage and its circumstances are not recorded in Lorde's writing and therefore little is known of it. Then, in 1968, *The First Cities*, her first book of poetry, was scheduled for publication by the Poet's Press. Her old high school friend Diane Di Prima was instrumental in its being published. At about the same time, Lorde was invited to Tougaloo College in Mississippi to be poet-in-residence.

Lorde was at Tougaloo for only six weeks, but during that time her life changed suddenly and radically. Public recognition of her poetry in the form of her book's publication was one of the foremost reasons; another was her experience teaching the students of Tougaloo—a historically black institution—about poetry, an experience that she wrote of movingly in the poem "Blackstudies"; the third significant factor was meeting Frances Clayton. The two women would become life partners.

Upon her return to New York City, Lorde continued teaching: She gave courses in writing at City College and on racism at Lehman College and John Jay College. Her second book of poetry, *Cables to Rage*, came out in 1970.

In 1971, Lorde publicly read a lesbian love poem; the subject had never before appeared in her public work. The same poem was published later in *Ms*. It was not, however, included in her next volume of poetry, *From a Land Where Other People Live*, having been rejected by the editor of the volume. In 1974, the book was nominated for a National Book Award, bringing Lorde greater recognition for her work and,

after two more publications with small presses, a contract with W.W. Norton.

Norton brought out *Coal*, a collection of new poems and poems from her first two, hard-to-find books, with a jacket blurb written by Adrienne Rich; Rich was at that time one of Norton's most prominent poets, and the association between Lorde and Rich continued over the years. The same blurb appeared on Lorde's second book with Norton, *The Black Unicorn*, published in 1978. In the summer of 1981, Rich published an interview with Lorde in *Signs: Journal of Women in Culture and Society*, thereby introducing her to a large white readership.

The Black Unicorn is probably Lorde's most successful poetic attempt to merge her different worlds. She uses the image of the unicorn (which she believes Europeans took from the African agricultural goddess Chi-Wara, a one-horned antelope) to explore the influences of European and African cultures upon each other. She delves into the sexual significances of the symbol, pointing out how the European myth divides meaning into the masculine—the phallic horn—and the feminine—the pale virgin who alone can tame the animal. In contrast, African culture combines those meanings to emphasize the power of growth.

With the appearance of *The Black Unicorn*, Lorde became an acknowledged, widely reviewed poet. Critical articles began to be written about her work, often alongside that of other poets belonging to one of her "categories" and sometimes alone. Her prose, too, though published by small presses, began to command attention and respect. *Zami* was published in 1982 and reviewed in the *New York Times*. A different audience grew out of the publication of a collection of essays titled *Sister Outsider*

(1984). It was widely adopted in women's studies courses and quickly achieved the status of a feminist classic.

During the 1970s, Lorde traveled in Africa, the Caribbean, Europe, and Russia. In 1980, her autobiographical work *The Cancer Journals* was published. In it, she describes her feelings during and after her affliction with breast cancer. The experience had added yet one more identity to her long list. In another prose work, *A Burst of Light* (1988), she recounts her decision not to undergo further surgery after a return of the disease and her experience with alternative methods of treatment. Again, during this time, Lorde traveled extensively, teaching and giving readings.

The stubborn reality of her own experiences and her own feelings serves as the basis of Lorde's worldview. Where political oversimplifications collide with her personal affections and loyalties, she sees a reason to challenge the politics, as in her essay "Man Child: A Black Lesbian Feminist's Response." In that work, she explores, among other issues, the ramifications of her motherhood of a son in a cultural milieu in which her primary identification is lesbian.

Lorde's focus as a writer and a person has been to strive for unity by embracing diversity. She challenges all political and social actions that arbitrarily separate one individual from another, that exclude and ostracize. She has done this by fervently defending the individual's right to define herself and her possibilities: In her prose, this position has often been set forth explicitly; in her poetry, she has created a world of eroticism, sensuality, and symbolism that ultimately aspires to the same goal.

She died of cancer at her home on St. Croix on November 17, 1992.

MARGARET HOMANS

M

Madgett, Naomi Long (1923–)

With seven volumes of her own poetry published by 1988, two edited collections of poems by other African-American poets published by 1991, and two textbooks—one college-level creative writing (1980) and one secondary-level language and literature (1967)—Naomi Long Madgett belongs to the long tradition of African-American women writers who work as hard on their own literary career as on teaching and encouraging others to be artists. Her poems have been included in more than 100 anthologies, as early as 1949 in *The Poetry of the Negro, 1746–1949* edited by Langston Hughes and Arna Bontemps, and as recently as 1992 in *Adam of Ife: Black Women in Praise of Black Men*, which she edited and published herself through her own Lotus Press. Madgett's poetry has appeared in journals and magazines such as *Callaloo, Essence, Michigan Quarterly Review, Sage,* and *Obsidian.*

Born in Norfolk, Virginia, on July 5, 1923 Naomi Cornelia Long spent her early childhood in East Orange, New Jersey, where her father, Clarence Marcellus Long, served as a Baptist minister. Madgett's mother, Maude (Hilton) Long, was a schoolteacher. Both of her parents taught her to value education and encouraged her to read at an early age. She often sat on the floor of her father's study reading Aesop's fables or Robert T. Kerlin's anthology *Negro Poets and Their Poems* (1923). In the autobiographical foreword to her *Phantom Nightingale: Juvenilia* (1981), Madgett lists many American and English poets whose work she read as a child and whom she then unwittingly imitated as she progressed through her own poetry-writing phases: Edgar A. Guest, Longfellow, Langston Hughes, **Georgia Douglas Johnson,** Tennyson, and Robert Browning.

Madgett's parents moved the family from East Orange to St. Louis, Missouri, in December 1937, a move that the poet considers an important transition in her life because in St. Louis she attended the all-black Sumner High School, where her knowledge of African-American achievement was expanded; the school's academic standards were high, and Naomi Long's efforts to write poetry were encouraged. Following her high school graduation at age seventeen in June 1941, she published her first volume of poetry, *Songs to a Phantom Nightingale,* as Naomi Cornelia Long. She entered her mother's alma mater, Virginia State University, that same year; during her years at Virginia State, Long visited the African-American poet Countee Cullen, who encouraged her to continue writing.

When reflecting in a 1992 interview on her long career as a poet, Naomi Long Madgett assessed the first twenty-two years, between 1934 and 1956, as a lonely time: "I didn't know other black poets. I didn't follow trends. I just tried to write honestly but my own timing was against me." At this early stage in her career, Madgett had followed her own interests in writing lyrical and romantic poetry on a range of topics, while publishers at the time sought poems emphasizing the African-American experience. Her numerous poems written during these years and published in her first two volumes, *Songs to a Phantom Nightingale* (1941) and *One and the Many* (1956), and in one comprehensive collection, *Phantom Nightingale: Juvenilia (Poems 1934–1943)* (1981), repeat the theme of loneliness to characterize her early childhood, adolescence, and young adult years through the mid-1950s. Her repeated references to the small, melodious, Old World migratory bird, the nightingale, in her poems reflect her preoccupation with lyrical poetry as well as her belief that the bird "was a phantom . . . as elusive as my dream of happiness, as otherworldly as my youthful fantasies" (*Phantom Nightingale: Juvenilia*).

Long earned her B.A. from Virginia State in 1945; she then began graduate school at New York University, withdrawing after one semester to marry Juan F. Witherspoon on March 31, 1946. She moved with him to Detroit that same year, where she worked as a reporter and copyreader for the *Michigan Chronicle,* an African-American weekly, until the birth of her child, Jill, in 1947. During this time, some of her poems began to appear in anthologies under the name Naomi Long Witherspoon.

In 1948, she started divorce proceedings at the same time that she began to work in an all-black branch office of the Michigan Bell Telephone Company in Detroit as a service representative. She was granted a divorce in 1949 and continued working for the telephone company until 1954. She married William H. Madgett on July 29, 1954; in 1960, this second marriage also ended in divorce, but the poet continues to publish under the name Madgett.

She began to teach in the Detroit public junior high and high schools in 1955. While working as a teacher in Detroit, Madgett completed a master's degree in English education at Wayne State University in 1956 and in 1961 and 1962 took postgraduate courses at the University of Detroit. She introduced a course in creative writing and the first structured African-American literature course in Detroit public schools in 1965.

During the academic year 1965–66, Madgett was awarded a $10,000 Mott Fellowship to work as a resource associate at Oakland University in Rochester, Michigan. During this year, she published the third collection of her own poems (*Star by Star*) and wrote an African-American literature textbook (with Ethel Tincher and Henry B. Maloney), *Success in Language and Literature/B* for use in high schools. It was published in 1967, the same year that she was honored by the Metropolitan Detroit English Club as the Distinguished English Teacher of the Year. One of Madgett's high school students, **Pearl Cleage**, is a recognized author of short stories and poetry and has acknowledged Madgett as having first recognized her talent and encouraged her to consider a writing career. Madgett resigned from the Detroit public schools in 1968 to accept a position as associate professor of English at Eastern Michigan University in Ypsilanti. There, she taught courses in creative writing and African-American literature in the Department of English Language and Literature until 1984, when she retired as a full professor.

In 1972, three of Madgett's friends who were interested in publishing her fourth book of poetry, *Pink Ladies in the Afternoon,* founded Lotus Press; two years later, Naomi Madgett arranged to take over the existing stock of books and name. In 1978, Lotus Press published Madgett's fifth book of poetry, *Exits and Entrances.* Along with her third husband Leonard Andrews and her daughter Jill W. Boyer, Madgett, in 1980, incorporated the press as a nonprofit, tax-exempt corporation. Retirement in 1984 allowed Madgett to devote full attention to the growth and development of Lotus Press. The press had gained a reputation as one of the few companies in the country dedicated to keeping black poetry alive and has published seventy-five titles, sixty-six of which are still in print. Madgett runs the press by herself, reading and responding to each manuscript personally. Many African-American writers (Houston Baker, Tom Dent, James Emmanuel, Ronald Fair, Lance Jeffers, **Gayl Jones**, Pinkie Gordon Lane, and Paulette Childress White) were first published by Madgett's Lotus Press. In commemoration of the twentieth anniversary of Lotus Press in 1992, Madgett edited an anthology of poems by black women to pay tribute to the black American man: *Adam of Ife: Black Women in Praise of Black Men.*

In 1980, Naomi Long Madgett earned a Ph.D. in literature and creative writing from the International Institute for Advanced Studies. Between 1982 and 1988, she was honored by the Detroit City Council, the Michigan state legislature, the Black Caucus of the National Council of Teachers of English, the Stylus Society of **Howard University**, Your Heritage House with the Robert Hayden Runagate Award, the College Language Association with its Creative Achievement Award, and Wayne State University with the Arts Achievement Award.

Madgett received a Creative Artist Award from the Michigan Council for the Arts in late 1986, to underwrite her seventh book of poetry, *Octavia and Other Poems.* Published by Third World Press in Chicago in 1988, *Octavia and Other Poems* is divided into three sections, the first of which contains a sequence of thirty-three poems that explore Madgett's family history. The title poem, "Octavia," is based on Madgett's great-aunt, Octavia Cornelia Long, who died of tuberculosis at the age of thirty-four in Charlottesville, Virginia, three years before Madgett was born. The emphasis in the entire collection is on the lives of Madgett's grandparents, uncle, aunts, and father during the first two decades of the twentieth century. The appendix consists of family pictures, biographies, and a family tree that provides a context for the poems about her family. In some ways, *Octavia and Other Poems* is a narrative of the experiences of many African-American families at that time.

In the course of her more than fifty years as a poet, publisher, and teacher, Naomi Long Madgett has either been influenced by or participated in the Harlem Renaissance, the civil rights movement, the Black Arts Movement, and the women's movement in the United States. When she began to write poetry in early 1940, there were few if any other African-American women publishing poetry; by the mid-1960s, Madgett was part of a circle of black poets in Detroit and other cities who encouraged one another's development. Since the mid-1970s, she has been contributing to the tradition of African-American poetry both as poet and as an independent publisher. She currently lives with her husband, Leonard Andrews, in Detroit, Michigan.

ALICE A. DECK

Marshall, Paule (1929–)

"We (as people of African descent) must accept the task of 'reinventing' our own images and the role which Africa will play in the process will be essential." This statement summarizes the content as well as the ideological thrust of Paule Marshall's fiction, for although she focuses primarily on the experiences of English- and French-speaking African peoples from the Caribbean, she also writes about the black experience in North and South America. Her writing as a whole explores and reconstructs the African presence throughout the diaspora.

She was born Valenza Pauline Burke on April 9, 1929, in Brooklyn, New York, the daughter of Ada (Clement) and Samuel Burke, emigrants from Barbados, and she grew up in a tightly structured West Indian–American community. At nine years of age, she visited the homeland of her parents and wrote a series of poems reflecting her impressions. However, it was not until her young adult life, when she began to write serious fiction, that she drew upon the power of Barbadian speech to describe a distinct racial and ethnic heritage.

Marshall graduated cum laude and Phi Beta Kappa from Brooklyn College in 1954. From her first marriage to Kenneth Marshall (1950), she has one son, Evan Keith, who is a naval architect living in London; she divorced Kenneth Marshall in 1963. In 1970,

Paule Marshall draws upon her experience as the daughter of emigrants from Barbados to examine in her fiction what she calls "the task of 'reinventing'" the image of people of African descent. (SCHOMBURG CENTER)

she wed for the second time, marrying Nourry Menard, a Haitian businessman.

Marshall's fiction writing began when she started to compose short vignettes at the end of her workday as a researcher and staff writer for *Our World* magazine in New York City. These exercises later developed into her first short story, "The Valley Between" (1954). Her subsequent fiction includes *Brown Girl, Brownstones* (1959), *Soul Clap Hands and Sing* (1961), "Reena" (1962), "Some Get Wasted" (1964), "To Da-Duh: In Memoriam" (1967), *The Chosen Place, the Timeless People* (1969), *Praisesong for the Widow* (1983), and *Daughters* (1991).

Marshall combines a writing career with teaching and currently holds an appointment as professor of English and creative writing at Virginia Commonwealth University in Richmond. She has received several prestigious awards, including a Guggenheim fellowship (1960), the Rosenthal Award (1962), a Ford Foundation grant for fiction writers (1964–65), the National Endowment for the Arts and Humanities Award (1967–68 and 1978–79), the American Book Award (1984), the Langston Hughes Medallion Award (1986), the New York State Governor's Award for Literature (1987), the John Dos Passos Award for Literature (1989), and John D. and Catherine T. MacArthur Fellowship (1992).

With her multicultural background, Marshall is uniquely suited to examine points of convergence and divergence between various cultures, and her emphasis on black female characters addresses contemporary feminist issues from an Afrocentric perspective. The ultimate objective of Marshall's fiction is to dismantle all forms of personal, social, and political oppression and to celebrate the triumph of the human spirit.

DOROTHY L. DENNISTON

McElroy, Colleen J. (1935–)

Colleen McElroy began as a dancer. As a poet, she desires to make words dance. With eleven volumes of poetry and prose, her work has been widely anthologized. She has also won awards and fellowships that have sent her to the far reaches of the globe.

McElroy was born in St. Louis, Missouri, on October 30, 1935, the daughter of Jesse O. Johnson, an army officer, and Ruth (Long) Johnson. She went to segregated schools in St. Louis, where she had to walk across town to attend the black high school. She knew little about black writers, except for a few famous ones who were read on Negro History Day. It didn't occur to her to dream of writing.

Instead, McElroy began on the path toward becoming a speech pathologist: She attended Harris Teacher's College, where she acquired her associate of arts degree in 1956; received her bachelor of science from Kansas City State University in 1958; did graduate work at the University of Pittsburgh and Western Washington State College; and finally received her Ph.D. from the University of Washington in 1973.

McElroy was the first black woman to become a full professor at the University of Washington. Her first book was a college text—*Speech and Language Development of the Preschool Child: A Survey*. It was not until her thirties that McElroy began to find herself as a poet.

McElroy wrote because of a yearning for words, not fame or glory. As she has said, "There was never any question in my head of whether writing would gain me stardom because I didn't have those role models. I went into writing thinking I was one of three black women in the whole country writing, since I'd not been exposed to any."

She has written nine books of poetry with such titles as *The Mules Done Long Since Gone* (1973), *Looking for a Country Under Its Original Name* (1985), *Queen of the Ebony Isles* (1985), *Bone Flames* (1987), *Lie and Say You Love Me*, (1988), and *What Madness Brought Me Here: New and Selected Poems*, (1990).

Her short story collections include *Jesus and Fat Tuesday and Other Short Stories* (1987), and *Driving Under the Cardboard Pines* (1990). She co-wrote a play with Ishmael Reed, *In the Wild Gardens of the Loup Garou.*

McElroy has been awarded a number of fellowships to further her studies, including a Rockefeller Fellowship to study in Italy, a Fulbright Scholarship to Yugoslavia (1988), and a Fulbright Research Scholarship to Madagascar (1993).

As a poet, Colleen J. McElroy has used her travels and her artist's flair to mine the possibilities of sound and language. "You can make language elastic," she says, "... I mean you can acknowledge there are different ways of saying the same thing, that language is not fixed. You can explore it and use it in different ways."

ANDRA MEDEA

McMillan, Terry (1951–)

Funny, outspoken, and able to communicate with and move her readers, Terry McMillan is a serious and successful novelist.

Born October 18, 1951, in Port Huron, Michigan, to Madeline Washington Tilman and Edward McMillan, McMillan's father, a sanitation worker, died when she was sixteen; her mother held a variety of jobs from auto worker to domestic to pickle-factory employee. According to McMillan, her mother was responsible for "teaching me and my five siblings how to be strong and resilient. She taught us about taking risks."

McMillan attended public schools in Port Huron and, when she was sixteen years old, worked in the public library; there, she discovered black writers when she was shelving a book by James Baldwin. "I remember feeling embarrassed," she admits now, "and did not read his book because I was too afraid. I couldn't imagine that he'd have

anything better or different to say than Thomas Mann, Henry Thoreau, Ralph Waldo Emerson." Eventually, she did read Baldwin as well as other classic black writers; she was amazed and moved.

From 1973 to 1979, McMillan attended the University of California at Berkeley, graduating with a bachelor's degree in journalism; while there, she wrote and published her first short story, "The End." After Berkeley, she moved to New York to study film at Columbia University, where she earned a master's degree. She made her living as a word processor and enrolled in a

Terry McMillan proved that black people do buy books when she successfully undertook the marketing of her first novel, Mama, *by reaching out to black readers through direct-mail advertising.* (MARION ETTLINGER)

writing workshop at the Harlem Writers Guild. During this time, her son, Solomon Welch, was born. In 1983, McMillan was accepted at the MacDowell Colony where she wrote the first draft of her first novel, *Mama*, which was published in 1987.

McMillan took the marketing of *Mama* into her own hands: She sent out thousands of letters, primarily to black organizations, asking them to promote her book and offering to read from it to their members. Conventional wisdom among white publishers had been that black people do not buy books; McMillan proved that when someone reaches out to them, black readers are indeed there. Her second novel, *Disappearing Acts* (1989), did even better than her first, and *Waiting to Exhale* (1992) was on *The New York Times* best-seller list for months; the paperback rights were sold for $2.64 million. McMillan has been hailed as a "crossover" success, but the book buyers, according to her, are mostly black. "I've had 1,500 people show up for a reading of *Waiting to Exhale*. Twelve hundred in Chicago, a thousand people waiting in line in Washington. I think I've signed more than 10,000 books, and the people who come are 90 percent black. In some cities 98 percent."

After the publication of *Disappearing Acts*, McMillan was involved in a landmark legal battle. Her former living partner sued her for defamation of character, charging that the central male character in the novel was recognizably himself and that the depiction was injurious. Fiction writers around the country breathed a sigh of relief when his claim was dismissed in court.

In 1988, McMillan became associate professor at the University of Arizona and retains her tenure there even though she has moved to Danville, California. She tours extensively, reading from her work and teaching workshops. In 1990, she was a judge for the National Book Award for fiction; the same year, she edited *Breaking Ice: An Anthology of Contemporary African American Fiction*, an anthology of African-American writing that showcased the fiction of more than fifty contemporary authors.

When reviewing *Disappearing Acts*, Robert G. O'Meally made an astute estimate of McMillan as a writer: "... with eloquence and style, McMillan gives her work a voice that is her own, one tough enough to speak across color and class lines, daring enough to make a statement about our country and our times."

In 1995, *Waiting to Exhale* was made into a movie starring Whitney Houston and Angela Bassett and directed by Forest Whitaker. The screenplay was written by McMillan and Ronald Bass.

KATHLEEN THOMPSON

Meriwether, Louise (1923–)

"I have been deeply concerned for many years by the way African Americans fell through the cracks of history," writes Louise Meriwether, "and I reacted by attempting to set the record straight" (In Letter to Rita Dandridge 1981). Her attempt was to involve herself with race issues and to write about the remarkable exploits of African Americans, which, she insists, are not black history but American history.

Louise Meriwether was born May 8, 1923, in Haverstraw, New York, to Marion Lloyd Jenkins and Julie Jenkins, South Carolinians who had migrated to New York via Philadelphia in search of a better life. The only daughter and the third of five children, she had moved with her family to Brooklyn and later to Harlem, where, trapped by the Great Depression, her father became a numbers runner. She grew up on welfare and attended P.S. 81. Meriwether graduated from Central Commercial High School in downtown Manhattan, received a B.A. in English from New York University, and an M.A. in journalism from the University of California in Los Angeles, where she moved with Angelo Meriwether, her first husband. That marriage ended in divorce, and so did her second marriage, to Earl Howe. Meriwether currently lives in New York City with her mother.

Primarily as a writer, Meriwether has raised the consciousness of black Americans about their history. While a newspaper woman for the *Los Angeles Sentinel* from 1961 to 1964, she published articles on significant but little-known African Americans (**Grace Bumbry**, a singer; Audrey Boswell, an attorney; and Vaino Spencer, a Los Angeles judge) who overcame great odds to achieve success; she also published an article on Matthew Henson, the African American who was the first man to stand atop the North Pole. She revised and published one of her graduate theses as "The Negro: Half a Man in a White World" in the October 1965 issue of *Negro Digest*. In 1970, her first novel, *Daddy Was a Numbers Runner*, which documents the corrosive effects of the economic depression on the Coffins, a black Harlem family on welfare, was published. The novel received favorable reviews and was reissued by the Feminist Press in its black-women-writers series. It garnered two grants for Meriwether in 1973: one from the National Endowment for the Arts in Washington, D.C., and the other from the Creative Arts Service Program, an auxiliary of the New York State Council on the Arts.

In addition to a number of history-related short stories and essays, Meriwether has published three children's books on historical figures: *The Freedom Ship of Robert Smalls* (1971), *The Heart Man: Dr. Daniel Hale Williams* (1972), and *Don't Ride the Bus on Monday: The Rosa Parks Story* (1973). Her *Fragments of the Ark* (1994) is a Civil War novel told from the point of view of several slaves and deals with, perhaps for the first time, the 150,000 black soldiers and the thousands of field hands who deserted their masters' plantations—crippling the Confederacy—to work as laborers for the Union army.

Meriwether has frequently interrupted her writing to participate in civil-rights activities. In 1965, she trekked to Bogalusa, Louisiana, to work with the Congress of Racial Equality (CORE) and tote guns for the Deacons, a black coalition that maintained a twenty-four-hour patrol to secure the area's black citizens from the forays of the Ku Klux Klan. Two years later, she opposed Hollywood director Norman Jewison and Twentieth Century-Fox producer David L. Wolper, who wanted to make a movie about Nat Turner based on William Styron's *The Confessions of Nat Turner* (1967); because Styron's book emasculated the insurrectionist and distorted historical truths, Meriwether and Vantile Whitfield, founder of Performing Arts Society of Los Angeles (PASLA), formed the Black Anti-Defamation Association to protest the making of the film. Tremendous support came from the black community, including that of John Henrik Clarke, noted historian, who edited a volume of essays entitled *William Styron's Nat Turner: Ten Black Writers Respond* (1968). As a result of these efforts, the motion picture was not made.

In the early 1970s, Meriwether and others formed Black Concern, a committee to protest South Africa's offering large sums of money to American black entertainers to break the boycott of the Organization of African Unity (OAU) and perform in that country. Meriwether and John Henrik Clarke wrote and distributed "Black Americans Stay Out of South Africa," a pamphlet detailing the flagrant injustices against black South Africans. She carried her message to radio audiences and to the United Nations, receiving support from their Committee Against Apartheid, the United Council of Churches, and other national organizations. Black Concern was instrumental in persuading Muhammad Ali, then heavyweight boxing champion, to cancel a match in Johannesburg and in convincing other black entertainers to uphold the OAU's boycott.

The crisis over, Meriwether returned to her writing, publishing short stories and articles. From 1979 to 1985, she was a faculty member at Sarah Lawrence College in Bronxville, New York (and one semester, while on leave, an instructor at the University of Houston), teaching creative writing. During that time, she received a grant from the Mellon Foundation through Sarah Lawrence College to assist her in researching a Civil War novel, which required several trips to the Sea Islands, Charleston, and North Carolina.

Meriwether's "weakness" has been in taking time away from her writing to organize the community in political activities that she felt were of prime importance. While trying to write, she has actively protested the Gulf War, the Vietnam War, the invasions of Panama and Grenada, and the covert actions of the United States in Chile and Cuba.

RITA DANDRIDGE

Moody, Anne E. (1940–)

Social activist Anne E. Moody made a significant contribution to the literature of black women when, in 1968, she published *Coming of Age in Mississippi*. This remarkable autobiography tells of the hardships and joys of growing up in the Deep South. It also explains how Moody came to an awareness of herself as a black woman in a racist society.

The book is also important as history: In telling how she became involved in the civil rights movement, Moody describes landmark events in that movement. *Coming of Age in Mississippi* had a great impact when it was published in the sixties and remains a moving story as well as an important document. Anne E. Moody's biographical entry is in the *Social Activism* volume of this encyclopedia.

Morrison, Toni (1931–)

"I felt I represented a whole world of women," said Toni Morrison, "who either were silenced or who had never received the imprimatur of the established literary world." One of the great writers of our time, Morrison was describing her emotions in Stockholm, Sweden, when she accepted the Nobel Prize in literature, the highest honor the literary world has to offer.

"I felt the way I used to feel at commencements," she went on in a *New York Times* interview, "when I'd get an honorary degree: that it was very important for young black people to see a black person do that. . . . Seeing me up there might encourage them to write one of those books I'm desperate to read. And *that* made me happy. It gave me license to strut."

It would be difficult to find anyone with more "license to strut" than Toni Morrison: A brilliant writer, charismatic personality, and inspiring leader, she is at the forefront of a remarkable school of black women writers who are sweeping through American literature like a hurricane of talent and heart. Her creative rigor, her intellectual and critical depth, and her prophetic vision of the role of literature in interpreting the African-American experience in the United States are unsurpassed. Morrison has written six novels, one short story, one play, and numerous critical essays and has come to be regarded as one of the preeminent writers of our time. In all of her writings, Morrison is concerned about crafting a special, clarifying angle for remembering the past and making it a useful mechanism for survival in the contemporary world. "I think long and hard about what my novels should do," says Morrison. "They should clarify the roles that have become obscured, they ought to identify those things in the past that are useful and those things that are not and they ought to give nourishment."

Morrison began to write during the 1970s when there was a ready audience in the United States for works by women, particularly black women. Although she has been concerned in her works with a female quest for selfhood, the major thrust of the Morrison canon has been the "elaborately socialized world" of black people as a whole. Her women protagonists have been representatives of the challenges that face all those within the black community. For Morrison, the major challenge in the late twentieth century in the aftermath of the civil rights movement and integration is forgetfulness. Morrison wants to record and restore in her works the sustaining values

that she believes were part of the cohesive black communities of the past. Through penetrating and enhancing analyses of historical experience and creative use of the myths, music, language, and worldview of African Americans, Morrison has created a body of work that is as well regarded for its pure aesthetic beauty as for the magnitude of its interpretive power.

Born Chloe Anthony Wofford on February 18, 1931, Morrison grew up in the small midwestern town of Lorain, Ohio. She was the second of George and Ramah Wofford's four children. Her parents had migrated from the South with their families in the early 1900s; her maternal grandparents, who had been sharecroppers in Greenville, Alabama, had lost their land in the late 1890s and were never able to get out of debt. Her father's family were Georgia sharecroppers, and the racial strife they endured left him with painful memories of the South and a bitter attitude toward white people.

With both parents from migrant families, Morrison was brought up—as many in such families were—with a strong distrust of whites and an understanding that the only tangible or emotional aid on which she could depend would come from her own community. Group loyalty was among the earliest values she was taught as a child. It was, her parents believed, one of the most important lessons that she could learn in order to survive in the harsh racial environment of the 1930s and 1940s.

In the Wofford household, the distinctiveness of black cultural life was richly lived and affirmed by Morrison's parents on a daily basis. Her growing years were filled with the jokes, lore, music, language, and myths of African-American culture. Her mother sang to the children, her father told

Toni Morrison won the Nobel Prize in literature in 1993. (SCHOMBURG CENTER)

them folktales, and they both told "thrillingly terrifying" ghost stories. It was at their knee that she heard tales of Br'er Rabbit and of Africans who could fly; heard the names, the imagery, the rhythms of the language; and observed the naming ritual that would become a significant part of her later work as a novelist.

Education was also expected and encouraged during her growing years. Morrison was taught to read at home by her parents before she entered first grade. During her adolescent years, she read Dostoyevsky, Jane Austen, and Tolstoy—they wrote so specifically about their culture, Morrison remembers, that even a little black girl in Lorain, Ohio, could enjoy their stories. Later, as a beginning writer, Morrison

wanted to bring that kind of specificity to the experiences of her culture as well.

In 1949, Morrison graduated with honors from Lorain High School and the following fall entered **Howard University,** where she was an English major and a classics minor. As a member of the Howard Repertory Theater, she had the opportunity to make her first trips to the South, where she was able to see, firsthand, the harsh realities of southern life for blacks that her father had recounted; more important, in the black communities that she visited, she saw the similarities between core black cultural life in the North and South. The knowledge of that shared worldview of black people in both the North and the South would help her later to achieve the group cultural resonance in her works for which she has become famous.

In 1953, Morrison graduated from Howard and entered graduate school in English at Cornell University. She wrote a dissertation on Woolf and Faulkner and graduated from Cornell in 1955. Morrison taught briefly in the English department at Texas Southern University in Houston and then returned to Howard in 1957; while at Howard she joined a writers' group, where she first began to work seriously on her writing. She also met and married Jamaican architect Harold Morrison. The couple lived in Washington and had two sons, Slade Kevin and Harold Ford. The marriage, challenged by the differing cultural expectations of the roles of each partner, ended in divorce in 1964.

With two children to support alone, Morrison accepted a job in 1966 as a textbook editor with a subsidiary of Random House in Syracuse, New York. During the 1960s, many publishing companies, as a result of demands by civil rights groups, were trying to revise their textbook selections, and Morrison thought that she could make a contribution. It was in Syracuse during the nights after the children were asleep that she began to work on a story she had started in her writers' group at Howard about a little black girl who wanted blue eyes. Morrison sent the story to Holt; it was published in 1970 as *The Bluest Eye*. Still considered a favorite by many of her readers, *The Bluest Eye* tells the story of a young girl, Pecola Breedlove, and her family who fall victim to the debilitating effects of racism, poverty, urban life, and—most significantly for this novel—the Anglo-Saxon standards of physical beauty, accepted not only by the larger society but by the black community as well. The family destruction and the consequent madness of Pecola were a stinging indictment by Morrison of what happens to individuals whose personhood and beauty are negated summarily by the society in which they live.

In 1968, Morrison moved from Syracuse to New York City to become a trade-book editor in the New York office of Random House. During the next sixteen years, Morrison would rise to become senior editor at Random House, one of few blacks and the only black woman to hold such an esteemed position. Morrison was a highly regarded editor and oversaw the publication of black writers such as **Gayl Jones, Toni Cade Bambara**, John McCluskey, Muhammad Ali, and Andrew Young.

Working as an editor by day and a writer by night, Morrison completed her second novel, *Sula*, in 1973. In this novel, the protagonist is not a passive victim of the imposed values of the larger society that take her away from the true values of her culture,

as was Pecola; Sula, in a search for an existential self, defies the values of the community willingly. Unlike her childhood friend, Nel, who gives up the rebellion and quest for self of adolescence and settles into womanhood in the same way as the others in her community, Sula never conforms. She comes to church suppers without underwear, she sleeps with Nel's husband, she puts her grandmother in a nursing home, and—worst of all for the people in her community—Sula sleeps with white men. Her words to Nel on her deathbed are a commentary on the restricted lives she sees black women living: "I know what every Black woman in the country is doing. . . . Dying. Just like me. But the difference is they dying like a stump. Me I'm going down like one of those redwoods." While Morrison understands the desire for self-definition outside the community, she believes it is a futile effort. Racism and sexism in the society allowed no such definition for the Sulas of the 1950s, and so ultimately they had to depend on their communities, even if they did so in defiance. The community ostracizes Sula and keeps its distance from her, but despite her defiance of their values, she is never put out of the community. In her characterization of Sula, Morrison demonstrates the larger values of the black community regarding evil: "They let it run its course, fulfill itself and never invented ways either to alter it, annihilate it or prevent its happening again." She also affirmed, as she would do in all of her novels, the value of community allegiance over the desire for an existential self.

During the early 1970s, Morrison also was involved in the publication of a unique pictorial history of African-American life in the United States called *The Black Book*.

Although her name appears nowhere on the work and her official capacity on the project was that of in-house editor, *The Black Book* was Morrison's idea, and she participated as much in collecting materials as did the official editors of the project: Middleton Harris, Morris Levitt, Robert Furman, and Ernest Smith. The book chronicles black life from slavery to roughly the 1940s. It contains newspaper clippings, bills of sale, sheet music, announcements, dream books, definitions, letters patent, crafts, photographs, sport files, and other memorabilia taken largely from the collection of its editors, but it also includes an array of contributions from attics, scrapbooks, and trunks gathered by Morrison and other supporters of the project. In explaining her desire to do this kind of book, Morrison says she had gotten tired of histories of black life that focused only on leaders, leaving the everyday heroes to the "lump of statistics." She wanted to bring those lives to the forefront—to create a genuine black history book "that simply recollected life as lived." *The Black Book* was not a major commercial success, but Morrison's work on the project, which exposed her to the firsthand documents of the everyday lives of black people—their joys, triumphs, and creations—would be invaluable to her work as a novelist. Here, she saw head braces used on slaves, read the newspaper account of a slave woman who killed her children rather than have them returned to slavery, saw the patents of unsung accomplishments, and saw the photographs of Harlem life and the loves that grew and died there. The kernel of many of the conflicts that would appear in her later novels had been suggested through the view of black life she gained from compiling the materials for this project.

Perhaps nowhere was the evidence of her work on *The Black Book* more prevalent than in her next novel, *Song of Solomon*. Filled with the lore, the songs, and the myths of African Americans, *Song of Solomon*, published in 1977, was a treasury of history and culture. It is the story of Milkman Dead, a young man who, in his attempts to find a family fortune in the caves of Virginia, finds instead the songs, myths, lore, and love of his ancestors. It is a redemptive tale of a young boy who has been cut off from his family and knowledge of his ancestry by his father, who believes that the way to achieve manhood in this country is to own things. The only link Milkman has to his ancestry in the town where he grows up is his Aunt Pilate, a wise old woman who sings the stories of her history. She lives with very little, supporting herself and her daughters with only the bootleg wine she sells from her house, and her special joy is loving and caring for the living and the dead of her family. In an ironic twist that has Milkman finding the treasury of his ancestry rather than a bag of gold, *Song of Solomon*, more dramatic than any previous Morrison novel, affirms the value of connecting with the past. Morrison also explores material wealth and violence as solutions to problems in contemporary society, but she affirms, once again, the validity, the richness, and the empowerment of a knowledge of ancestral heritage.

Song of Solomon was received with much fanfare and high critical acclaim. It sold more than three million copies and was on *The New York Times* best-seller list for sixteen weeks, won the American Academy and Institute of Arts and Letters Award and the National Book Critics' Circle Award in

1978, and was chosen as a Book-of-the-Month Club selection, the only novel by a black writer since *Native Son* (1940) to have achieved such recognition.

Tar Baby, Morrison's fourth novel, was published in 1981. It was an instant commercial success, appearing on *The New York Times* best-seller list less than one month after it was published. With a *Newsweek* cover story and a stunning lineup of promotional tours, *Tar Baby* had made Morrison, said one reviewer, "the toast of the literary world." In the novel, Morrison focused on the effects that access to material success and its trappings can have on the viability of the village values that had been a sustaining part of the African-American past.

Set in the Caribbean on the fictional Isle de Chevalier, the novel combines mythical landscape, traditional peasant and patrician class culture, a black male longing to return to the past, and a black woman enjoying the material benefits of money and fame. The relationship between Son and Jadine turns into a romantic Armageddon between old ways and the new. The novel dramatizes the way in which the larger sociopolitical choices of blacks during the late 1970s manifested themselves on a personal level. The outcome of this debate, however, is not hopeful. Unable to resolve their differences, Son and Jadine end the romance as individuals who understand more about the value of each other's outlook on life but who are unable to reconcile these ways into a unifying relationship. Morrison not only sets up a thematic argument against Jadine, pointing out that she is one who has "forgotten her ancient properties," but she also unravels the story against a natural landscape so mythically rendered that the setting, too,

suggests the superiority of that which is timeless, rooted, and unshaken by contemporary realities.

With the financial and critical success of *Song of Solomon* and *Tar Baby*, Morrison was able to leave her position at Random House. In 1984, she was named to the Albert Schweitzer Chair in the Humanities at the State University of New York (SUNY) at Albany. While at Albany, she taught courses in literature and was commissioned by the New York State Writers Institute to write a play in honor of the first national observance of the birthday of Dr. Martin Luther King, Jr. The play, *Dreaming Emmett*, was based on the life of the young boy Emmett Till, who was killed by a lynch mob in Mississippi in 1954. The play was performed by the Capital Repertory Theater of Albany, New York, on January 4, 1986.

While at Albany, Morrison also completed writing her fifth novel, *Beloved*, which was published in 1987. The writing of *Beloved* suggested a settling period for Morrison: A minority writer, she had said, must go through four stages: a period of anger, a period of self-discovery, a period of celebratory use of the culture, and finally an arrival at a "conceptual notion of the ethnic experience." With the writing of *Beloved*, Morrison had come through all of these stages: She was not just writing the story of the effects of slavery on the rights and responsibilities of the mother-love of one woman, but she was trying, through the characterization of Sethe, to understand the full human meanings and implications of the slave experience.

Motherhood and infanticide provided a powerful medium through which to reveal the effects of the horror of slavery on the humanity of individuals. The story is based on the life of Margaret Garner, a Kentucky slave who, with her four children, escaped to Cincinnati, Ohio; when caught, she tried to kill all of the children but succeeded in killing only one, by cutting her throat.

When Morrison read this story while working on *The Black Book*, she was deeply moved by the humanistic and symbolic nature of this story. Here was a woman who did a courageous thing, says Morrison: "She took the lives of her children into her own hands." This incident proved not only how slavery robbed individuals of their most basic human rights, but it also demonstrated the way in which slaves, sometimes in violent and paradoxical ways, insisted on their humanity in spite of slavery's horror. Even as she reveals the most brutal and humiliating aspects of slavery, Morrison does not explain away Sethe's deed; in fact, the story is largely about how Sethe accepts her guilt and seeks forgiveness. In the novel, Sethe is revisited by what she believes is the ghost of her daughter; the story pivots around Sethe, her family, and her community coming to terms with this awful deed and finding the strength and courage to live clearer, fuller lives as a result of it.

Beloved has been called Morrison's most successful novel, technically and thematically. The complexity that it assigns to slavery, an event too often "summarized away" in American history, gives the novel its greatest moral and historical merit. Full of intertwining plots and layered time sequences, the novel keeps readers challenged and attentive. The order of revelation, always out of chronological sequence in Morrison's novels, is doubly complicated in this novel by characters "remembering what they were remembering in a time past." The infanticide that is the cause of the action in the story gives way to the labor of working out symbolic meanings of the ghost's presence and understanding the quests for psychological and moral wholeness that it inspires in all the characters.

Beloved touched a major chord in the American reading public. It has been a widely read and studied text, taught in history courses and literature courses as well as courses in women's studies and creative writing. Never before had Morrison been so successful in achieving her own standard for good literature: *Beloved* was a novel that was "unquestionably political and irrevocably beautiful at the same time." It won the Pulitzer Prize for fiction.

In 1989, Morrison was named the Robert F. Goheen Professor in the Council of the Humanities at Princeton University, where she teaches courses in American literature and is writer-in-residence in the humanities. With her professorships at both SUNY and Princeton, Morrison began to write critical essays as highly regarded as her fictional works. Her essays in critical anthologies and for such journals as the *Michigan Quarterly* and *Thought* have been widely read and have provided useful insights for interpretations of her works and of American literature in general.

Morrison delivered the prestigious Massey Lectures in American Civilization at Harvard University and the Clark Lectures at Trinity College, Cambridge in 1990. The Massey Lectures, which explore the presence of blackness or "Africanism" in literature by white writers and the reflexive implications of that presence on the writers themselves and the culture out of which they wrote, were published by Harvard University Press in 1992 (*Playing in the Dark: Whiteness and the Literary Imagination*).

While at Princeton, Morrison's artistic works also continued to flourish. She was commissioned by Carnegie Hall to write the lyrics for the operatic piece *Honey and Rue*, which was performed there in January 1992 featuring soprano **Kathleen Battle** with music by André Previn. In the spring of 1992, she completed her sixth novel, *Jazz*, her intricate and improvisational telling of the story of black city life in the 1920s and 1930s. *Jazz* is the second in a trilogy, which began with *Beloved*; it mythologizes black life throughout various periods in history.

Morrison has served as a trustee of the New York Public Library and of the National Humanities Center, as cochair of the Schomburg Commission for the Preservation of Black Culture, and for six years as a member of the National Council of the Arts. She is a member of the American Academy and Institute of Arts and Letters and the American Academy of Arts and Sciences and has received honorary degrees from Harvard, the University of Pennsylvania, Sarah Lawrence College, **Oberlin College, Spelman College**, Dartmouth College, and Yale, Georgetown, Columbia, and Brown universities. In 1978, Morrison received the Distinguished Writer Award from the American Academy of Arts and Letters, was the first recipient of the Washington College Literary Award in 1987, and was a New York State governor's awardee in 1986. She has also been a subject of the highly regarded PBS interview series *A World of Ideas with Bill Moyers*. She was the recipient in 1990, of the Modern Language Association of America Common Wealth Award in Literature and the Sara Lee Corporation Front Runner Award in the Arts and in 1992 edited and introduced a collection of essays entitled *Race-ing Justice and En-gendering Power: Essays on Anita Hill, Clarence Thomas, and the Construction of Social Reality*.

Because the challenge in Morrison's writing is one undertaken in service to her people and not to herself, and because she sincerely believes that the story, the novel, is the mode through which African Americans can be led out of the cultural confusion and complexity of contemporary society, Morrison has become a kind of literary Moses. In her works, she strips away the idols of whiteness and of blackness that have prevented blacks in the United States from knowing themselves and gives them their own true, mythical, remembered words to live by. She takes on the whole culture and seeks to restore the mythos and the ethos that will clarify the meaning of the journey of African Americans in the United States. She is healer and prophet; she is nurturer and guide; and because she achieves these tasks with such grace, such love, and such confidence, courage, and skill, Morrison holds an indelible position of prominence in African-American history and in the history of great writers throughout the world.

CAROLYN DENARD

N

Naylor, Gloria (1950–)

Gloria Naylor has become widely associated with a line from her novel, *The Women of Brewster Place* (1982): "All the good men are either dead or waiting to be born." While Naylor explores the violence inflicted upon black women by their men, she also writes about the possibilities of transformation of

Gloria Naylor, author of The Women of Brewster Place, *has made a commitment to illuminate the condition of black women in America.* (SCHOMBURG CENTER)

men. Primarily, however, Naylor has made a commitment to illuminate the condition of black women in America.

A short-story writer and novelist, Gloria Naylor was born on January 25, 1950, to Roosevelt, a transit worker, and Alberta McAlpin Naylor, a telephone operator, in Brooklyn, New York. Born and reared in the South, her parents left her a rich legacy from which to draw fictional characters. Naylor earned a bachelor's degree in English from Brooklyn College of the City University of New York in 1981 and a master's degree in Afro-American Studies from Yale University in the early 1980s.

Before choosing writing as a primary career, Naylor worked as a missionary for Jehovah's Witnesses in New York, North Carolina, and Florida from 1968 to 1975. Between 1975 and 1981, she worked for several hotels, including the Sheraton City Square in New York City, as a telephone operator. Since the 1980s, Naylor has taught at George Washington University, New York University, Boston University, and Cornell University.

Naylor achieved national acclaim with the publication of her first novel, *The Women of Brewster Place*, which won the American Book Award for first fiction in 1983. Her novel centers on the lives of seven black women of different backgrounds and ages who find themselves on a dead-end ghetto street that seems to have a life of its own. The novel weaves together such broad topics as sex, birth, death, love, and grief to convey the common burden that black women experience because of their race and gender. With their backs literally up against a brick wall, these women act as mothers to each other as they share their trials and triumphs.

Naylor's second novel, *Linden Hills* (1985), explores the lives of affluent but spiritually dead African Americans who are trapped by the American dream. While these upwardly mobile African Americans pride themselves on having arrived, their achievements are undermined by their disdain for the more humanistic values—mutual support of family and kindness to others—and their preoccupation with material possessions.

With the support of a grant from the National Endowment for the Arts, Naylor wrote her third novel, *Mama Day* (1989).

Steeped in mysticism, the novel resembles **Toni Morrison**'s *Beloved* (1987), **Sherley Anne Williams**'s *Dessa Rose* (1987), and **Alice Walker**'s *The Temple of My Familiar* (1990). In a timeless world where traditionalists practice herbal medicine and worship their ancestors, Mama Day, a stalwart matriarch, has magical powers that she must conjure up in order to save her great niece from the island's evil forces. A compelling generational saga, *Mama Day* tells a story of pride, pain, and woman-healing. Her 1992 novel *Bailey's Cafe* was a best-seller. It is set in the 1940s in an American diner where neighborhood prostitutes congregate.

Winner of a Guggenheim fellowship in 1988, Gloria Naylor joined the ranks of the select few black women who have won the coveted creative writing award. Naylor's novels have established her as one of the most talented contemporary fiction writers in America.

ELIZABETH BROWN-GUILLORY

P

Petry, Ann Lane (1908–)

If working in the family drugstore had not been, literally, a 365-days-a-year job, Ann Petry once speculated to a class of young pharmacy students, she might have applied for a license from the state of New York rather than seek a job in journalism when she moved there in the late 1930s. Had that happened, the world would have missed an acclaimed novelist. As it is, Ann Petry's writing captures the full scope of her life and heritage, including her brief career in pharmacy.

Ann Lane was born in Old Saybrook, Connecticut, on October 12, 1908. Her father, Peter C. Lane, was one of the first black pharmacists registered in Connecticut and the only black pharmacist in the nearly all-white Old Saybrook of the early 1900s. He built a successful practice, despite early threats from some members of the community—harassment that extended to young Ann and her sister as well. Her mother, Bertha James Lane, owned several businesses at various times, and two of her aunts received college educations. One of them, Anna L. James, the first black woman pharmacist in Connecticut, practiced with her brother in the family drugstore. "I don't think it ever occurred to them there were things they could not do because they were women," Petry remembers.

It was to her father's drugstore that Ann Lane went upon her graduation from Connecticut College of Pharmacy in 1931. Petry's childhood, drugstore life, and New England life—and their particular tensions for black professional families—are fictionalized in *Country Place* (1947), "Miss Muriel" (1971), and "The New Mirror" (1965).

Ann Lane married George Petry and moved to New York City. Her early fiction found regular publication in the *Crisis*, a

The Street, *Ann Lane Petry's novel about the Harlem she knew as a newspaper reporter, sold 1.5 million copies in 1946.* (MOORLAND-SPINGARN)

black journal that particularly nurtured promising writers. Her experiences as a reporter in Harlem taught her stark lessons that have been captured in such works as "Like a Winding Sheet" (1946), "In Darkness and Confusion" (1947), and Petry's first novel, *The Street* (1946), which sold 1.5 million copies and won a Houghton Mifflin Literary Fellowship Award in 1946. (Houghton Mifflin reissued the novel as a paperback in 1992.)

Petry has also written historical novels for young readers that reflect her desire to nurture knowledge of and pride in the achievements and humanity of black women throughout history. Her books for children include *The Drugstore Cat* (1949), *Harriet Tubman, Conductor of the Underground Railroad* (1955), *Tituba of Salem Village* (1964), and *Legends of the Saints* (1970).

Petry's contribution to literature has been acknowledged by membership in the Authors' Guild and American PEN (Association of Poets, Playwrights, Editors, Essayists, and Novelists) and by honorary doctorates from several colleges and universities. Literary critics have praised her writing for various qualities, some seeing her as a chronicler of New England, referring primarily to *The Narrows* (1953), which tells of a doomed interracial love affair in a closed New England community; others classify her as the most successful follower of the "Richard Wright school" of urban realism; still others praise her hard-hitting short stories about the tragedies and ironies of black life. More recent critics, who look at her work within the tradition of black women writers, compare her strong urban women characters with **Zora Neale Hurston**'s characterizations of strong rural women.

Ann and George Petry have one child, a daughter, Elizabeth. They live today in Old Saybrook, a short distance from the James Pharmacy, which still bears her aunt's name. In 1989 Beacon Press republished Petry's short fiction collection, *Miss Muriel and Other Stories*, which had originally been issued in 1971.

SUZANNE POIRIER

Polite, Carlene (1932–)

Carlene Polite is among the most talented and versatile black artists to emerge from the "second renaissance" of black culture in the

The remarkably talented and versatile Carlene Polite emerged from the "second renaissance" of black culture in the 1960s and 1970s as an innovative novelist, an accomplished dancer, and a committed political activist.
(SCHOMBURG CENTER)

1960s and 1970s. An innovative novelist, an accomplished dancer, and a political activist, Polite has been firmly committed to the cultural and political liberation of black Americans.

Born in Detroit on August 28, 1932, to John and Lillian (Cook) Hatcher, Carlene Polite attended Sarah Lawrence College and the Martha Graham School of Contemporary Dance before embarking on her multifaceted career. From 1955 to 1963, Polite concentrated her energies on dance; in addition to performing with the Concert Dance Theater of New York City (1955–59), the Detroit Equity Theater (1960–62), and the Vanguard Playhouse (1960–62), she taught modern dance at the Detroit Young Men's Christian Association (1962-63) as well as at Wayne State University.

In the early 1960s, Polite was one of numerous black artists and intellectuals who turned to political activism. During this period, which she later described as her freedom-fighter days, Polite held a number of political positions, including organizer of the Northern Negro Leadership Conference in 1963, elected member of the Michigan State Central Committee of the Democratic party from 1962 to 1963, and coordinator of the Detroit Council for Human Rights in 1963. She participated in the historic June 23, 1963, Walk for Freedom and the Freedom Now rally in November 1963 to protest the Birmingham bombings.

After the Detroit Council for Human Rights closed in 1964, Polite worked briefly in a nightclub and then moved to Paris, where she lived for the next seven years. During these years, Polite focused on her writing. Her first novel, *The Flagellants*, was published in French in 1966 and in English the following year. While residing in Paris, Polite sustained her preoccupation with the political condition of black Americans: in an article entitled "Speak, Brother!" that appeared in *Mademoiselle* in January 1968, Polite presented four different approaches to the issue of black power in four distinct black speech styles. Her second novel, *Sister X and the Victims of Foul Play*, was published in 1975, four years after her return to the United States. Polite is currently a full professor in the English department at the State University of New York at Buffalo, which she joined as an associate professor in 1971. Divorced from Allen Polite, she has two daughters, Glynda Bennett and Lila Polite.

In keeping with the Black Nationalist aesthetic of the 1960s and 1970s, Polite's work urgently conveys the need for political liberation from the disabling stereotypes of matriarchs and emasculated black men portrayed in *The Flagellants* and from the oppressive cultural and political system of capitalism portrayed in *Sister X*. Polite's novels have not achieved the recognition they deserve; their dense prose and uneven style are offset by the dazzling originality and exuberance of her writing. In her attempt to introduce the rhythms of black oral expression into her novels, and in her playful experimentation with form, Carlene Polite helped to shape the development of black fiction, opening the way for later innovators such as **Gayl Jones** and Ishmael Reed.

MADHU DUBEY

Prince, Lucy Terry   (c. 1730–1821)

Lucy Terry Prince was a remarkable figure in the early history of African-American women. Her importance to literature lies in her poem "Bars Fight," which was written in 1746 and is, so far as we know, the first poem written by a black person in America; it was not published, however, until 1855.

"Bars Fight" describes a raid by Native Americans on August 25, 1746, on a part of Deerfield, Massachusetts, called "The Bars." Prince's poem is considered the most accurate description of the event that exists.

Prince's daughter Durexa also gained a reputation as a poet, but no work of hers has come down to us. Lucy Terry Prince's biographical entry is in the first volume of this encyclopedia, *The Early Years, 1619–1899*.

R

Rollins, Charlemae Hill (1897–1979)

Noted librarian Charlemae Rollins Hill was dedicated to the development of literature for black children; besides researching, writing bibliographies, and encouraging others to write for this precious audience, she wrote for them herself.

In 1963, she edited *Christmas Gifts*, an anthology of black folklore about Christmas. In the years that followed, she wrote biographies for children of African Americans, which included *They Showed the Way:* *Forty American Negro Leaders* (1964), *Famous American Negro Poets for Children* (1965), *Famous Negro Entertainers of Stage and Screen* (1967), and *Black Troubador: Langston Hughes* (1970); for her Langston Hughes biography, she won the Coretta Scott King Award.

Hill's biographies were noted for being accurate, straightforward, and respectful of their subjects. Her biographical entry is in the *Business and Professions* volume of this encyclopedia.

S

Sanchez, Sonia (1934–)

Uh Huh, But How Do It Free Us, the title of Sonia Sanchez' 1970 drama, best sums up her commitment to improving the life of black Americans. Sanchez was a leading activist during the civil rights movement of the 1960s who—like her contemporaries, Imamu Amiri Baraka, Addison Gayle, Don L. Lee, **Nikki Giovanni**, Tom Dent, and Lorenzo Thomas—called for a change in American politics. She became a spokesperson for the millions who demanded a revamping of a society in which the masses of African Americans were impoverished and undereducated. When meager gains were made by select black politicians, many of whom she believed had been bought, Sanchez was quick to ask, "Uh huh, but how do it free us?"

Sonia Sanchez was born on September 9, 1934, in Birmingham, Alabama, to Wilson L. and Lena Jones Driver. She earned a bachelor's degree from Hunter College in 1955 and holds an honorary doctorate from Wilberforce University. The mother of three children, Anita, Morani, and Mungu, Sanchez held several faculty positions since 1965 in California, New York, New Jersey, and Massachusetts before moving to Philadelphia in the late 1970s to teach English and write at Temple University. She has been the recipient of several major awards, including the PEN Writing Award in 1969, the National Institute of Arts and Letters Grant in 1970, a National Endowment for the Arts fellowship, and an American Book Award for poetry in 1978–79.

Evocative, moving, and *militant* are words that best describe the poetry and plays of Sonia Sanchez, who manipulates black street speech to illuminate the deplorable conditions that the black masses

Sonia Sanchez' uncompromising view of black life is skillfully presented in her evocative, moving, and militant poetry and plays. (SCHOMBURG CENTER)

151

endure. Sanchez also writes about imperialism, capitalism, racism, sexism, child abuse, ineffectual and womanizing men, initiation rites for women, drug abuse, the destruction of great black leaders, black-on-black crime, and generational conflicts.

A leading poet since the 1960s, Sanchez has published several major collections: *Homecoming* (1969), *We a BaddDDD People* (1970), *It's a New Day: Poems for Young Brothers and Sisters* (1971), *Love Poems* (1973), *A Blues Book for Blue Magic Women* (1974), *I've Been a Woman* (1978), *Home Girls and Handgrenades* (1984), and *Generations: Selected Poetry, 1969–1985* (1986). In many of these collections, Sanchez calls for new black heroes and heroines to lead a revolution that will save black children from destruction.

Sanchez's uncompromising vision of the meaning of black life is as pervasive in her plays as it is in her poetry: She warns African Americans against moving toward a vacuous America that places value on material possessions and devalues human life. Sanchez also warns white Americans that African Americans will no longer tolerate disenfranchisement and degradation and that blood will be spilled as a corrective measure. Blending poetry with drama, Sanchez has published several poem-plays, including *The Bronx Is Next* (1970), *Uh Huh, But How Do It Free Us?* (1970), *Sister Son/ji* (1972), *Dirty Hearts* (1972), *Malcolm/Man Don't Live Here No Mo* (1972), and *I'm Black When I'm Singing, I'm Blue When I Ain't* (1982).

Sonia Sanchez was one of the leading proponents of the black arts movement. Increasingly since the 1960s, she has concerned herself with racism on a global scale, recognizing that the unjust treatment of one black person anywhere threatens black people everywhere. Her poetic voice of the 1960s expressed the violence and turmoil of the period, but Sanchez' voice continues to appeal to audiences nationally and internationally as she warns that tumultuous times may come again if women and people of color continue to be victimized by capitalist America.

ELIZABETH BROWN-GUILLORY

Sanders, Dori (19??–)

Peaches and fiction have in common Dori Sanders, author of the novels *Clover* and *Her Own Place:* Not only does she produce and sell both (as well as watermelons and okra), she also likes to compare the reaping of a story, good or bad, to that of a similar peach crop.

Dori Sanders was born near Filbert, South Carolina, the eighth of ten children. Her mother was a homemaker, and her father both a farmer and an elementary school principal. His insistance that his children report any complaints in writing had results: In so doing, Dori was to recall, "I think I honed my fictional skills." Himself author of a 1924 county history, her father encouraged the children's reading and study.

As a writer, Sanders was a late bloomer, or late cropper, and came to write not by design but to silence a boss who insisted that she had talent. She had been a college dropout and—her word—an "underachiever" who never took a creative writing class and had spent a lifetime near Filbert on one of York County's oldest black-owned farms, which was started by her father in 1915.

As a child, Sanders had a speech impediment that discouraged her from talking freely before strangers; yet, as she and her brothers and sisters grew up, she enjoyed their story-swapping sessions around a big, mushroom-shaped rock on the farm. In time, however, everyone moved off the farm, except Dori and her brother Orestus; they continued growing peaches and selling them at their roadside stand, Sanders' Peach Shed, up to the present.

During World War II, Sanders joined many black farm women who were hired to work in a nearby munitions plant. She put her factory earnings into the purchase of more land for the farm, and much later she would put her factory experiences and her reflections upon those other women so like herself to use for the background and plot of *Her Own Place*.

Sanders married at some point in her life but was later divorced, and she never had children. During the winters, she took jobs away from the farm, such as that of assistant banquet manager for a Maryland motel in the early 1980s. Her supervisor, seeing that she had jotted notes on the back of a menu, prodded her to take her writing seriously.

Her first undertaking, a novel about sharecroppers and migrant farmers, was turned down by North Carolina's Algonquin Press, but in the meantime, she had conceived another story. It was inspired by two funeral corteges she saw from her stand—one with a black girl waving from a car window, another with a white woman passing by a few hours later. She imagined the woman as the girl's white stepmother and decided to explore their attempts to live and cope with each another. The result was *Clover*. The book, published by Algonquin in 1990, was on the *Washington Post's* fiction best-seller list for ten weeks, won the Lillian Smith Award, and was optioned by Walt Disney Studios as a possible film.

In the years that followed, Sanders spent winters writing not far from the farm in a leased Charlotte, North Carolina, office, but her ideas continued to flow from the substance of her memories and ongoing observations of people, black and white, on the farm and at the stand. Writing her impressions on whatever scrap of paper was handy, she harvested in 1993 the result—the equally successful, more complex *Her Own Place*. She has since been at work on such projects as a children's book, another novel, and a cookbook concerning, not surprisingly, peaches.

GARY HOUSTON

Shockley, Ann Allen (1927–)

Ann Allen Shockley, librarian, novelist, newspaper columnist, teacher, and feminist political activist, has made contributions in a wide range of fields; yet, she remains one of countless black women whose achievements remain invisible to most of mainstream America. The subjects of her major writings illuminate some of the reasons for this lack of recognition, as do the social and political environments in which she has written.

Shockley was born June 21, 1927, in Louisville, Kentucky, the daughter of Bessie Lucas and Henry Allen, both social workers. She was encouraged by her parents to pursue her love for reading and writing at an early age, became the editor of her junior-high-school newspaper and, later, a fiction editor and columnist for the *Fisk University Herald* during her undergraduate years. She received her B.A. from Fisk University (1944–48) and a master's degree in library science from Case Western Reserve University (1959–60). In August 1949, she married William Shockley, a teacher; they had two children, William Leslie, Jr. and Tamara Ann.

In 1945, at eighteen and still an undergraduate at Fisk, Shockley became a staff writer for the *Louisville Defender*, which published some of her earliest writings, among them teen columns and short stories. In 1949, she began to write a weekly column called "Ebony Topics" for Maryland's white-owned *Federalsburg Times*; for about three years beginning in 1950, she wrote a similar weekly column for the *Bridgeville News* in Delaware, where she lived with her husband, and also published articles in the *Afro-American* (Baltimore) and *Pittsburgh Courier* newspapers.

In 1959, Shockley wrote *A History of Public Library Services to Negroes in the South, 1900–1955* (unpublished), the first of several works in the area of librarianship that had special emphasis on black collections, and in 1969, she began to work at the Fisk University Special Negro Collection. Since then, she has coauthored *Living Black American Authors: A Biographical Directory* (1973) and published her well-received *Handbook of Black Librarianship* (1977), both significant works to the fields of black librarianship and African-American history, as well as numerous essays and articles in the professional journals of her field.

Shockley is also a prolific short-story writer and novelist: Before the appearance of her first published novel, *Loving Her*, in 1974, she had published more than thirty short stories in newspapers and periodicals. In most of her stories, she grapples with such socially and politically charged issues as racism, sexism, homophobia, interracial relationships, and the everyday trials and tribulations of being black in America. These themes reflect some of her personal experiences as a black feminist

as well as the larger collective experiences of the political and social struggles of the 1960s and 1970s. The influences of civil rights, Black Power, the second wave of women's liberation in North America, and the lesbian and gay liberation movements echo through the pages of her stories, where they are interpreted and challenged.

Of particular historical, political, and social significance have been Ann Allen Shockley's published novels and collections of short stories. *Loving Her* was the first novel written by a black woman that has a black lesbian as its central character and explores a lesbian relationship in depth: Renay, the protagonist, flees a physically and emotionally abusive husband to pursue a relationship with Terry, a wealthy white woman. Shockley's second novel, *Say Jesus and Come to Me* (1982), confronts the issue of homophobia in the black church in a satirical and biting manner: The main character, Reverend Myrtle Black, a black lesbian minister, uses her power from the pulpit like her male heterosexual counterpart to seduce young women in the congregation. Shockley wrote that the intent of this piece was to "bring out the homophobic hypocrisy of the black church, which is filled to the pulpit with closet gays and lesbians from all walks of life. . . . I wanted to expose the conservatism and snobbishness of the black middle class and academicians, which I see all the time; black male oppression of women; [and] the superior attitudes and opportunism of some white women towards black women in the women's liberation movement." In her collection of ten short stories, *The Black and White of It* (1980), Shockley offers glimpses into relationships between lesbians living within the constraints of a racist and heterosexist society.

Although her plots and themes incorporate many different living situations and relationship issues, Shockley has been criticized for her overall negative outlook regarding the possibility of lesbians finding fulfilling and enduring loving relationships. Her two novels have been extensively reviewed in lesbian, third world, and women's publications, receiving mixed responses that including favorable yet critical assessments from **Alice Walker**, Barbara Smith, and Rita Dandridge, as well as a scathingly homophobic response to *Loving Her* from Frank Lamont Phillips. Her three major works nonetheless represent important steps toward exposing and confronting important issues both within and outside of black communities.

TRACYE A. MATTHEWS

Southerland, Ellease (1943–)

"I got a horn / You got a horn / All God's Children got a horn" describes the talent, spirituality, and sense of communality that characterize the work of Ellease Southerland. "I Got a Horn, You Got a Horn" is the title of an autobiographical essay in which Southerland describes what she most remembers growing up the oldest daughter in a family of fifteen, a family she describes as "plagued by brilliant minds on fire." This musician, poet, novelist, teacher, and ex-social worker remembers herself at five years of age singing hymns with her family—hymns such as "O Mary Don't You Weep," "Onward, Christian Soldiers," and, especially, "I Got a Horn."

Ellease Southerland was born on June 18, 1943, in Brooklyn, New York, to Ellease Dozier and Monroe Penrose Southerland. She earned a B.A. from Queens College of the City University of New York in 1965 and an M.F.A. from Columbia University in 1974. Southerland's mother was born in North Carolina and her father in Florida, as were her two oldest brothers. Southerland says that the roots of her parents in the black South, with its lost, but identifiable, ties to Africa, defined her family's life. Her father was a minister and a baker; her mother, a homemaker. The memories of her upbringing are the materials from which her poetry and fiction are shaped.

In "I Got a Horn," Southerland tells of the family growing to a full brass band, using horns bought by her father in a pawnshop. The gift of music evident in the family takes specific form in her poetry. She won the Gwendolyn Brooks Award from *Black World* magazine in 1972 for her poem "Warlock," which is in her first volume of poetry, *The Magic Sun Spins*, published by Paul Breman in 1975.

The Magic Sun Spins takes its title from the poem "Black is," which celebrates Blackness, ending with the words, "And the magic sun is beautiful. / Beautiful / because / Black is." Three poems—"Ellease," "Two Fishing Villages," and "Nigerian Rain"—celebrate Southerland's love and affinity for the people and traditions of Nigeria; "That Love Survives" addresses the lessening of pain after four years of grieving for her dead mother with whom she had a deep spiritual and psychic bond. Southerland, in the essay "I Got a Horn," describes coming of age with her mother's intimate guidance and understanding the depth of love of her mother for her father—in spite of their problematic relationship. Southerland says she felt like a "co-mother" rather than a daughter, an observation that foreshadows her role as mother to her brothers and sisters after her mother's death from cancer at age forty-five.

Music, religion, and family solidarity are the themes most evident in Southerland's extraordinary first novel, *Let the Lion Eat Straw* (1979), in which the protagonist, Abeba Williams, born out of wedlock in the rural South, is raised by the midwife who delivered her. Abeba is eventually claimed by her natural mother and transported to Brooklyn, New York, where she experiences traditional family life with her mother and kindly stepfather. Her exceptional musical abilities are encouraged, and she graduates from high school with honors. Against her mother's wishes, Abeba abandons a promising career as a concert pianist to marry a man who will experience recurring bouts of madness; nevertheless, she will bear fifteen children and preside over a household of exuberant, creative people. The story of Abeba is a bittersweet account of Southerland's own mother. *Let the Lion Eat Straw* was a Book-of-the-Month Club alternate selection.

After the death of her mother, Southerland became a social worker in order to help support her brothers and sisters. Her second novel in progress, a sequel to the first, tentatively titled *A Feast of Fools*, introduces Abeba's daughter, who continues the family saga. (The novel is excerpted in *Breaking Ice*, an anthology edited by **Terry McMillan**.) In an interview, Southerland indicates that this daughter, in love with a Nigerian, is the link between African Americans and Africans. The story is a counterbalance to *Lion*, ending with a wedding and acknowledging the human need for ceremony. The novel reflects Southerland's love of Africa and her early sense of black heritage originating in Africa.

In addition to this novel, she is working on a collection of short stories entitled *Before the Cock Crows Twice*. Southerland has already published short fiction and poetry in such periodicals as *Black World*, *Massachusetts Review*, *Présence Africaine*, and *Journal of Black Poetry*. Her excellent critical essay, "The Influence of Voodoo on the Fiction of Zora Neale Hurston," is published in *Sturdy Black Bridges*, an anthology of essays on the literature of black women.

Ellease Southerland lives in Jamaica, New York, and is an adjunct professor and poet-in-residence at Pace University. She says she writes so that readers can dream their own dreams, believing that her story should not be so heavy as to overwhelm the reader's story. She has traveled five times to Nigeria and once to Egypt, is interested in Egyptology and hieroglyphics, and teaches people in workshop sessions to understand the principles of this ancient form and to write their names in it. The themes in her poetry and fiction speak to family, church, and community values; her forthcoming work reflects her love for Africa. Though Southerland works slowly, publishing only when she senses her work is ready, she is a major voice in contemporary black literature.

CAROLYN MITCHELL

Spencer, Anne (1882–1975)

Of the many women who distinguished themselves as poets during the Harlem Renaissance, Anne Spencer may be the most original and unconventional.

Annie Bethel was born in Henry County, Virginia, on February 6, 1882. Her parents, Joel Cephus and Sarah Louise, separated when she was five; Annie then moved with her mother to Bramwell, West Virginia, a mining town. While Sarah worked to support them, Annie lived with another family, the Dixies. When she was eleven, her father learned that she had never received a formal education—her mother had not wanted her to attend school in a mining town. He threatened to take Annie, and so her mother enrolled her in the Virginia Seminary in Lynchburg as Annie Bethel Scales—under Sarah's maiden name. She was the youngest student ever to attend school there.

Annie excelled in humanities courses but did not fare as well in the sciences; for these she recruited a tutor, Edward Spencer. Soon, she performed well in all her courses and in 1899 graduated from the seminary, receiving the honor of delivering the valedictory address. After teaching school for two years in West Virginia, Annie returned to Lynchburg in 1901 to marry Edward Spencer.

Spencer soon became the mother of two daughters, Bethel Calloway (Stevenson) and Alroy Sarah (Rivers), and a son, Chauncey Edward (who grew up to become a pioneer in black aviation). Others assisted in their care; she spent most of her time writing and working in her garden.

When James Weldon Johnson became the guest of the Spencers, arriving in Lynchburg in 1917 to help organize a chapter of the **National Association for the Advancement of Colored People,** he saw some of Spencer's poetry, helped her find a publisher, and suggested the pen name Anne Spencer. At thirty-eight, Anne Spencer published her first poem, "Before the Feast of Shushan," in the February 1920 *Crisis,* and Johnson published five of her poems in *The Book of American Negro Poetry* (1922). By 1927, ten of her poems were published in Countee

Cullen's *Caroling Dusk,* and it had become clear that she was an important new poet.

From the 1920s through the 1940s, Anne Spencer was represented in every volume of black poetry and in *American Negro Poetry since 1900.* Her poems, receiving favorable reviews, were often characterized as private or ironic, yet conventional in structure and nonracial in theme; focusing on recurring themes such as friendship, love, and freedom, Spencer had more in common with nineteenth-century American poets than with her contemporaries in Harlem.

Her home at 1313 Pierce Street became an important resting place for black travelers when hotels would not allow them accommodations. W. E. B. DuBois, Paul Robeson, Langston Hughes, George Washington Carver, and Sterling Brown were often guests in her home as Spencer participated in the New Negro cultural and intellectual awakening. Writers solicited her criticism of their works and exchanged ideas during their visits.

As Anne Spencer's popularity grew outside of Lynchburg, she became notorious locally: She forced the ouster of white teachers at the all-black high school, which led to the hiring of black teachers; she boycotted segregated public transportation and rode the trolley in defiance—refusing to move or be moved; in 1923 she walked two miles to the town's library and requested a job as librarian, thus initiating the opening of the only black library in Lynchburg in which she served as librarian from 1923 to 1945.

Spencer's local fame also was based on her gardening abilities: Her garden became well known for its varied plants and flowers. She spent eight years developing a pink candy-striped Chinese peony from seed. Her devotion to her garden matched her devotion to her poetry; indeed, she uses a garden as image or setting in many of her poems. In the last published poem of her lifetime, "For Jim, Easter Eve" (written in memory of James Weldon Johnson, who died in a car accident in 1938 shortly after visiting her home), Anne Spencer states, "if ever a garden was Gethsemane . . . this, my garden has been to me."

By 1940 Anne Spencer had become a recluse. After Edward's death in 1964, she began to work on a number of historical pieces and to prepare her poems for publication. When she died July 12, 1975, at the age of ninety-three, she left behind approximately fifty poems and her famous garden. Most of these poems have been compiled in J. Lee Greene's *Time's Unfading Garden: Anne Spencer's Life and Poetry* (1977), and her garden and its cottage, "Edankraal," have been placed on the National Register of Historic Places.

PAULA C. BARNES

T

Taylor, Mildred (1943–)

In 1990, among the best-sellers in children's literature was one book by an African American; that book, *Roll of Thunder, Hear My Cry*, was written fourteen years before by Mildred Taylor. Immediately hailed in 1976 as a beautifully written work of great insight, it has since established itself as a classic and its author as one of the foremost writers of children's literature in the country.

Mildred Delois Taylor was born in Jackson, Mississippi, in 1943. Three months after her birth, her family moved out of the South because of a potentially violent quarrel between her father, Wilbert Lee Taylor, and a white man. They settled in Toledo, Ohio, eventually buying a large house that served as a haven for relatives and friends escaping the racial hostilities of the South. As a child, Taylor visited the South with her parents many times; the culture, rhythms, sights, and sounds of her birthplace entered her consciousness during those visits, but she never lived in Mississippi again.

Taylor's childhood was apparently very happy, filled with the love of her family and relatively free of the pain of bigotry. Attending public schools that were segregated in elementary grades and integrated in high school, she was an excellent student, a class officer, editor of the school newspaper, and a member of the honor society. After graduating from the University of Toledo, Taylor joined the Peace Corps, a dream since high school, and characterized the two years she spent in Ethiopia teaching history and English as one of the happiest periods of her life.

Immediately hailed in 1976 as a beautifully written work of great insight, Roll of Thunder, Hear My Cry *has since established itself as a classic and its author, Mildred Taylor, as one of the foremost writers of children's literature in the country.* (SCHOMBURG CENTER)

On her return to the United States, Taylor taught in a Peace Corps training school and recruited for the organization. After a year, she entered the University of Colorado, where, in the atmosphere of the 1960s, she became a political activist: She helped found the Black Student Alliance and lobbied for a black studies department. After receiving an M.A. in English, she remained at the university, working as coordinator of the study-skills center.

The urge to write, however, was strong. Taylor quit her job and moved to Los Angeles, taking a position that did not tax her intellectual or creative energies so that she could write at night. The stories she wanted to write were about her family; in an article for *Booklist* in 1990, she explained why:

> As the years passed I felt a growing need for others to know these people, too. I felt a growing need to put the stories on paper for I wanted to show the black world as I knew it, a world different from that so often portrayed. I wanted to include the teachings of my own childhood, the values and principles upon which I and so many other black children were reared. I wanted to show a family united in love and self-respect, as parents strong and sensitive who attempted to guide their children successfully, without harming their spirits, through the hazardous maze of living in a discriminatory society. I wanted to show happy, loved children, about whom other children of all colors, or all cultures, could say, 'I really like them, I feel what they feel.'

Taylor's father was her primary source of inspiration: Throughout their childhood, he told his children stories about strong men and women who were proud of their race and history; when Taylor tried to share these stories with her white teachers and classmates, they were often dismissed as fanciful, but Taylor believed them and wanted to tell them to others.

Starting in 1975, Taylor published a series of seven novels about the Logan family in the years before and after World Wars I and II, just prior to the convulsive period of the 1960s civil rights movement. The first book, *Song of the Trees*, won a contest sponsored by the Council on Interracial Books for Children in 1973 and was published two years later; the second, *Roll of Thunder, Hear My Cry*, won the Newbery Medal in 1977 for Taylor, who became the second African American to receive the award. The book also was nominated for a National Book Award and was made into a film.

The third book in the series, *Let the Circle Be Unbroken*, won the Coretta Scott King Award in 1983 and was nominated for an American Book Award. The fourth Logan family book, *The Friendship*, also was given the Coretta Scott King Award, in 1984. The next two, *Mississippi Bridge* (1990) and *The Road to Memphis (1990)*, were named Notable Children's Books in the Field of Social Studies. The last installment in the Logan sagas is *The Well*, which was published in 1995. In addition to this seven-part series, Taylor has written *The Gold Cadillac* (1987) about the vicissitudes of a family that visits the South in a gaudy, prestigious car.

Taylor's awards assure her reputation, but children do not select a book and make it a best-seller because of its critical pedigree; they want characters who are recognizable and have traits that appeal to them. Themes must resonate without didacticism, and the action must not be contrived. Taylor's books meet these criteria, and children have taken them to their hearts, sharing in the lives of the Logans and coming away renewed, challenged, educated, entertained, and, one suspects, hopeful. Taylor's family represents, to a great extent, the best in African-American families; thus, she makes African Americans visible and places their lives in the center of life in the United States.

VIOLET J. HARRIS

Thomas, Joyce Carol (1938–)

"I use my pen to carve voices," says Joyce Carol Thomas, "as technicolor as the voices of my father's radio quartet. When it comes to showing anger I work until I can hear thunder, see icicles hanging from the ceiling."

Born in 1938 in Ponca City, Oklahoma, the fifth of nine children of bricklayer Floyd Dave Haynes and housekeeper Leona Haynes, Thomas worked in the fields as a child but says, "even though we missed the first part of school because of the necessity for work, we made up for it by telling stories." Her fundamentalist mother and her father who sang in a religious quartet gave her inspiration that has lasted throughout her career.

When Thomas was still young, her family moved to Tracy, California, another small rural town. She went to San Francisco City College and a number of other small colleges in the Bay area, receiving her B.A. from San Jose State College in 1966 and her M.A. in 1967 from Stanford University.

In the late sixties and early seventies, Thomas made her living teaching, but after stints at San Jose State College, Contra Costa College, St. Mary's College, and San Jose State University, she left teaching in 1983 to become a full-time writer. By that time, Thomas was already established as a poet and as a playwright. Her first book of poetry was *Bittersweet,* published in 1973; next came *Crystal Breezes* (1974) and *Blessings* (1975).

As her reputation grew in San Francisco and Berkeley, Joyce Carol Thomas turned to theater. Her plays *A Song in the Sky* (1976), *Look! What a Wonder!* (1976), *Magnolia* (1977), *Ambrosia* (1978), and *Gospel Roots* (1981) were all produced by San Francisco area theaters.

Thomas published two more volumes of poetry before writing the book in 1982 that would bring her to national attention: *Marked by Fire,* a novel for young adults, tells the story of Abyssinia Jackson, a young black girl growing up in Ponca City, Oklahoma. She is, according to the town's wise woman, "marked for unbearable pain and unspeakable joy." Described as a hauntingly and beautifully written novel and named outstanding book of the year by the *New York Times* and a best book for young adults by the American Library Association, it became required reading in high school and universities across America.

Thomas' next novel was a sequel to the first: *Bright Shadow* (1984) follows Abyssinia Jackson to pre-med school, where she meets a young man and falls in love. While this second work did not receive the critical acclaim of the first, it won the Coretta Scott King Award of the American Library Association. Thomas' next books were *Water Girl* (1986), *The Golden Pasture* (1986), *Amber* (1986), *Journey* (1988), *A Gathering of Flowers* (1990), and *When the Nightingale Sings* (1992).

Her remarkable gift for capturing the lives of small-town black people and recreating the rhythms of their speech led Thomas to comment: "I find myself now going back to black churches to listen to the music, to hear again those I used to hear as a child. And I think that is my quest in the writing also. I work at recreating those sounds, that kind of melody that I hear in the voices."

ANDRA MEDEA

V

Vroman, Mary Elizabeth (c. 1924–1967)

"Writing School Marm: Alabama Teacher Finds Literary, Movie Success with First Short Story" is the title of an article about Mary Elizabeth Vroman that appeared in the July 1952 edition of *Ebony* magazine. The story, titled "See How They Run," had been published in *Ladies' Home Journal* and depicted the real-life struggles of a rural schoolteacher trying to educate poor black children. An immediate success, the story received the prestigious Christopher Award and was later adapted as the movie *Bright Road*, starring Harry Belafonte and **Dorothy Dandridge**. Vroman wrote the screenplay and became the first black woman to gain membership in the Screen Writers Guild.

Born in Buffalo, New York, Vroman was a twenty-seven-year-old Alabama schoolteacher at the time the *Ebony* article was written. She had grown up in the West Indies and was a graduate of Alabama State Teachers College in Montgomery. A devoted educator, she later taught in Chicago and New York City.

Vroman's literary accomplishments also included two novels and one work of nonfiction. *Esther*, published in 1963, portrays the life of Esther Kennedy, the granddaughter of a midwife who overcomes seemingly insurmountable obstacles to become a nurse in a segregated hospital. Vroman's second novel, *Harlem Summer*, was published in 1967, the year of her death; written for young adult readers, the work recounts the experiences of sixteen-year-old John who visits relatives in Harlem. Both works celebrate black people as overcomers, attesting to their unwavering will to succeed.

Mary Elizabeth Vroman died from complications following surgery in 1967. She was survived by her husband, Oliver M. Harper.

SHIRLEY JORDAN

W

Walker, Alice (1944–)

The title of Alice Walker's 1983 collection of essays, *In Search of Our Mothers' Gardens*, best sums up the perspective that dominates nearly everything she writes; in this collection of essays, Walker argues that black women can survive whole only by recovering the rich heritage of their ancestors, particularly their black sister warriors. Walker urges women to look to their mothers to find ways to heal themselves; her message is that black women's personal salvation hinges upon recognizing their connectedness to women who historically have built bridges for them with their indomitable and independent spirit. From these sister warriors, black women can develop respect for possibilities.

Grange Copeland in Walker's *The Third Life of Grange Copeland* (1970) expresses Walker's vision about women and their mothers when he says that, regardless of the cost, human beings have the capacity to enjoy spiritual health and that poor, black, uneducated people have the potential to blossom. Walker suggests that although black women often find themselves in the harshest of environments—ones that are physically, spiritually, economically, and mentally debilitating—they can soar by finding in their mothers' gardens the roots that can bind, nurture, guide, and sustain them.

Although Walker writes about the restrictions placed on black women because of sexism and racism, she also writes about the transformations that are possible. In her novel, *Meridian* (1976), the civil-rights workers express Walker's vision when they say that fighting is sometimes necessary to keep from becoming overwhelmed with bitterness. Walker repeatedly makes the point in her writings that black women can ameliorate the loneliness of their lives by armoring themselves with the knowledge of the heroic lives of their foremothers and cogently argues that when a woman goes in search of her mother's garden, she will ultimately find her own.

Novelist, poet, short-story writer, essayist, educator, biographer, and editor, Alice Walker was born the last of eight children to sharecroppers Willie Lee and Minnie Tallulah (Grant) Walker on February 9, 1944, in rural Eatonton, Georgia. Growing up with five brothers, Walker learned how to defend herself. She also learned to make her way in a world of cotton fields, hogwire fences, sharecroppers' shacks, overpriced food in white-owned commissaries, and landlords who believed that black men were invisible, black women could be theirs for the taking, and black children did not need an education.

Walker's early childhood in abject poverty led to feelings of loneliness and

For years a prolific and highly respected writer, Alice Walker became internationally known with the publication of The Color Purple *in 1982. The book won the Pulizer Prize and the American Book Award and was made into a blockbuster movie starring Whoopi Goldberg and Oprah Winfrey.* (SCHOMBURG CENTER)

alienation that were magnified when her brother accidentally shot her in the eye with a BB gun. Losing vision in one eye and developing what seemed to her like a monstrous white film over it, Walker became reclusive and dreamed of suicide. She discovered books and began to read texts by some of the world's master writers.

Walker has recalled that her mother, perhaps because of the sympathy she felt when she looked into the disfigured eye, allowed her time to read without interruption, even when there were chores that needed attending to. When she was growing up, Walker's mother gave her three gifts that she considered the most significant of her life, gifts that were particularly meaningful because her mother had never owned such items and had bought them for Walker on a salary of less than $20 a week earned as a maid. One was a sewing machine so that Walker could

make her own clothes, communicating the message to be self-sufficient and independent; the second was an exquisite suitcase, better than most people in Eatonton owned, giving her permission to travel the world and to come home whenever she needed to touch base with her family and community; the third was a typewriter, which Walker saw as a mandate to write not only her own but also her mother's stories.

Armed with her three gifts, a "rehabilitation" scholarship from the state of Georgia awarded to her as senior class valedictorian, and $75 collected from her poor community, Walker marched off to **Spelman College** in Atlanta, where she studied from 1961 to 1963. At the all-woman college, Walker's consciousness was raised as she interacted with black females from across the country who wanted to change the world, particularly the politics of racism. While at Spelman, Walker became an activist and also became disillusioned with the middle-class preoccupation with respectability and material possessions. During the 1960s, Spelman's aim was to produce "ladies," and Walker had learned that she did not want to sit upon a pedestal; she wanted to be a sister warrior like her foremothers.

Walker transferred to Sarah Lawrence College in Bronxville, New York, in 1963, a move that allowed her an opportunity to distance herself from the South and to begin to see the world as a global village. She traveled to Africa in her senior year, storing up experiences that would later appear in her literary works.

One experience at Sarah Lawrence that spawned Walker's writing career was an unplanned pregnancy. Her recurrent childhood dreams of suicide returned as she struggled with her options. She knew that if she committed suicide her parents would be devastated but that if they learned of her pregnancy they would be disappointed and ashamed. She chose to have an abortion, which led her to write a series of poems about her ordeal, published in 1968 in *Once*.

After graduating from Sarah Lawrence with a bachelor's degree in 1965, Walker returned to the South to work in voter registration and to promote welfare rights in Georgia. On March 17, 1967, she married white civil-rights lawyer Melvyn Rosenman Leventhal. Her work in Georgia put her in contact with the state's poorest and least educated African Americans and allowed her to observe the impact of poverty on the relationships between black men and women, namely their cruelty to family members and to each other. Funded by a National Endowment for the Arts grant, Walker completed her first novel, *The Third Life of Grange Copeland*, in 1969, three days before the birth of her daughter Rebecca Grant.

Perhaps her most passionately written work, *Grange Copeland* centers on a father and son, Grange and Brownfield, who turn to alcohol and violence as they try to survive life in a state of powerlessness. Incapable of loving, they abuse their women. Grange's wife kills herself and her child when Grange abandons her; when Brownfield's wife, Mem, tries to elevate her family out of poverty, he blows her head off. Brownfield is probably the least redeemable male character in Walker's canon, particularly because he is arrogant, cruel, unfaithful, and jealous of Mem's college training; he literally beats the newly acquired education out of Mem, which parallels the flesh that falls from her bones and the teeth and hair she loses. An emaciated, toothless nag whose newborn baby Brownfield places on the porch to freeze to death, Mem is spiritually dead long before Brownfield drunkenly sends her head flying in one direction and her body spastically hopping in another. Walker leaves only Ruth, Mem's daughter, with a possibility of surviving whole. Ironically, it is her grandfather, Grange, who makes a commitment to save Ruth from destruction by both her evil father and white people. He teaches Ruth that she must cling tightly to a place inside her where white people cannot go, essentially an inviolable place. More important, Grange is transformed or redeemed when he teaches Ruth independence and self-love.

Walker held several teaching jobs early in her writing career, including writer-in-residence and teacher of black studies at Jackson State University (1968–69) and Tougaloo College (1970–71). Leaving the South in 1971 to assume a two-year Radcliffe Institute fellowship, Walker continued to reach back to her native state for characters. She worked as a lecturer in literature at Wellesley College and at the University of Massachusetts in Boston in 1972–73.

In 1973, Walker published a second volume of poetry, *Revolutionary Petunias and Other Poems*, which won the Lillian Smith Award and was nominated for a National Book Award. While the poems in this collection point to the decline of the Southern revolution, there are heroines whose acts of rebellion establish black women's role in the civil rights movement.

In the same year, she published a collection of short stories, *In Love and Trouble: Stories of Black Women*, for which she won a Richard and Hinda Rosenthal Award from the National Institute of Arts and Letters. This collection focuses on the violence that dominates the lives of black women and the mechanisms they use to fight back. One story in the collection that is frequently anthologized is "The Revenge of Hannah Kemhuff," in which a black woman has a conjurer cast a spell on a white woman who had denied her commodities during the Depression; the spell results in the deaths of the white woman's children. Obsessed with the curse, the white woman goes mad and begins to collect her own hair, fingernails, feces, and so on. She eventually dies from stress or, perhaps, from the curse.

An artist who believes in recovering the lives and texts of African Americans, Walker wrote *Langston Hughes, an American Poet* (1974), a biography for children. Later she would research and recover **Zora Neale Hurston**'s rich legacy to American literature. Walker's second novel, *Meridian*, takes up where *Grange Copeland* leaves off in terms of the civil rights movement, with the main character devoting her life to freeing her people. Meridian goes against stereotypical images of black mothers in that she is so terrified of failing at motherhood that she gives up her son, has her tubes tied, and becomes an activist to help change a society that places restrictions on women and African Americans. Walker elevates Meridian to the symbolic mother of the black race.

Walker's career was well on its way by the time she was awarded the prestigious Guggenheim Fellowship in 1977–78. In 1979, she moved from New York City to a ranch outside San Francisco, where she currently resides and writes full time.

A third collection of poetry, *Good Night Willie Lee, I'll See You in the Morning* (1979), treats love relationships by restructuring them to include a healthy love of self for women. Walker's second collection of short stories, *You Can't Keep a Good*

Woman Down (1981), looks closely at pornography, abortion, interracial rape, and politicization of relationships; unlike heroines in her previous works, the women in these stories are more optimistic, spirited, and tenaciously committed to surviving whole.

Walker became internationally known with the publication in 1982 of *The Color Purple*, which was nominated for a National Book Critics Circle Award and which won the Pulitzer Prize and the American Book Award in 1983. The book was made into a movie in 1985 and had mass appeal. Using the epistolary style, Walker has Celie write to God, Nettie to Celie, and Celie to Nettie. What occurs in these letters is the story of gross abuse of black women, subjugated by their men in both America and Africa. Focusing on incest, women's explorations of their bodies and souls, wife beating, and other violence, *The Color Purple* illustrates the dehumanization of women.

Becoming more prolific with each passing year, Walker has completed several projects since winning the Pulitzer. A collection of essays, *In Search of Our Mothers' Gardens* (1983), introduced the term *womanist*, as opposed to *feminist*, to separate black feminists or feminists of color from white feminists, who often differ ideologically on issues of race and gender. These essays essentially bring together her ideas about art and its relationship to life, namely, that a bad person cannot write a good book because art must improve life.

Several other texts have followed, including *Horses Make the Landscape Look More Beautiful* (1984), a book of poems; *To Hell with Dying* (1987), a book for children; and *Living by the Word: Selected Writings, 1973–1987* (1988), a book of essays. Her

1990 novel, *The Temple of My Familiar*, was a Book-of-the-Month Club featured alternate. Steeped in mysticism, employing a dreamlike structure, and filled with ample symbols, myths, legends, and fantasy, the novel addresses issues of self-knowledge, humanity, and human destiny.

One of America's most prolific and profound writers, Walker treats a host of subjects, including individual and collective freedom for black people and women, the endurance or will to survive, ancestral worship, the transformation of impoverished illiterate people, and the impact of racism and sexism on black relationships. With the releasing of the movie *The Color Purple*, Walker's vision for women and black people became accessible to millions. Perhaps no other black author has touched as many lives as Walker. Walker often writes about possibilities, and her very life gives testimony to the blossoms that can grow strong and tall when a woman finds her own in her mother's garden.

Her descriptively titled book *The Same River Twice: Honoring the Difficult: A Meditation on Life, Spirit, Art, & the Making of the Film* The Color Purple *Ten Years Later* was published in 1996.

ELIZABETH BROWN-GUILLORY

Walker, Margaret Abigail (1915–)

"I taught nearly forty years," says Margaret Walker, "and I taught my students that every person is a human being. Every human personality is sacred, potentially divine. Nobody is any more than that and nobody can be any less." This simple statement comes very close to encapsulating Walker's poetry.

Margaret Abigail Walker was born on July 7, 1915, in Birmingham, Alabama. Her father, Sigismund C. Walker, was a Methodist minister, a well-educated theologian who could speak five languages and read three more. Her mother, Marion Dozier Walker, was a music teacher who also had a college education. Because of her parents' love of learning, Walker grew up surrounded by music and books. Because of their passion for achievement, she was under constant pressure to excel. Her mother taught her to read by the time she was four years old; she finished elementary school at eleven, high school at fourteen, and college at nineteen. (She would have finished earlier, but she had to stay out a year.) Her father was determined that she complete a Ph.D. by twenty-one. "Luckily," as she later put it, "neither health nor finances would permit it."

Walker had begun to write poetry when she was eleven. Her family had moved to New Orleans, where her parents were both professors at New Orleans University. Walker attended Gilbert Academy and then enrolled at the university where her parents taught. When she was sixteen, Langston Hughes read his work at the school, and Walker approached him afterward with her own. He encouraged her to keep writing and to get out of the South.

At Northwestern University, where she did her undergraduate work, Walker again found encouragement. W. E. B. DuBois published her poetry in *Crisis*, and E. B. Hungerford, her creative writing teacher, arranged for her to be admitted to the Northwestern chapter of the Poetry Society of America. After graduating, Walker lived in Chicago for several years and joined the Federal Writers Project, which was funded by the Works Progress Administration (WPA). At the time, she did not realize how much less money she was receiving than the men in the project; she did realize, however, that she was working with and enjoying the company of such writers as **Gwendolyn Brooks**, Arna Bontemps, and Richard Wright. Her exposure to life for Chicago's urban black population proved to be an important ingredient in her writing.

When funding for the project stopped, Walker went to the University of Iowa to work on a master's degree. While she was there, she completed her first book of poetry, *For My People* (1942). Its publication has been called one of the most important events in black literary history. Not since **Georgia Douglas Johnson** had a black woman published a book of poetry, and Walker was the first black poet to be chosen for Yale University's Series of Younger Poets. *For My People* is a powerful work of poetic excellence; written with strong rhythm and imagery, it presents a world of emotions that are both personal and mythic.

Poets, however, do not often support themselves through book sales. In the twentieth century, most of them look to academia for financial support, and this was the avenue Walker chose. When she received her master's degree, she went to teach, first at Livingstone College in Salisbury, North Carolina, and then at West Virginia State College. She also married Firnist James Alexander, on June 13, 1943. In 1945, she went back to Livingstone for a year and then to Jackson State College, where she taught until 1979 and beginning in 1968 was director of the college's Institute for the Study of the History, Life, and Culture of Black People.

Walker did not publish a book between 1942, when *For My People* appeared, and 1966, when her novel *Jubilee* and another book of poetry, *Ballad of the Free*, came out;

she did, however, write poetry and essays and received a Rosenwald Fellowship in 1944 and a Ford Fellowship in 1954. She completed work on her Ph.D. in creative writing at the University of Iowa in 1966, submitting *Jubilee* as her final creative work. She also had four children and supported her family financially because her husband was disabled.

Jubilee was well received, both critically and commercially. It was translated into six languages, was made into an opera, and is still in print. A fictionalized reconstruction of the life of Walker's great-grandmother, the book describes a woman who maintains her own positive spirituality in the face of tremendous oppression. Walker says that this aspect of the book, which has been criticized by those who see forgiveness as weakness, accurately portrays her great-grandmother, who "realized that hatred wasn't necessary and would have corroded her spiritual well-being."

Walker's third volume of poetry, *Prophets for a New Day*, published in 1970, is filled with reflections on the civil rights movement, tributes to its leaders, and poetic indictments of the racist world in which black people live. In 1972, Walker published *How I Wrote Jubilee*, describing the thirty-year process of writing that book and the obstacles that she and other women writers face. Eighteen years later, she published *How I Wrote Jubilee and other Essays on Life and Literature*, a group of essays in which she reveals much of her anger and frustration about the lives of women, especially black women.

Walker has written two other volumes of poetry, *October Journey* (1973) and *This Is My Century: New and Collected Poems* (1989). She and poet **Nikki Giovanni** collaborated on the book *A Poetic Equation:*

Conversations between Nikki Giovanni and Margaret Walker (1974). In *This Is My Century*, Walker's voice is that of an elder, one who teaches, heals, and admonishes. It is a rich and satisfying book in which wisdom is often cut with bitterness and frustration, but faith and humanity prevail. Walker is also the author of a biography, *Richard Wright, Daemonic Genius: A Portrait of the Man, a Critical Look at His Work* (1987).

Whether or not Margaret Walker has ever received the critical attention she deserves, there is another standard that anyone who has taught young people will recognize: the smudged and ragged pages of an often-read literary anthology. Margaret Walker belongs to an elite group of poets who qualify for this award.

KATHLEEN THOMPSON

Wallace, Michele (1952–)

Michele Wallace was born on January 4, 1952, in New York City to musician Robert Earl and eminent artist Faith Ringgold. She received a B.A. from City College of the City University of New York (CUNY), in 1974 and after graduation took a job as book review researcher for *Newsweek* magazine. A year later, she became a journalism instructor at New York University.

Wallace was only twenty-six years old when she published the book that would cause such tremendous controversy in the black community: *Black Macho and the Myth of the Superwoman* appeared in 1979, while black male writers and critics were still in a ferment about **Ntozake Shange's** *for colored girls who have considered suicide/when the rainbow is enuf*, produced in 1978. In that play, Shange dealt with the unhappiness and pain that black women

experience, not only as a result of racism, but as a result of the sexism of black men. It spoke to something profound in the experience of black women and was extremely successful.

Quivering with indignation at what they called Shange's disloyalty and divisiveness, these same men picked up *Black Macho* and read Wallace's sharp analysis of what she considered a distorted relationship between black men and black women. In the course of this analysis, she attacked black men, civil-rights organizations, white women, feminism, and American society as a whole. Understandably, she was attacked in return. Black men and women were sharply divided in their reactions to the book, but no one

Michele Wallace was only twenty-six years old when she published a book that would cause tremendous controversy in the black community—Black Macho and the Myth of the Superwoman. (MICHELE WALLACE)

could deny that it stimulated discussion about the issues it raised.

In the years following this first book, Wallace taught at the University of California at San Diego, the University of Oklahoma, the State University of New York (SUNY) at Buffalo, and the City College of New York. She wrote essays and articles that appeared in the *Village Voice*, the *New York Times*, and a number of art magazines. She edited a book on her mother's work.

Then, in 1990, Wallace hit the publishing scene with another book. Released with a reissue of *Black Macho*, *Invisibility Blues: From Pop to Theory* again addressed the politics of race and gender in American culture. In its review of the book, *American Visions* magazine wrote that Wallace is a "sharp-eyed cultural sniper. She sights her targets with the assistance of black feminist cross hairs. . . . Wallace understands that her job is to make readers squirm, to make them think anew."

In talking about *Invisibility Blues*, Wallace explained how some of the reactions to her first book affected her: Hurt and embarrassed by many of the comments, she was also shocked and completely unprepared for the spotlight in which she found herself; she was just too young. The result was a nervous breakdown. However, she has clearly recovered and is once again making powerful and controversial comments about black women, black men, and the nature of their struggles.

West, Dorothy (1907–)

As an author and journalist, Dorothy West has critically engaged the social and political issues of her day, and her early literary ca-

reer was emblematic of the much celebrated Harlem Renaissance of the 1920s.

The only child of Rachel Pease Benson and Isaac Christopher West, Dorothy West was born on June 2, 1907, in Boston, Massachusetts. Her formal education began at age two under the tutelage of Bessie Trotter, sister of Monroe Nathan Trotter, then editor of the *Boston Guardian*. At age four, West entered Farragut School in Boston and proved herself already capable of doing second-grade work; her elementary education was completed at Matin School in Boston's Mission District. At age seven, she began to write short stories; her first, "Promise and Fulfillment," was published in the *Boston Globe*, a paper to which West became a regular contributor and one that awarded her several literary prizes. After graduating from Girl's Latin High School in 1923, West continued her education at Boston University and later at the Columbia University School of Journalism.

West's long association with Harlem began as a teenager when she and her cousin, Helen Johnson, accepted an invitation to attend *Opportunity* magazine's annual awards dinner in New York and stayed at the Harlem **Young Women's Christian Association** (YWCA). West later moved to New York into an apartment that previously had been the residence of **Zora Neale Hurston**. West's writing career flourished in New York, and she quickly became a part of the Harlem Renaissance, surrounded by such luminaries as Hurston, Wallace Thurman, Aaron Douglas, and Langston Hughes. In 1926, West's short story "The Typewriter" won second place in a competition run by *Opportunity* magazine, an award she shared with Hurston.

In 1927, West traveled to London with the original stage production of *Porgy*, in which she had a small part. During the 1930s, West's involvement in the production of the film *Black and White* led her to the Soviet Union. The film was never completed, but West extended her visit for another year. Back in New York in 1934, she began to publish a literary magazine called *Challenge*, which was devoted to promoting the work of established Harlem Renaissance figures as well as that of lesser-known writers. In 1937, West founded *New Challenge*, with Richard Wright as associate editor; only one issue was published, but the magazine reflected West's increasing interest in class issues as well as the struggles of black people generally.

After her two magazines folded due to financial and editorial difficulties, West became a welfare investigator in Harlem for one and a half years. She then joined the Federal Writers Project of the Works Progress Administration (WPA) until its demise in the 1940s. West never stopped writing in this era, and several of her short stories were published, such as "Hannah Byde," "An Unimportant Man," "Prologue to a Life," and "The Black Dress." From the 1940s to the 1960s, she was a regular contributor to the *New York Daily News*. In 1945, West moved to Martha's Vineyard in Massachusetts, where she has since written weekly for the *Martha's Vineyard Gazette*.

In her novel, *The Living Is Easy*, published in 1948, West satirized affluent black Bostonians who allowed class differences to separate them from the concerns of working-class black communities. Although the novel received mixed reviews in the late 1940s, it became a significant influence in later decades on rising authors such as

Dorothy West dedicated her 1995 novel The Wedding *to her editor at Doubleday, Jacqueline Onassis. "To the memory of my editor, Jacqueline Kennedy Onassis. Though there was never such a mismatched pair in appearance, we were perfect partners."* (MOORLAND-SPINGARN)

Paule Marshall. In 1982, it was reprinted by the Feminist Press, and its reemergence elicited the interest of critics and readers who are more inclined toward issues related to women, black people, and the working class. Among the novel's original supporters was Robert Bone, who described it as a work of "primarily Renaissance consciousness" and "a diamond in the rough . . . bitingly ironic."

In 1995 West published *The Richer, The Poorer: Stories, Sketches, and Reminiscences* and a novel, *The Wedding*. She was egged on to write her long-stalled second novel by her summer neighbor on Martha's Vineyard, Jacqueline Onassis, who had read West's pieces in the *Vine-*

yard Gazette. Onassis, an editor at Doubleday, contracted for the novel and began to visit West once a week. The dedication to *The Wedding* speaks volumes about their relationship: "To the memory of my editor, Jacqueline Kennedy Onassis. Though there was never such a mismatched pair in appearance, we were perfect partners."

The talent and social awareness of Dorothy West have rightly earned her a place both as a member of the Harlem Renaissance and as a writer of enduring significance.

FENELLA MACFARLANE

Williams, Sherley Anne (1944–)

In one of Sherley Anne Williams' poems, "I See My Life," the speaker explains that in her male child she sees herself, her parents, her grandparents, and all her ancestors melding into a symbol of courage, strength, and wisdom. This poem is representative of Williams' philosophy that family and ancestors are crucial subjects in writing. Her writing frequently deals with both the individual and collective past of African Americans; she feels that it is her obligation to tell the truth about black life and to leave behind numerous models of heroes to help African Americans understand themselves.

Literary critic, poet, and novelist Sherley Anne Williams was born in Bakersfield, California, on August 25, 1944, to Jesse Winson and Lena Silver Williams. One of four sisters, Williams grew up in the low-income housing projects where her family battled poverty. She and her sisters (Ruby, Jesmarie, and Lois) were very

close and stored up ways to survive by observing their parents' indomitable spirit.

Williams attended junior high and high school in Fresno, California; after earning a bachelor's degree in history at California State University in 1966, she moved to Washington, D.C., where she spent one year in graduate school at **Howard University**. After working at Federal City College in Washington, D.C., for several years, she transferred to Brown University in Providence, Rhode Island, where she taught in the black studies department and earned a master's degree in 1972. She then returned to California State University as associate professor of English; In 1975, she joined the faculty of the University of California, San Diego, where she is currently a professor of literature. As a teacher, administrator, and mother of one son, John Malcolm, she has had to carve time to write.

Williams began her writing career in 1967 with the publication of the short story "Tell Martha Not to Moan." Her first major work appeared in 1972, a literary study entitled *Give Birth to Brightness: A Thematic Study in Neo-Black Literature*, in which she analyzes works by Amiri Baraka, James Baldwin, and Ernest Gaines and concludes that true black heroes have their origins in the black folkloric tradition. Her own vision emerged three years later with the publication of *The Peacock Poems* (1975), which was nominated for the National Book Award in Poetry in 1976. A second collection of poems, *Someone Sweet Angel Chile* (1982), established Williams as a major African-American poet in the blues tradition. Both poetry volumes explore the struggles and triumphs of lower-income black women, upon whose backs many professional women have stood.

The mysticism of Williams' debut novel, *Dessa Rose* (1987), links her to **Toni Morrison** and **Alice Walker**. An illuminating neo-slave narrative, the book focuses on a black woman, Dessa, who leads an insurrection; she and her companions not only escape hanging but also become successful entrepreneurs. Rufel, a white plantation mistress abandoned by a gambling husband, joins with Dessa and her friends to dupe white planters by selling them into slavery, helping them escape, and reselling them in other locations.

In 1992 Williams' one-woman play, "Letters from a New England Negro," premiered in Chicago, and her 1993 children's book, *Working Cotton*, was a Caldecott Honor Book.

Williams' literary criticism, poetry, and fiction are extraordinary and place her among the most highly regarded neo-Black American writers.

ELIZABETH BROWN-GUILLORY

Wilson, Harriet E.   (b. c. 1827)

On August 18, 1859, Harriet E. Wilson registered the copyright of her novel, a fictional third-person autobiography titled *Our Nig: or, Sketches from the Life of a Free Black, in a Two-Story White House, North. Showing That Slavery's Shadows Fall Even There*. The novel's publication date was September 5. In her preface, Wilson asked her "colored brethren" to purchase her book so that she might support herself and her child. Just five months and twenty-four days later, the Amherst, New Hampshire, *Farmer's Cabinet* recorded in its obituary section the death of George Mason Wilson, seven years old, the only son of H. E. Wilson. The "color" of the child is recorded on his death certificate as "Black."

Harriet Wilson wrote a sentimental novel so that she could regain the right to care for her only son. Six months later, her son died of that standard disease, "fever." The record of his death, alone, proved sufficient to demonstrate his mother's racial identity and authorship of the book, and so Harriet Wilson entered history as probably the first African American to publish a novel in the United States, the fifth African American to publish fiction in English, and one of the first two black women to publish a novel in any language.

Despite their importance to the African-American literary tradition, however, Wilson and her text seem to have been ignored or overlooked both by her "colored brethren" universally and by even the most scrupulous scholars for more than a century for reasons as curious and as puzzling as they are elusive.

Reconstructing the life and times of Harriet E. Wilson is a challenge. Even her exact birthdate and date of death are unknown. Information in the 1850 federal census of the state of New Hampshire indicates that she was born Harriet Adams in 1827 or 1828. However, the 1860 federal census of Boston, to which she had moved, indicates that she was born in Fredericksburg, Virginia, in 1807 or 1808.

It seems definite, however, that in 1850 Harriet Adams lived with a white family, the Boyles, in Milford, New Hampshire. Because the Boyles had four adult nonfamily members living with them, the home probably was a kind of boardinghouse, and the Boyles may very well have been remunerated by the county for sheltering aged and disabled persons.

One year after the census, in 1851, Harriet Adams married Thomas Wilson. In late May or early June 1852, George Mason Wilson was born in Goffstown, New Hampshire, the first and apparently only child of the Wilsons. In Goffstown was located the Hillsborough County Farm; one of the letters appended to Wilson's novel states that, abandoned by her husband, the author of *Our Nig* was forced—after "days passed; weeks passed"—to go to the "County House," where she gave birth to a child.

It also is fairly certain that Wilson had moved to Boston by 1855 and, according to the Boston City Directory, that she remained there through 1863.

These are the bare bones of Wilson's life, drawn from public documents. They correspond dramatically to assertions about the life of the author of *Our Nig* that were made by three acquaintances who endorsed her novel in an appendix. Another source of confirmation is the plot of *Our Nig*—described as autobiographical by Wilson's supporters—which parallels those major events of her life that have been verified.

These sources help us put flesh on the biographical skeleton. According to the letter of Margareta Thorn, one of the three corroborating acquaintances, Wilson was hired out as a very young child to a family that put her to work "both in the house and in the field," allegedly ruining her health by unduly difficult work. By the time she was eighteen, her health was seriously impaired. For a time, according to the letter of an acquaintance calling herself Allida, the young woman worked as a straw sewer in Massachusetts, most probably in the area around Worcester, living in the home of a Mrs. Walker. Wilson was adept at her work, but her health prevented her from working continuously, a condition that forced Mrs.

Walker to nurse her "in a room joining her own chamber."

This was the best part of Wilson's life, a time of comparative comfort with the support of kind friends. Unfortunately, she then met Thomas, whom she soon married. The two left Massachusetts and briefly made their home in New Hampshire; then Thomas went to sea, abandoning his young, pregnant wife. It was at this point that she entered the county farm, which, according to George Plummer Hadley's *History of the Town of Goffstown*, consisted of a large farm house, a barn, a "small dwelling-house near the oak tree," and some smaller buildings. The "paupers" were "scattered through different buildings, which were heated by wood fires." Conditions were apparently horrid: in 1853, some of the inmates "were stricken with smallpox, and it was necessary to build a pesthouse" for their proper isolation and care.

Wilson remained at the county home until her baby was born. Then her errant husband returned just long enough to take his family out of the farm and move them to another town. For a time he supported his family well enough, but then he left again. Soon, Wilson's poor health made it necessary for her to give up her child to kind, apparently white, foster parents. Oddly, at this point, having been given by a compassionate stranger a recipe for getting rid of grey hair, Wilson entered the beauty business until her health broke down again. It was at this point that, confined to bed, she turned to literature as a method of supporting herself and getting back her child.

Our Nig is based on this life story, but it is definitely a work of fiction; it also is definitely the work of Harriet Wilson. It is quite unlike **Harriet Jacob**'s *Incidents in the Life of a Slave Girl*, whose prefatory authenticator, Lydia Maria Child, admits minimal "revision," "condensation," and "arrangement." Not one of the three letters appended to *Our Nig* questions that Wilson wrote all the words in the text in their exact order. A letter of Wilson's, which Allida quotes at length, reveals the same attention to detail and event that is evident in the text of the novel; that is, it is written in the same style, giving further evidence of Wilson's authorship. Her accomplishment is all the more astonishing because the novel reads so much more fluidly and its plot seems so much less contrived than the novels published before *Our Nig* in the African-American tradition. Astonishment grows when we take into consideration that the authors of two of those novels, William Wells Brown and Martin R. Delany, traveled widely, published extensively, lectured regularly, and educated themselves diligently. Delany even studied medicine at Harvard.

Moreover, *Our Nig* is significant in its form. Wilson used the plot structure of her contemporary white female novelists; yet, she abandoned that structure when it failed to satisfy the needs of her well-crafted tale. In other words, she revised significantly what was known as the white woman's novel and thereby made the form her own. By this act of formal revision, she *created* the black woman's novel, not merely because she was the first black woman to write a novel in English, but because she *invented* her own plot structure through which to narrate the saga of her orphaned mulatto heroine. In this important way, Wilson inaugurated the African-American literary tradition in a fundamentally *formal* manner.

Nonetheless, this remarkable accomplishment was virtually ignored for a century after its publication: A systematic search of all extant copies of black and reform newspapers and magazines that were in circulation contemporaneously with the publication of *Our Nig* yielded not one notice or review, nor did searches through the Boston dailies and the Amherst *Farmer's Cabinet*. Other black fiction of the time, though not popularly reviewed, was reviewed on occasion. That such a significant novel, the very first written by a black woman, would remain unnoticed in Boston in 1859, a veritable center of abolitionist reform and passion, and by a growing black press eager to celebrate all black achievements in the arts and sciences, remains one of the troubling enigmas of African-American literary history. The list of people and publications who do *not* mention Wilson and her book is too long to insert here, but it includes DuBois' three important bibliographies, Murray's *Preliminary List of Books and Pamphlets by Negro Authors* (prepared for the American Negro Exhibit at the Paris Exhibition of 1900), and all of the late-nineteenth- and early-twentieth-century black biographical dictionaries.

If the historians, bibliophiles, and bibliographers overlooked Harriet Wilson, the literary historians fared only a bit better. The only references to *Our Nig* that have been discovered give the book little importance: John Herbert Nelson mentions the title only in passing in his 1926 study, *The Negro Character in American Literature*; Herbert Ross Brown, in *The Sentimental Novel in America, 1789–1860* (1940), implies that H. E. Wilson is a white male! Monroe N. Work, in his monumental compilation, *A Bibliography of the Negro in Africa and America*, does indeed list both author and title but under the category, "Novels by White Authors Relating to the Negro"; in his 1972 dissertation on miscegenation in the American novel, James Joseph McKinney discusses the novel's plot; Wilson is listed in Geraldine Matthew's bibliography, *Black Writers, 1771–1949*, and in Fairbanks and Engeldinger's *Black American Fiction: A Bibliography*, but with no information beyond that found in the second column of Lyle Wright's three-volume listing of American fiction.

Curiously enough, the most complete entry for the title was made in a 1980 catalogue of the Howard S. Mott Company of Sheffield, Massachusetts, a company well regarded among antiquarians. The listing, prepared by Daniel Mott, asserted that Wilson's novel was the first by an African-American woman. Mott decided that Wilson was a black woman because of evidence presented in the letters appended to the text.

That Wilson's novel was, to all intents and purposes, lost to the tradition for more than a century seems clear, but the question of why it was so ignored is difficult to answer. Herbert Ross Brown, though mistaking the race and gender of the author, made an insightful comment in his 1940 study: "The author of *Our Nig*," he writes, "dared to treat with sympathetic understanding the marriage of Jim, a black, to a white woman who had been seduced and deserted." This reference to the marriage of the heroine's parents may point up one of the causes of the book's neglect—the absolute horror of interracial marriage, even among most abolitionists. It also may lead us to the more general cause.

Harriet E. Wilson's preface to *Our Nig* is an extraordinary document in the African-American literary tradition, being, if not unique, one of the rare instances in which a black author has openly anticipated a hostile reaction to her text from antislavery forces. She warns, in effect, that her book is not about the horrors of slavery in the South but about the horrors of racism in the North. Moreover, she states that

> I do not pretend to divulge every transaction in my own life, which the unprejudiced would declare unfavorable in comparison with treatment of legal bondmen: I have purposely omitted what would most provoke shame in our good anti-slavery friends at home.

The villains of *Our Nig* are not slaveholders and overseers; they are instead the women of a Northern white household. Their crimes will not be destroyed by the abolition of slavery but only by a complete reexamination and amendment of the economic and social position of black women in American society.

Literarily, Wilson's achievement was that she combined the received conventions of the sentimental novel with certain key conventions of the slave narrative to create a new form, of which *Our Nig* is the unique example. Had subsequent black authors had this text to draw upon, perhaps the black literary tradition would have developed more quickly and more resolutely than it did. It seems possible that, by challenging racism directly and unequivocally in a society that was not yet prepared to come to terms with the issue on that level, Harriet Wilson, through no fault of her own, condemned herself to obscurity and unwittingly slowed the emergence of a distinctive black voice in American fiction.

HENRY LOUIS GATES, JR.

Chronology

1746

Lucy Terry Prince writes "Bar's Fight," a poem commemorating the Deerfield Massacre. This is the first poem known to be written by a black person in the United States and later published (1895).

1767

Phillis Wheatley writes "A Poem by Phillis, a Negro Girl, on the Death of Reverend George Whitefield." It is her first work and will be published in 1770.

1773

Phillis Wheatley's *Poems on Various Subjects, Religious and Moral* is published. It is the first book published by an African American and the second by a woman in North America.

1831

The first slave narrative by a black woman in the United States is published. It is Mary Prince's *The History of Mary Prince, a West Indian Slave, Related by Herself, with a Supplement by the Editor, to Which is Added the Narrative of Asa-Asa, a Captured African.*

1832

Memoir of Chloe Spear, a Native of Africa, Who Was Enslaved in Childhood: By a "Lady of Boston" is published.

1833

Appeal in Favor of That Class of Americans called Africans by Lydia Maria Childs is published.

1835

Productions of Mrs. Maria Stewart is published in Boston.

1838

Narrative of Joanna, an Emancipated Slave of Surinam is published in Boston.

The Memoirs of Elleanor Eldridge is published. It is one of the few early nineteenth-century autobiographies written by a free black woman.

1841

Ann Plato's *Essays, including Biographies and Miscellaneous Pieces in Prose and Poetry* is published.

1843

In New Orleans, African Americans begin to publish *L'Album Littéraire, Journal des Jeunes Gens, Amateurs de la Littérature*, a monthly review in French that includes poems, stories, and articles.

1845

Forest Leaves, the first book by **Frances Ellen Watkins Harper**, is published.

1850

Sojourner Truth's *Narrative of Sojourner Truth, a Northern Slave, Emancipated from Bodily Servitude by the State of New York in 1828, Narrated to Olive Gilbert, including Sojourner Truth's Book of Life and a Dialogue* is published.

1852

Mary Ann Shadd Cary publishes *A Plea for Emigration.*

1853

A Narrative of the Life and Travels of Mrs. Nancy Prince is published.

Mary Ann Shadd Cary becomes editor and publisher of the *Provincial Freeman*. She is the first black woman editor of a newspaper in the United States.

1854

Frances Ellen Watkins Harper's *Poems on Miscellaneous Subjects* is published.

1855

Charlotte Forten Grimke's poem "A Parting Hymn" is published and wins a number of prizes.

1858

Aunt Sally; or The Cross the Way to Freedom by Sally Williams is published in Cincinnati.

1860

Narrative of the Life of Jane Brown and Her Two Children is published in Hartford.

1861

Incidents in the Life of a Slave Girl Written by Herself by **Harriet Jacobs** is published under the name Linda Brent. It was believed to be fiction by a white writer until 1987.

1868

The first "Behind-the-Scenes-at-the-White House" book is published by **Elizabeth Keckley**, dressmaker to Mary Todd Lincoln and former slave. It's full title is *Behind the Scenes by Elizabeth Keckley, Formerly a Slave, but More Recently a Modiste and Friend to Mrs. Abraham Lincoln; or Thirty Years a Slave and Four Years in the White House.*

A biography entitled *The Life and Times of Martin Robinson Delaney* is published under the pseudonym Frank Rollins by Frances Anne Rollins.

1869

Scenes in the Life of Harriet Tubman, as told by Sarah Bradford, is published.

1872

Frances Ellen Watkins Harper's *Sketches of Southern Life* is published.

1876

The **Hyers** Sisters Concert Company becomes the first black repertory company when it changes its format to the presentation of musical plays.

1883

Rebecca Lee Crumpler, the first black woman physician in the United States, writes *A Book of Medical Discourses in Two Parts*, which includes advice to potential woman doctors.

1885

In the first issue of T. Thomas Fortune's *Freeman*, **Gertrude Mossell** begins her column "Our Woman's Day."

1888

William J. Simmons founds the magazine *Our Women and Children*, which will publish the work of **Lucy Wilmot Smith**, Mary V. Cook, **Ida B. Wells**, and Ione E. Woods.

1889

Ida B. Wells becomes editor, and part owner, of the *Memphis Free Speech and Headlight*.

1890

The House of Bondage by **Octavia R. Albert** is published.

1891

An illustrated magazine for black women, *Ringwood's Afro-American Journal of Fashion*, is founded by **Julia Ringwood Coston**, who will be editor and publisher.

Lucy Parsons founds the newspaper *Freedom: An Anarchist-Communist Monthly*.

1892

Anna Julia Cooper publishes *A Voice from the South by a Black Woman of the South*.

Frances Ellen Watkins Harper's *Iola Leroy: or Shadows Uplifted* is published.

1893

Julia Ringwood Coston founds *Ringwood's Home Magazine*.

1894

The Women's Era begins publication.

The Work of Afro-American Women by **Gertrude Mossell** is published.

1895

Alice Dunbar-Nelson publishes her first book, *Violets and Other Tales*.

1898

A Slave Girl's Story by **Kate Drumgold** is published.

1900

Pauline Hopkins publishes *Contending Forces: A Romance Illustrative of Negro Life North and South*.

1902

Susie King Taylor, first black nurse in the U.S. Army, publishes *My Life in Camp with the U. S. Colored Troops*.

1907

C. M. Hughes and Minnie Thomas found *Colored Woman's Magazine*.

1918

The Heart of a Woman by **Georgia Douglas Johnson** is published. It is her first book.

1919

Columnist **Delilah Beasley** publishes *The Negro Trail-Blazers of California*.

1920

Anne Spencer's first poem, "Before the Feast of Sushan," is published in *Crisis*.

1926

Hallie Quinn Brown publishes *Homespun Heroines and Other Women of Distinction.*

1927

In this year, Bessie Smith is the highest paid black artist in the world.

1928

Georgia Douglas Johnson's *An Autumn Love Cycle*, a book of poetry, is published.
  Nella Larsen's first novel, *Quicksand*, is published.

1930

Nella Larsen is the first African American to win a creative writing award from the Guggenheim Foundation.
  Zora Neale Hurston collaborates with Langston Hughes on a play called *Mule Bone*. When the authors disagree, the play remains unfinished.

1935

Zora Neale Hurston's *Mules and Men* is published.

1937

Their Eyes Were Watching God by Zora Neale Hurston is published.

1942

Margaret Walker's first book of poetry is published. With *For My People*, Walker becomes the first African-American poet to be published in the Yale University Press' Series of Younger Poets.

1945

The first book of poetry by Gwendolyn Brooks, *A Street in Bronzeville*, is published.
  African Journey, a memoir by Eslanda Goode Robeson, is published.

1946

Ann Petry's first book, *The Street*, sells 1.5 million copies.

1950

Gwendolyn Brooks wins the Pulitzer Prize for her book of poetry, *Annie Allen*. She is the first African American to win in any category.

1951

Anna Julia Cooper's *Personal Recollections of the Grimké Family* and *The Life and Writings of Charlotte Forten Grimké* are published.

1953

Maud Martha, an autobiographical novel by Gwendolyn Brooks, is published.

1954

Paule Marshall's first short story, "The Valley Between," is published in the magazine *Our World.*

1956

The Negro in American Culture by Margaret Just Butcher is published.

1959

Paule Marshall's *Brown Girl, Brownstones,* is published.

1966

Margaret Walker's *Jubilee* is published. The novel is her first book since her 1942 book of poetry, *For My People*.

1967

Nikki Giovanni's first book of poetry, *Black Feeling, Black Talk*, is published.

1968

Alice Walker's first book of poetry, *Once*, is published.

1969

Sonia Sanchez' first book of poetry, *Homecoming*, is published.

Good Times by **Lucille Clifton** is published and later chosen as one of *The New York Times'* ten best books of the year.

Gwendolyn Brooks is named Poet Laureate of Illinois.

1970

Toni Morrison's first novel, *The Bluest Eye*, is published.

Maya Angelou's *I Know Why the Caged Bird Sings*, the first volume of her five-volume autobiography, is published.

Essence begins publication. It is the most important magazine for black women since *Ringwood's Afro-American Journal of Fashion* in 1891.

Louise Meriwether's *Daddy Was A Numbers Runner*, is published.

The Black Woman: An Anthology, edited by **Toni Cade Bambara**, is published. It contains the work of many of the new wave of black women writers.

1971

Maya Angelou's *Just Give Me a Cool Drink of Water 'fore I Die*, is published. It will later be nominated for the Pulitzer Prize in poetry.

Gemini: An Extended Autobiographical Statement on My First Twenty-Five Years of Being a Black Poet by Nikki Giovanni is published.

1974

Virginia Hamilton's *M. C. Higgins, the Great* is published. It will win the Newbery Medal, the National Book Award, the Lewis Carroll Shelf Award, and the International Board on Books for Young People Award.

Ann Allen Shockley's *Loving Her*, is published. It is the first known book by a black woman to have a lesbian main character.

1977

Toni Morrison's *Song of Solomon* is published. It sells more than three million copies and will win the National Book Critics Circle Award.

1978

Mildred Taylor wins the Newbery Medal for *Roll of Thunder, Hear My Cry*.

Sonia Sanchez wins the American Book Award for her poetry in *I've Been a Woman*.

1979

Barbara Chase-Ribaud's *Sally Hemings*, is published.

Lucille Clifton is named Poet Laureate of the state of Maryland.

1980

Lucille Clifton is nominated for the Pulitzer Prize in poetry for *Two-Headed Woman*.

Toni Cade Bambara wins the American Book Award for *The Salt Eaters*.

1981

Toni Morrison's *Tar Baby* is published and makes the *New York Times* best-seller list within a month.

1983

Alice Walker wins the Pulitzer Prize for her novel, *The Color Purple*.

Gloria Naylor wins the National Book Award for *The Women of Brewster Place*.

1984

Octavia Butler wins the Hugo Award for excellence in science fiction writing.

1985

Gwendolyn Brooks becomes poetry consultant to the Library of Congress.

Rita Dove wins the Pulitzer Prize for poetry for *Thomas and Beulah*.

1988

Toni Morrison wins the Pulitzer Prize for fiction for *Beloved*.

1992

Terry McMillan's *Waiting to Exhale* becomes a best-seller.

1993

Toni Morrison wins the Nobel Prize for literature.

Rita Dove is named Poet Laureate of the United States.

Maya Angelou reads her specially commissioned poem "On the Pulse of Morning" at the inauguration of Bill Clinton as President, the first time a poet participated in this ceremony since President-Elect John F. Kennedy invited Robert Frost in 1962.

1994

Barbara Chase-Riboud's *The President's Daughter* is published.

1995

Dorothy West's *The Wedding* is published after the writer is rediscovered by Doubleday editor Jacqueline Kennedy Onassis.

Terry McMillan's novel *Waiting to Exhale* is made into a major motion picture, starring **Angela Bassett** and **Whitney Houston**.

Bibliography

GENERAL BOOKS USEFUL TO THE STUDY OF BLACK WOMEN IN AMERICA

Reference' Books

African-Americans: Voices of Triumph. Three volume set: *Perseverance, Leadership*, and *Creative Fire*. By the editors of Time-Life Books, Alexandria, Virginia, 1993.

Estell, Kenneth, ed., *The African-American Almanac*. Detroit, Michigan, 1994.

Harley, Sharon. *The Timetables of African-American History: A Chronology of the Most Important People and Events in African-American History*. New York, 1995.

Hine, Darlene Clark. *Hine Sight: Black Women and The Re-Construction of American History*. Brooklyn, New York, 1994.

Hine, Darlene Clark, ed., Elsa Barkley Brown and Rosalyn Terborg-Penn, associate eds. *Black Women in America: An Historical Encyclopedia*. Brooklyn, New York, 1993.

Hornsby, Alton, Jr. *Chronology of African-American History: Significant Events and People from 1619 to the Present*. Detroit, Michigan, 1991.

Kranz, Rachel. *Biographical Dictionary of Black Americans*. New York, 1992.

Lanker, Brian. *I Dream a World: Portraits of Black Women Who Changed America*. New York, 1989.

Logan, Rayford W., and Michael R. Winston, eds. *Dictionary of American Negro Biography*. New York, 1982.

Low, W. Augustus, and Virgil A. Clift, eds. *Encyclopedia of Black America*. New York, 1981.

Salem, Dorothy C., ed. *African American Women: A Biographical Dictionary*. New York, 1993.

Salzman, Jack, David Lionel Smith, and Cornel West. *Encyclopedia of African-American Culture and History*. Five Volumes. New York, 1996.

Smith, Jessie Carney, ed., *Notable Black American Women*. Two Volumes. Detroit, Michigan, Book I, 1993; Book II, 1996.

General Books about Black Women

Giddings, Paula. *When and Where I Enter: The Impact of Black Women on Race and Sex in America*. New York, 1984.

Guy-Sheftall, Beverly. *Words of Fire: An Anthology of African-American Feminist Thought*. New York, 1995.

Hine, Darlene Clark, Wilma King, and Linda Reed, eds. *"We Specialize in the Wholly Impossible": A Reader in Black Women's History*. Brooklyn, New York, 1995.

Jones, Jacqueline. *Labor of Love, Labor of Sorrow: Black Women, Work, and the Family from Slavery to the Present*. New York, 1985.

183

Lerner, Gerda, ed. *Black Women in White America: A Documentary History.* New York, 1972.

BOOKS THAT INCLUDE INFORMATION ON BLACK WOMEN WRITERS

African American Writers. Valerie Smith, Consulting Editor; Lea Baechler and A. Walton Litz, General Editors. New York, 1991.

Daughters of Africa: An International Anthology of Words and Writings by Women of African Descent from the Ancient Egyptian to the Present. Edited with an introduction by Margaret Busby. New York, 1992.

Lewis, David. L. *When Harlem Was in Vogue.* New York, 1981.

Wagner, Jean. *Black Poets of the United States: From Paul Laurence Dunbar to Langston Hughes.* Urbana, Illinois, 1973.

Contents of the Set

Burroughs, Margaret
Butler, Octavia E.
Campbell, Bebe Moore
Cary, Lorene
Chase-Riboud, Barbara
Cleage, Pearl
Cliff, Michelle
Clifton, Lucille
Cooper, J. California
Cortez, Jayne
Danner, Margaret Essie
Davis, Thadious
Davis, Thulani
Delaney Sisters, The
DeVeaux, Alexis
Dove, Rita
Drumgold, Kate
Dunbar-Nelson, Alice
Dunlap, Ethel Trew
Fauset, Jessie Redmon
Giddings, Paula
Giovanni, Nikki
Golden, Marita
Greenfield, Eloise
Guy, Rosa
Hamilton, Virginia Esther
Harper, Frances Ellen Watkins
hooks, bell
Hopkins, Pauline Elizabeth
Hunter, Kristin
Hurston, Zora Neale
Johnson, Georgia Douglas
Jones, Gayl
Jordan, June
Kincaid, Jamaica
Larsen, Nella
Lorde, Audre
Madgett, Naomi Long
Marshall, Paule
McElroy, Colleen J.
McMillan, Terry
Meriwether, Louise
Morrison, Toni
Naylor, Gloria
Petry, Ann Lane
Polite, Carlene
Sanchez, Sonia
Sanders, Dori
Shockley, Ann Allen

Southerland, Ellease
Spencer, Anne
Taylor, Mildred
Thomas, Joyce Carol
Vroman, Mary Elizabeth
Walker, Alice
Walker, Margaret Abigail
Wallace, Michele
West, Dorothy
Williams, Sherley Anne
Wilson, Harriet E.

Dance, Sports, and Visual Arts

Dance
Asante, Kariamu Welsh
Baker, Josephine
Blunden, Jeraldyne
Brown, Joan Myers
Collins, Janet
DeLavallade, Carmen
Dunham, Katherine
Forsyne, Ida
Hinkson, Mary
Jamison, Judith
Johnson, Virginia
Primus, Pearl
Turney, Matt
Waters, Sylvia
Yarborough, Sara
Zollar, Jawole Willa Jo

Sports
Ashford, Evelyn
Bolden, Jeanette
Brisco-Hooks, Valerie
Brown, Alice
Brown, Earlene
Cheeseborough, Chandra
Coachman, Alice
Daniels, Isabel
Dawes, Dominique
DeFrantz, Anita
Devers, Gail
Edwards, Teresa
Faggs, Mae
Ferrell, Barbara

Franke, Nikki
Gallagher, Kim
Garrison, Zina
Gibson, Althea
Glenn, Lula Mae Hymes
Harris-Stewart, Lusia
Hudson, Martha
Hyman, Flora
Jacket, Barbara J.
Jackson, Nell Cecilia
Jones, Barbara
Jones, Leora "Sam"
Joyner, Florence Griffith
Joyner-Kersee, Jackie
Love, Lynette
Matthews, Margaret
McDaniel, Mildred
McGuire, Edith
Miller, Cheryl
Mims, Madeleine Manning
Murray, Lenda
Patterson-Tyler, Audrey
  (Mickey)
Pickett, Tydie
Powell, Renee
Rudolph, Wilma
Stokes, Louise
Stone, Lyle (Toni)
Stringer, C. Vivian
Thomas, Debi
Thomas, Vanessa
Tyus, Wyomia
Washington, Ora
White, Willye B.
Williams, Lucinda
Woodard, Lynette

Visual Arts
Beasley, Phoebe
Blount, Mildred E.
Brandon, Barbara
Burke, Selma
Catlett, Elizabeth
Fuller, Meta
Gafford, Alice
Humphrey, Margo
Hunter, Clementine
Jackson-Jarvis, Martha
Jackson, May Howard

Education

Religion and Community

National Urban League Guild
Neighborhood Union, Atlanta
New Era Club
Oblate Sisters of Providence
Phyllis Wheatley Homes and Clubs
Porter, Diane M.
Prout, Mary Ann
Rankin, Marlene Owens
Ransom, Emma
Roberts, Ruth Logan
Saddler, Juanita
Saint Frances of Rome Academy, Baltimore
Sanctified Church
Saunders, Cecelia Cabaniss
Sigma Gamma Rho Sorority
Sisters of the Holy Family
Smith, Amanda Berry
Smith, Celestine Louise
Southeastern Association of Colored Women's Clubs
Sprague, Fredericka and Rosabelle Jones
Stewart, Ella Phillips
Stewart, Sallie Wyatt
Stokes, Ora Brown
Tanneyhill, Ann
Thomas, Cora Ann Pair
Waddles, Charleszetta
Walker, A'Lelia
Walker, Maggie Lena
White Rose Mission, New York City
Williams, Fannie Barrier
Williamson, Sarah
Woman's Loyal Union of New York and Brooklyn
York, Consuella
Young Women's Christian Association
Zeta Phi Beta Sorority

Law and Government

Alexander, Sadie
Anderson, Violette N.
Atkins, Hannah Diggs

Barrett, Jacquelyn H.
Bass, Charlotta Spears
Belton, Sharon Sayles
Berry, Mary Frances
Bethune, Mary McLeod
Black Women Mayors' Caucus
Bolin, Jane Mathilda
Brown, Corrine
Burke, Yvonne Brathwaite
Carson, Julia
Carter, Eunice Hunton
Carter, Pamela Fanning
Chisholm, Shirley
Clayton, Eva
Collins, Barbara-Rose
Collins, Cardiss
Congresswomen
Delco, Wilhelmina R.
Elliott, Daisy
Fauset, Crystal Bird
Federal Judges
Fisher, Ada Lois Sipuel
Guinier, Lani
Hall, Katie
Hamilton, Grace Towns
Harris, Patricia Roberts
Harvard, Beverly
Hedgeman, Anna Arnold
Herman, Alexis M.
Hill, Anita
Ingram, Edith J.
Johnson, Eddie Bernice
Johnson, Norma Holloway
Jones, Elaine
Jones, Star
Jordan, Barbara Charline
Kearse, Amalya Lyle
Kelly, Sharon Pratt Dixon
Kidd, Mae Street
Lafontant-Mankarious, Jewel Stradford
Lawson, Marjorie McKenzie
Lee, Sheila Jackson
McKinney, Cynthia
Meek, Carrie
Mitchell, Juanita Jackson
Morris, Carolyn
Moseley-Braun, Carol
Motley, Constance Baker

National Organization of Black Elected Legislative Women
National Political Congress of Black Women
Norton, Eleanor Holmes
O'Leary, Hazel Rollins
Payton, Carolyn Robertson
Perry, Carrie Saxon
Phillips, Velvalea Rogers
Poe, L. Marian Fleming
Powers, Georgia
Ralston, Elreta Alexander
Ray, Charlotte
Sampson, Edith
Sears-Collins, Leah
Smythe-Haithe, Mabel Murphy
Stout, Juanita Kidd
Taylor, Anna Diggs
Tucker, C. DeLores
Waters, Maxine
Watson, Diane Edith
Welcome, Verda Freeman
Williams, Margaret
Williams, Patricia J.

Theater Arts and Entertainment

Alice, Mary
Allen, Billie
Allen, Debbie
American Negro Theater
Andrews, Regina M. Anderson
Archer, Osceola
Avery, Margaret
Bassett, Angela
Baxter, Karen
Beavers, Louise
Belgrave, Cynthia
Bentley, Gladys
Berry, Halle
Bowman, Laura
Burke, Georgia
Burrill, Mary P.
Burrows, Vinie
Bush, Anita
Canty, Marietta

Social Activism

Science, Health, and Medicine

Contents of the Set

(LISTED ALPHABETICALLY BY ENTRY)

Index

Page numbers in **boldface** indicate main entries. *Italic* page numbers indicate illustrations.